Quotation Index to Children's Literature

Quotation Index to Children's Literature

Melanie Axel-Lute

2001
LIBRARIES UNLIMITED, INC.
Englewood, Colorado

For Paul, and Miriam, and Gregory
I'm never *afraid with you*

Libraries Unlimited, Inc.
P.O. Box 6633
Englewood, CO 80155-6633
1-800-237-6124
www.lu.com

Library of Congress Cataloging-in-Publication Data

Quotation index to children's literature / [compiled by] Melanie Axel-Lute.
        p. cm.
    Includes bibliographical references and index.
    ISBN 1-56308-809-6 (pbk.)
    1. Quotations, English. 2. Children's literature. I. Axel-Lute, Melanie.

PN6081 .Q593 2001
808.8'0083--dc21   00-066308

CONTENTS

INTRODUCTION

A statue of Peter Pan stands in Central Park, one of Paddington in Paddington Station, and the whole family from *Make Way for Ducklings* in Boston's Public Garden. There is a portrait of Eloise in the Plaza Hotel lobby. The mayor of New York City and a British Member of Parliament recently engaged in a verbal battle over where Winnie-the-Pooh and his friends (the original stuffed animals) will reside. Children's books are more than just stories for kids. They have become part of our culture.

Quotations from children's literature have also found their way into everyday speech. References to the Grinch, to Mr. McGregor's garden, to "the old house in Paris that was covered with vines" appear in print as well as in conversation. We've all muttered "I think I can, I think I can," and know that 11:00 is Time-for-a-little-something.

The Quotation Index to Children's Literature is designed to identify and locate quotations and phrases found in books, tales, and poetry commonly considered to be works for children, few of which have been indexed in the standard quotation indexes. It is not merely a collection of inspirational lines or quotations selected by topic. This is the place to find out where "Always winter and never Christmas" and "Christmas won't be Christmas without any presents" come from. It will help identify books that are set in fictional towns like Who-ville and Chewandswallow and those that feature characters like the Lost Boys and the Assistant Pig-Keeper. It will also answer specific questions about a book, such as "What did Charlotte write about Wilbur in her web?" and "What is Pippi Longstocking's full name?" Using the keyword and subject entries in the index, you can find quotations from children's literature on a particular topic.

Quotations in this book come from popular, classic, and award-winning books for children. Folk and fairy tales and nursery rhymes are also included in the section called "Quotations from Traditional Sources." The emphasis is on books originally written in English, but you will also find books familiar to American readers in translation, such as *Pippi Longstocking* and *Babar*. Only poetry collections by a single author have been included, not poetry anthologies. The quotations themselves were chosen because they were familiar, representational of the book, or simply interesting, useful, or thought-provoking.

It is important to note that many of these quotations are not original. L. Frank Baum was probably not the first to state, "There's no place like home," and "It was a dark and stormy night" was a well-worn cliché long before *A Wrinkle in Time*. This index does not attempt to track down the first source of any phrase. Its purpose is to identify which children's work is popularly associated with that phrase.

Main Body of Quotations

The "Quotations by Author" section is arranged alphabetically by the authors of the quotations. Authors' names are given as they appear in the book. If the name is a pseudonym, the author's "real" name follows in brackets. Under each author appear the quotations, numbered and arranged alphabetically by the title of the work in which they are found, with multiple quotes from the same work given in the order in which they appear in the work. Following each quotation is the name of the speaker (or thinker) of the quote, if relevant, the title of the work in which it appears, and the chapter number or title (if any), plus any explanatory information. For example:

❚ Barrie, J. M.

(7)   Boy, why are you crying?
   ▶ [Wendy, in *Peter Pan*, ch 3]

The quote is spoken by the character Wendy in chapter 3 of *Peter Pan* by J. M. Barrie.

If a short story or poem appears in a collection, its title is given first, then the title of the collection. For example:

❚ Kipling, Rudyard

(1)   The Law of the Jungle
   ▶ [in "Mowgli's Brothers," in *The Jungle Book*]

This line appears in the story "Mowgli's Brothers," which is found in *The Jungle Book* by Rudyard Kipling. It is not spoken by a particular character in the story, and there are no chapter numbers in this story.

This contrasts with a chapter title, which would appear after the book's title. For example:

◥ **Snyder, Zilpha Keatley**

(5)   Imagination is a great thing in long dull hours, but it's a real curse in a dark alley.

▶ [in *The Egypt Game*, "Fear Strikes"]

Following the author listing is a section called "Quotations from Traditional Sources," which contains anonymous works of three types: the Arabian Nights, fairy tales, and nursery rhymes. These quotations are arranged by title of the tale or first line of the nursery rhyme. There are, of course, many variations in these anonymous folk tales and rhymes, as well as many different translations. I have tried to include the most commonly used form of each quote and have provided a source for that variant, with the understanding that there are many other versions and many other sources. For example:

◥ **Fairy Tales**

(1)   Up stick and bang him.

▶ [in "The Ass, the Table, and the Stick," in Jacobs, *English Fairy Tales*]

This line is from the fairy tale "The Ass, the Table, and the Stick," as found in *English Fairy Tales*, collected by Jacobs. Complete bibliographic information for the collection can be found in the Bibliography.

Keyword Index

The keyword index is what makes *Quotation Index to Children's Literature* a useful reference tool instead of a random collection of quotations. It is the way to locate a quotation when you don't know its author. Each entry in the index is a keyword from the quotation, or a subject. Keyword entries come first, followed by subject entries, which are identified by "(subj.)" No attempt has been made to organize the quotations into general subject categories (family, happiness, school). The subject entries serve mainly to complete or clarify quotations that do not present their meaning in a keyword. For example, "They're everyone borrowed" is indexed under "Children (subj.)" because this is the unstated meaning of "they."

Under each entry, whether keyword or subject, an abbreviated part of the quotation is given, with the keyword represented by a boldface letter. This should enable you to identify the quote you are seeking. After that is the author's name, or a reference to Nursery rhymes, Fairy tales, or Arabian Nights, and the number of the quotation. Be sure to look at the main entry of the quotation to get its complete and correct wording and do not rely on the truncated version that appears in the index. For example:

---

dead
    if I was **d** I'd set up   Rawlings (6)

Under the keyword "dead," we find the partial quote "if I was dead I'd set up," referring to Rawlings, quote number 6. In the main body of quotations, under the author **Rawlings, Marjorie Kinnan**, at the sixth entry we find:

---

(6)   If I was dead, I'd set up and
      take notice, a day like this
      un.
      ▶ [Penny Baxter, in *The Yearling*, ch 30]

To find a quotation you remember or partially remember, using the keywords, look in the index under any word that you remember from the quotation. Distinctive words are, of course, most likely to find you what you want. If you do not locate your desired quotation under one keyword, try another. I have tried to index the most memorable words in each quotation, but your idea of memorable may differ from mine. It is also possible that you have misremembered a word ("bravery" instead of "courage" for example) or have looked under the wrong form of a word. (There are several entries between "cat" and "cats.") Possessives and contractions are listed under the main form of the word. For example, "wolf in sheep's clothing" is indexed under *sheep* and "an elephant's faithful" is indexed under *elephant*.

Title Index

All books, stories, and poems are listed alphabetically by title followed by the author's name, or the designation "Fairy tales" or "Arabian Nights." Nursery rhymes, which do not have titles, are not included, because they may be found alphabetically by first line in their section. Check the title index if you wish to find quotations from a particular book and do not recall its author. Also check here if a book does not appear in the main body of quotations where you expected it. For instance, you may be surprised not to find "Mary Had a Little Lamb" in the Nursery Rhymes section. A look at the title index will show that this poem has an author, Sara Josepha Hale, and it appears under her name.

Bibliography

All works cited are listed in the bibliography. It is here that you should check to find the complete reference for sources given in the Nursery Rhymes and Fairy Tales sections.

QUOTATIONS BY AUTHOR

❚ Aardema, Verna

(1) But because of this the mosquito has a guilty conscience. To this day she goes about whining in people's ears: "Zeee! Is everyone still angry at me?"

   When she does that, she gets an honest answer. KPAO!
   ▶ [in *Why Mosquitoes Buzz in People's Ears: A West African Tale*]

❚ Aesop

(1) Beware lest you lose the substance by grasping at the shadow.
   ▶ [in "The Dog and the Shadow," in *The Fables of Aesop*]

(2) Any excuse will serve a tyrant.
   ▶ [in "The Wolf and the Lamb," in *The Fables of Aesop*]

(3) Injuries may be forgiven, but not forgotten.
   ▶ [in "The Man and the Serpent," in *The Fables of Aesop*]

(4) Much outcry, little outcome.
   ▶ [in "The Mountain in Labor," in *The Fables of Aesop*]

(5) The Lion's Share
   ▶ [title of fable, in *The Fables of Aesop*]

(6) You have put your head inside a Wolf's mouth and taken it out again in safety; that ought to be reward enough for you.
   ▶ [wolf, in "The Wolf and the Crane," in *The Fables of Aesop*]

(7) Better beans and bacon in peace than cakes and ale in fear.
   ▶ [in "The Town Mouse and the Country Mouse," in *The Fables of Aesop*]

(8) Do not trust flatterers.
   ▶ [in "The Fox and the Crow," in *The Fables of Aesop*]

(9) Precious things are for those that can prize them.
   ▶ [in "The Cock and the Pearl," in *The Fables of Aesop*]

1

(10) Little friends may prove great friends.
  ▶ [in "The Lion and the Mouse," in *The Fables of Aesop*]

(11) It is easy to be brave from a safe distance.
  ▶ [in "The Wolf and the Kid," in *The Fables of Aesop*]

(12) One bad turn deserves another.
  ▶ [in "The Fox and the Stork," in *The Fables of Aesop*]

(13) No gratitude from the wicked.
  ▶ [in "The Woodman and the Serpent," in *The Fables of Aesop*]

(14) It is not only fine feathers that make fine birds.
  ▶ [in "The Jay and the Peacock," in *The Fables of Aesop*]

(15) The Wolf in Sheep's Clothing
  ▶ [title of fable, in *The Fables of Aesop*]

(16) Appearances are often deceiving.
  ▶ [in "The Wolf in Sheep's Clothing," in *Aesop's Fables*]

(17) Belling the Cat
  ▶ [title of fable, in *The Fables of Aesop*]

(18) Familiarity breeds contempt.
  ▶ [in "The Fox and the Lion," in *The Fables of Aesop*]

(19) The Dog in the Manger
  ▶ [title of fable, in *The Fables of Aesop*]

(20) Sour Grapes
  ▶ [alternate title of fable "The Fox and the Grapes," in *Tales from Aesop*]

(21) Love can tame the wildest.
  ▶ [in "The Lion in Love," in *The Fables of Aesop*]

(22) It is better to bend than to break.
  ▶ [in "The Oak and the Reed," in *Aesop's Fables*]

(23) Better one safe way than a hundred on which you cannot reckon.
  ▶ [in "The Fox and the Cat," in *The Fables of Aesop*]

(24) Yield to all and you will soon have nothing to yield.
  ▶ [in "The Man and His Two Wives," in *The Fables of Aesop*]

(25) United we stand, divided we fall.
  ▶ [in "The Four Oxen and the Lion," in *The Fables of Aesop*]

(26) Little by little does the trick.
  ▶ [in "The Crow and the Pitcher," in *The Fables of Aesop*]

(27) Please all, and you will please none.
  ▶ [in "The Man, the Boy, and the Donkey," in *The Fables of Aesop*]

(28) Do not count your chickens before they are hatched.
  ▶ [in "The Milkmaid and Her Pail," in *The Fables of Aesop*]

(29) Union gives strength.
  ▶ [in "The Bundle of Sticks," in *The Fables of Aesop*]

(30) The gods help them that help themselves.
> ▶ [in "Hercules and the Wagoner," in *The Fables of Aesop*]

(31) One good turn deserves another.
> ▶ [in "The Dove and the Ant," in *Tales from Aesop*]

(32) The Boy Who Cried Wolf
> ▶ [title of fable, in *Tales from Aesop*]

(33) Slow and steady wins the race.
> ▶ [in "The Hare and the Tortoise," in *Tales from Aesop*]

(34) Be sure to look before you leap!
> ▶ [fox, in "The Fox and the Goat," in *Aesop's Fables*]

❚ Ahlberg, Janet and Allan

(1) Each Peach Pear Plum
I spy Tom Thumb
> ▶ [in *Each Peach Pear Plum*]

❚ Aiken, Joan

(1) Trees are swayed by winds, men by words.
> ▶ [Dan, in "Think of a Word," in *The Last Slice of Rainbow and Other Stories*]

(2) Words are like spices. Too many is worse than too few.
> ▶ [old lady, in "Think of a Word," in *The Last Slice of Rainbow and Other Stories*]

❚ Alcott, Louisa May

(1) Christmas won't be Christmas without any presents.
> ▶ [Jo, in *Little Women*, ch 1, first line]

(2) If you mean *libel*, I'd say so, and not talk about *labels* as if papa was a pickle bottle.
> ▶ [Jo, in *Little Women*, ch 1]

(3) I am angry every day of my life, Jo, but I have learned not to show it; and I still hope to learn not to feel it.
> ▶ [Marmee, in *Little Women*, ch 8]

(4) I didn't beg, borrow, or steal it. I earned it, and I don't think you'll blame me, for I only sold what was my own.
> ▶ [Jo, on her hair, in *Little Women*, ch 15]

(5) Amy's nose still afflicted her, for it never *would* grow Grecian.
> ▶ [in *Little Women*, ch 25]

(6) As Beth had hoped, the "tide went out easily," and in the dark hour before the dawn, on the bosom where she had drawn her first breath, she quietly drew her last, with no farewell but one loving look, one little sigh.
> ▶ [in *Little Women*, ch 40]

(7) When women are advisers, the lords of creation don't take the advice till they have persuaded themselves that it is just what they intended to do; then they act upon it, and, if it succeeds, they give the weaker vessel half

the credit of it; if it fails, they generously give her the whole.

▶ [in *Little Women*, ch 41]

(8) Mothers have need of sharp eyes and discreet tongues when they have girls to manage.

▶ [Marmee, in *Little Women*, ch 42]

❚ Aldrich, Thomas Bailey

(1) Whenever a new scholar came to our school, I used to confront him at recess with the following words: "My name's Tom Bailey; what's your name?" If the name struck me favorably, I shook hands with the new pupil cordially; but if it didn't, I would turn on my heel, for I was particular on this point. Such names as Higgins, Wiggins, and Spriggins were deadly affronts to my ear; while Langdon, Wallace, Blake, and the like, were passwords to my confidence and esteem.

▶ [in *The Story of a Bad Boy*, ch 1]

(2) My father was a person of untiring energy and ability; but he had no luck. To use a Rivermouth saying, he was always catching sculpins when everyone else with the same bait was catching mackerel.

▶ [in *The Story of a Bad Boy*, ch 15]

(3) A translation of "The Sorrows of Werther" fell into my hands at this period, and if I could have committed suicide without

killing myself, I should certainly have done so.

▶ [in *The Story of a Bad Boy*, ch 19]

❚ Alexander, Lloyd

(1) Most of us are called upon to perform tasks far beyond what we believe we can do. Our capabilities seldom match our aspirations, and we are often woefully unprepared. To this extent, we are all Assistant Pig-Keepers at heart.

▶ [in *The Book of Three*, author's note]

(2) In some cases . . . we learn more by looking for the answer to a question and not finding it than we do from learning the answer itself.

▶ [Dallben, in *The Book of Three*, ch 1]

(3) Once you have courage to look upon evil, seeing it for what it is and naming it by its true name, it is powerless against you, and you can destroy it.

▶ [Gwydion, in *The Book of Three*, ch 19]

(4) Be glad you are a cat! . . . Let me tell you about men: Wolves are gentler. Geese are wiser. Jackasses have better sense.

▶ [Stephanus, in *The Cat Who Wished to Be a Man*, ch 1]

(5) Everything is more confusing on an empty stomach.

▶ [Dr. Tudbelly, in *The Cat Who Wished to Be a Man*, ch 11]

(6) One thing you should know about tears: they're utterly useless.

▶ [Dr. Tudbelly, in *The Cat Who Wished to Be a Man*, ch 16]

(7) I put you into human shape. You made yourself into a human being.

▶ [Stephanus, in *The Cat Who Wished to Be a Man*, ch 19]

(8) Rich you will surely be. . . . On one condition: that you earn large sums of money.

▶ [fortune-teller, in *The Fortune-Tellers*]

(9) A man's life weighs more than glory, and a price paid in blood is a heavy reckoning.

▶ [Taran, in *The High King*, ch 3]

(10) It is harsh enough for each man to bear his own wound. But he who leads bears the wounds of all who follow him.

▶ [Llassar, in *The High King*, ch 9]

(11) Of wisdom there are as many patterns as a loom can weave.

▶ [Taliesin, in *The High King*, ch 10]

(12) Learning is not the same as wisdom.

▶ [Taliesin, in *The High King*, ch 10]

(13) Theo, by occupation, was a devil.

▶ [in *Westmark*, ch 1, first line]

(14) Men give up many things willingly: their fortunes, their loves, their dreams. Power, never. It must be taken.

▶ [in *Westmark*, ch 19]

(15) For those who don't expect miracles, but hope for them anyway.

▶ [in *The Wizard in the Tree*, Dedication]

(16) Even in my day, mortals had a deplorable tendency to mix appearance with fact. I should hate to tell you how many numbskulls put crowns on their heads—as if a metal hoop had anything to do with being a king.

▶ [Arbican, in *The Wizard in the Tree*, ch 1]

(17) A tree draws its strength from the roots of the earth. That's beyond the power of any enchanter.

▶ [Arbican, in *The Wizard in the Tree*, ch 1]

(18) Do you seriously think anything worthwhile can be had merely for the wishing?

▶ [Arbican, in *The Wizard in the Tree*, ch 1]

(19) Magic can't work miracles.

▶ [Arbican, in *The Wizard in the Tree*, ch 2]

(20) The world is all one place, life is life, whatever form it happens to be in.

▶ [Arbican, in *The Wizard in the Tree*, ch 4]

(21) You're [mortals are] so busy wishing for good fortune you don't have time to find it for yourselves.

▶ [Arbican, in *The Wizard in the Tree*, ch 4]

(22) I create illusions, I don't mistake them for the way things are.
> ▶ [Arbican, in *The Wizard in the Tree*, ch 7]

▌ Alger, Leclaire. *See* Nic Leodhas, Sorche

▌ Aliki [Brandenberg, Aliki]

(1) My friend Peter used to come watch the tadpoles. He called them Inkywiggles.
> ▶ [in *We Are Best Friends*]

▌ Allard, Harry

(1) I am your new teacher, Miss Viola Swamp.
> ▶ [in *Miss Nelson Is Missing*]

(2) "This isn't heaven," said Grandfather. "This is Cleveland."
> ▶ [in *The Stupids Die*]

▌ Alsop, Mary O'Hara. *See* O'Hara, Mary

▌ Andersen, Hans Christian

(1) But he [the emperor] doesn't have anything on!
> ▶ [child, in "The Emperor's New Clothes," in *The Complete Fairy Tales and Stories*]

(2) Grownups are always talking, but they are not always worth listening to.
> ▶ [in "The Ice Maiden," in *The Complete Fairy Tales and Stories*]

(3) What makes the poet unique is that he has a spiritual memory. He can retain his thoughts and his feelings until he has clarified them in words.
> ▶ [in "The Magic Galoshes," in *The Complete Fairy Tales and Stories*]

(4) Once upon a time there was a prince who wanted to marry a princess, but she would have to be a real one.
> ▶ [in "The Princess and the Pea," in *The Complete Fairy Tales and Stories*]

(5) On the bare bedstead she put a pea. On top of the pea she put twenty mattresses; and on top of the mattresses, twenty eiderdown quilts.
> ▶ [in "The Princess and the Pea," in *The Complete Fairy Tales and Stories*]

(6) God knows what was in that bed; but it was something hard, and I am black and blue all over.
> ▶ [princess, in "The Princess and the Pea," in *The Complete Fairy Tales and Stories*]

(7) Only a real princess could be so sensitive!
> ▶ [in "The Princess and the Pea," in *The Complete Fairy Tales and Stories*]

(8) You shall dance . . . dance in your red shoes until you become pale and thin. Dance till the skin on your face turns yellow and clings to your bones as if you were a skeleton. Dance you shall from door to door, and when you pass a house where proud and vain children live, there you shall knock on the door so that they will see you and fear your fate. Dance, you shall dance. . . . Dance!

▶ [angel, in "The Red Shoes," in *The Complete Fairy Tales and Stories*]

(9) They [the tin soldiers] were all exactly alike except one, who was different from the others because he was missing a leg. He had been the last one to be cast and there had not been enough tin. But he stood as firm and steadfast on his one leg as the others did on their two. He is the hero of our story.

▶ [in "The Steadfast Tin Soldier," in *The Complete Fairy Tales and Stories*]

(10) You get over it when your beloved has lain in a gutter and oozed for five years. You never recognize her when you meet her in the garbage bin.

▶ [in "The Sweethearts," in *The Complete Fairy Tales and Stories*]

(11) The Ugly Duckling

▶ [title of story, in *The Complete Fairy Tales and Stories*]

(12) It does not matter that one has been born in the henyard as long as one has lain in a swan's egg.

▶ [in "The Ugly Duckling," in *The Complete Fairy Tales and Stories*]

(13) Life is the best fairy tale of all.

▶ [in "What the Whole Family Said," in *The Complete Fairy Tales and Stories*]

❧ Archambault, John. *See* Martin, Bill, Jr.

❧ Avi [Wortis, Avi]

(1) People have a right to be losers.

▶ [Radosh, in *S. O. R. Losers*, ch 17]

(2) Not every thirteen-year-old girl is accused of murder, brought to trial, and found guilty.

▶ [in *The True Confessions of Charlotte Doyle*, "An Important Warning"]

(3) In *my* world, judgments as to rights and wrongs are left to my Creator, *not* to children.

▶ [Mr. Gummage, in *The True Confessions of Charlotte Doyle*, ch 1]

(4) One always needs a final friend. . . . Someone to sew the hammock.

▶ [Zachariah, in *The True Confessions of Charlotte Doyle*, ch 2]

(5) We shall have no democracy here. No parliaments. No congressmen. There's but one master on this ship, and that is me.

▶ [Captain Jaggery, in *The True Confessions of Charlotte Doyle*, ch 2]

(6) A sailor chooses the wind that takes the ship from a safe port. . . . Be careful . . . of the wind you choose.

> ▶ [Zachariah, in *The True Confessions of Charlotte Doyle*, ch 22]

❧ Babbitt, Natalie

(1) The sea can swallow ships, and it can spit out whales like watermelon seeds. It will take what it wants, and it will keep what it has taken, and you may not take away from it what it does not wish to give.

> ▶ [in *The Eyes of the Amaryllis*, Prologue]

(2) Is it better to be wise if it makes you solemn and practical, or is it better to be foolish so you can go on enjoying yourself?

> ▶ [Uncle Ott, in *Knee-Knock Rise*]

(3) The cat attacked a bit of string
And dragged it by the head
And tortured it beside the stove
And left it there for dead.

"Excuse me, sir," I murmured when
He passed me in the hall,
"But that was only string you had
And not a mouse at all!"

He didn't even thank me when
I told him he was wrong.
It's possible—just possible—
He knew it all along.

> ▶ [Uncle Ott, in *Knee-Knock Rise*]

(4) The woldwellers, who were admired by the people for their knowledge, stayed in their trees and came down to answer questions from time to time, but after a while they grew irritated by the foolishness of these questions and wouldn't always answer.

> ▶ [in *The Search for Delicious*, Prologue]

(5) A lot of serious things start silly.

> ▶ [Prime Minister, in *The Search for Delicious*]

(6) People are so foolish. They waste their time even though they have so little of it. We have forever and yet we never waste a moment.

> ▶ [dwarf, in *The Search for Delicious*]

(7) Today is the day tomorrow becomes and yesterday used to be.

> ▶ [Decry, the shepherd boy, in *The Search for Delicious*]

(8) Delicious is a drink of cool water when you're very, very thirsty.

> ▶ [Prime Minister, in *The Search for Delicious*]

(9) The first week of August hangs at the very top of summer, the top of the live-long year, like the highest seat of a Ferris wheel when it pauses in its turning.

> ▶ [in *Tuck Everlasting*, Prologue]

(10) That water—it stops you right where you are. If you'd had a drink of it today, you'd stay a little girl forever. You'd never grow up, not ever.

> ▶ [Mae Tuck, in *Tuck Everlasting*, ch 7]

(11) You can't have living without dying. So you can't call it living, what we got. We just *are*, we just *be*, like rocks beside the road.

▸ [Tuck, in *Tuck Everlasting*, ch 12]

❚ Bagnold, Enid

(1) Pity she's getting a sort of enemy. . . . It's because she's in love. . . . It just turns you. Like drink.

▸ [Velvet and Meredith, discussing Edwina, in *National Velvet*, ch 9]

(2) They're [horses are] simply born . . . to try to get to know what one person thinks. Their backs and their mouths are like ears and eyes. That's why those [livery] horses move like that and hang their heads down from the wither like a steep hill. . . . They've got broken hearts. . . . It's like seeing the dead go by.

▸ [Velvet, in *National Velvet*, ch 9]

(3) Almost as soon as the ambulance was off the ground little breezes began to blow hither and thither bearing the fact. Without the name. A girl had won the Grand National.

▸ [in *National Velvet*, ch 14]

(4) There may be wonder in money, but, dear God, there is money in wonder.

▸ [in *National Velvet*, ch 16]

(5) And now, finished with that puzzling mixture of insane intimacy and isolation which is notoriety,

Velvet was able to get on quietly to her next adventures. For obviously she was a person to whom things happened, since in a year she had become an heiress, got a horse for a shilling, and won the Grand National.

▸ [in *National Velvet*, ch 17]

❚ Bailey, Carolyn Sherwin

(1) Miss Hickory had difficulty in turning her head. It was a hickory nut that had grown with an especially sharp and pointed nose.

▸ [in *Miss Hickory*, ch 1]

(2) The tilt of her sharp little nose, her pursed mouth and her keen eyes were not those of a doll. You and I would have known Miss Hickory as the real person that she was.

▸ [in *Miss Hickory*, ch 1]

(3) Keep your sap running!

▸ [Crow, in *Miss Hickory*, ch 3]

(4) In like a lion, out like a lamb, as they say of March. But between you and me, it's in like a crow, out like a bluebird.

▸ [Crow, in *Miss Hickory*, ch 11]

(5) Up-boughs went headless, heedless, happy Miss Hickory.

▸ [in *Miss Hickory*, ch 14]

(6) As for Miss Hickory, who had been a scion all along without knowing it, she felt completely happy. She would never have

to do any hard thinking again. She had a permanent home at last and some day she would give Ann, who had recognized her, a big red apple.

▶ [in *Miss Hickory*, ch 14]

❚ Balian, Lorna

(1) There was this witch. . . . And all of her was little Except her nose. That was very BIG.

▶ [in *Humbug Witch*]

(2) And she took off her long, stringy, red hair.

▶ [in *Humbug Witch*]

❚ Banks, Lynne Reid.
See Reid Banks, Lynne

❚ Bannerman, Helen

(1) . . . a beautiful little red coat, and a pair of beautiful little blue trousers . . . a beautiful green umbrella, and a lovely little pair of purple shoes with crimson soles and crimson linings.

▶ [in *The Story of Little Babaji*]

(2) Now I'm the grandest tiger in the jungle.

▶ [in *The Story of Little Babaji*]

(3) [The tigers] were so angry that they ran round the tree, trying to eat each other up, and they ran faster and faster . . . till they

all just melted away, and there was nothing left but a great big pool of melted butter round the foot of the tree.

▶ [in *The Story of Little Babaji*]

❚ Barrett, Judi

(1) The only thing that was really different about Chewandswallow was its weather. It came three times a day, at breakfast, lunch, and dinner. Everything that everyone ate came from the sky.

▶ [in *Cloudy with a Chance of Meatballs*]

❚ Barrie, J. M.

(1) All children, except one, grow up.

▶ [in *Peter Pan*, ch 1]

(2) Her [Mrs. Darling's] sweet mocking mouth had one kiss on it that Wendy could never get, though there it was, perfectly conspicuous in the righthand corner.

▶ [in *Peter Pan*, ch 1]

(3) It is the nightly custom of every good mother after her children are asleep to rummage in their minds and put things straight for next morning.

▶ [in *Peter Pan*, ch 1]

(4) There were odd stories about him [Peter Pan]; as that when children died he went part of

the way with them, so that they should not be frightened.

▶ [in *Peter Pan*, ch 1]

(5) They [night-lights] are the eyes a mother leaves behind her to guard her children.

▶ [Mrs. Darling, in *Peter Pan*, ch 2]

(6) Stars are beautiful, but they may not take an active part in anything, they must just look on forever. It is a punishment put on them for something they did so long ago that no star now knows what it was.

▶ [in *Peter Pan*, ch 2]

(7) Boy, why are you crying?

▶ [Wendy, in *Peter Pan*, ch 3]

(8) You just think lovely thoughts . . . and they lift you up in the air.

▶ [Peter Pan, teaching the children how to fly, in *Peter Pan*, ch 3]

(9) Second to the right . . . and then straight on till morning.

▶ [Peter Pan, when Wendy asks where he lives, in *Peter Pan*, ch 3]

(In the Disney version this is changed to "second star to the right . . .")

---

(10) the Lost Boys

▶ [in *Peter Pan*, ch 3]

(11) When the first baby laughed for the first time, its laugh broke into a thousand pieces, and they all went skipping about, and that was the beginning of fairies.

▶ [Peter Pan, in *Peter Pan*, ch 3]

(12) Every time a child says, "I don't believe in fairies," there is a fairy somewhere that falls down dead.

▶ [Peter Pan, in *Peter Pan*, ch 3]

(13) Do you know . . . why swallows build in the eaves of houses? It is to listen to the stories.

▶ [Peter Pan, in *Peter Pan*, ch 3]

(14) That crocodile would have had me before this, but by a lucky chance it swallowed a clock which goes tick tock inside it, and so before it can reach me I hear the tick and bolt.

▶ [Captain Hook, in *Peter Pan*, ch 5]

(15) Make-believe was so real to [Peter] that during a meal of it you could see him getting rounder.

▶ [in *Peter Pan*, ch 7]

(16) All [a child] thinks he has a right to when he comes to you to be yours is fairness. After you have been unfair to him he will love you again, but will never afterwards be quite the same boy.

▶ [in *Peter Pan*, ch 8]

(17) To die will be an awfully big adventure.

▶ [Peter Pan, in *Peter Pan*, ch 8]

(18) Do you believe in fairies?

▶ [chapter title in *Peter Pan*, ch 13]

(19) She [Tinker Bell] thought she could get well again if children believed in fairies.

▶ [in *Peter Pan*, ch 13]

(20) If you believe . . . clap your hands; don't let Tink die.
▶ [Peter Pan, in *Peter Pan*, ch 13]

(21) It was the terrible tick-tock of the crocodile.
▶ [in *Peter Pan*, ch 14]

(22) I'm youth, I'm joy. . . . I'm a little bird that has broken out of the egg.
▶ [Peter Pan, in *Peter Pan*, ch 15]

(23) Keep back, lady, no one is going to catch me and make me a man.
▶ [Peter Pan, in *Peter Pan*, ch 17]

❚ Baum, L. Frank

(1) Dorothy lived in the midst of the great Kansas prairies, with Uncle Henry, who was a farmer, and Aunt Em, who was the farmer's wife.
▶ [in *The Wizard of Oz*, ch 1]

(2) There's a cyclone coming, Em.
▶ [Henry, in *The Wizard of Oz*, ch 1]

(3) The road to the City of Emeralds is paved with yellow brick.
▶ [Witch of the North, in *The Wizard of Oz*, ch 2]

___

(The exact phrase "yellow brick road" does not appear in the book.)

___

(4) My name is Dorothy . . . and I am going to the Emerald City, to ask the great Oz to send me back to Kansas.
▶ [Dorothy, in *The Wizard of Oz*, ch 3]

(5) There is no place like home.
▶ [Dorothy, in *The Wizard of Oz*, ch 4]

(6) If your heads were stuffed with straw, like mine, you would all live in the beautiful places, and then Kansas would have no people at all.
▶ [Scarecrow, in *The Wizard of Oz*, ch 4]

(7) I shall ask for brains instead of a heart; for a fool would not know what to do with a heart if he had one.
▶ [Scarecrow, in *The Wizard of Oz*, ch 5]

(8) I shall take the heart, . . . for brains do not make one happy, and happiness is the best thing in the world.
▶ [Tin Woodman, in *The Wizard of Oz*, ch 5]

(9) "I am Oz, the Great and Terrible. Who are you and why do you seek me?" . . . "I am Dorothy, the Small and Meek. I have come to you for help."
▶ [in *The Wizard of Oz*, ch 11]

(10) I'm really a very good man; but I'm a very bad Wizard.
▶ [Oz, in *The Wizard of Oz*, ch 15]

(11) True courage is facing danger when you are afraid.
▶ [Oz, in *The Wizard of Oz*, ch 15]

(12) I think you are wrong to want a heart. It makes most people unhappy.
▶ [Oz, in *The Wizard of Oz*, ch 15]

(13) All you have to do is knock the heels together three times and command the shoes to carry you wherever you wish to go.

▶ [Glinda, in *The Wizard of Oz*, ch 23]

(14) The Wicked Witch of the West

▶ [in *The Wizard of Oz*, throughout]

(15) Cowardly Lion

▶ [in *The Wizard of Oz*, throughout]

(16) Munchkins

▶ [in *The Wizard of Oz*, throughout]

(Note: Many of the famous Wizard of Oz quotes are from the movie, not the book.)

◣ Baylor, Byrd

(1) The way to start a day is this—
Go outside and face the east and greet the sun with some kind of blessing or chant or song that you made yourself and keep for early morning.

▶ [in *The Way to Start a Day*]

(2) Some people say there is a new sun every day, that it begins its life at dawn and lives for one day only.

▶ [in *The Way to Start a Day*]

◣ Belloc, Hilaire

(1) As a friend to the children commend me the yak.

▶ [in "The Yak," in *The Bad Child's Book of Beasts*]

(2) Then tell your papa where the Yak can be got,
And if he is awfully rich
He will buy you the creature—
or else he will *not*.
(I cannot be positive which.)

▶ [in "The Yak," in *The Bad Child's Book of Beasts*]

(3) I shoot the Hippopotamus
with bullets made of platinum,
Because if I use leaden ones
his hide is sure to flatten 'em.

▶ [in "The Hippopotamus," in *The Bad Child's Book of Beasts*]

(4) Be kind and tender to the Frog

▶ [in "The Frog," in *The Bad Child's Book of Beasts*]

(5) No animal will more repay
A treatment kind and fair;
At least so lonely people say
Who keep a Frog (and, by the way,
They are extremely rare).

▶ [in "The Frog," in *The Bad Child's Book of Beasts*]

(6) Decisive action in the hour of need
Denotes the Hero, but does not succeed.

▶ [in *A Moral Alphabet*]

(7) If you were born to walk the ground,
Remain there; do not fool around.

▶ [in *A Moral Alphabet*]

(8) The law protects you. Go your gentle way:
The Other Man has always got to Pay.

▶ [in *A Moral Alphabet*]

(9) The waterbeetle here shall teach
A sermon far beyond your reach;
He flabbergasts the Human Race
By gliding on the water's face
With ease, celerity, and grace;
But if he ever stopped to think
Of how he did it, he would sink.

▶ [in *A Moral Alphabet*]

(10) Whereas the Indian Elephant
Will only read *The Times.*

▶ [in *More Beasts for Worse Children*, Introduction]

(11) A python I should not advise,—
It needs a doctor for its eyes,
And has the measles yearly.

▶ [in "The Python," in *More Beasts for Worse Children*]

(12) She died, because she never knew
These simple little rules and few;—
The Snake is living yet.

▶ [in "The Python," in *More Beasts for Worse Children*]

(13) The Vulture eats between his meals,
And that's the reason why
He very, very rarely feels
As well as you and I.

▶ [in "The Vulture," in *More Beasts for Worse Children*]

(14) Oh! let us never, never doubt
What nobody is sure about!

▶ [in "The Microbe," in *More Beasts for Worse Children*]

◣ Bemelmans, Ludwig

(1) In an old house in Paris
that was covered with vines
lived twelve little girls in two
    straight lines.
They left the house at half past
    nine.
The smallest one was Madeline.

▶ [in *Madeline, Madeline's Rescue, Madeline and the Bad Hat, Madeline in London, Madeline and the Gypsies*]

(2) To the tiger in the zoo
Madeline just said, "Pooh-pooh."

▶ [in *Madeline, Madeline's Rescue*]

(3) And nobody knew so well
How to frighten Miss Clavel.

▶ [in *Madeline, Madeline's Rescue*]

◣ Berenstain, Jan and Stan

(1) Down Spook Hill
Through the woods
Between the rocks
Around the lake
Under the bridge
Over the wall
Up the tree . . . In the window!
Back in bed.

▶ [in *Bears in the Night*]

(2) This is what you must never do.
Now let this be a lesson to you.

▶ [in *The Bike Lesson*]

❧ Blake, Quentin

(1) "What this bike needs," said Mrs. Armitage to herself.
   ▸ [in *Mrs. Armitage on Wheels*]

❧ Blos, Joan W.

(1) Once I might have wished for that: never to grow old. But now I know that to stay young always is also not to change. And that is what life's all about—changes going on every minute, and you never know when something begins where it's going to take you.
   ▸ [Catherine Hall Onesti, in *A Gathering of Days*, Prologue]

(2) Like charity, stealing begins at home.
   ▸ [Mr. Shipman, in *A Gathering of Days*, ch 4]

(3) Kindness must be the highest virtue.
   ▸ [Cassie Shipman, in *A Gathering of Days*, ch 4]

(4) They are wrong . . . about the swallows and Spring. It is *exactly* one of them that creates a season! Take a whole flock, overwhelming a meadow, and that is merely a lot of birds—and a good grain plundered besides!
   ▸ [Mammann, in *A Gathering of Days*, ch 13]

(5) She lived among us for a while And brought joy where she went. We thought she was a gift from God But learned she was but lent.
   ▸ [Cassie's epitaph, in *A Gathering of Days*, ch 15]

(6) O, I do think, as has been said, that if getting in the corn and potatoes are the prose of a farm child's life, then nutting's the poetry!
   ▸ [Catherine Cabot Hall, in *A Gathering of Days*, ch 17]

(7) Life is like a pudding: it takes both the salt and the sugar to make a really good one.
   ▸ [Catherine Hall Onesti, in *A Gathering of Days*, Epilogue]

❧ Blume, Judy

(1) Don't let New Jersey be too horrible.
   ▸ [Margaret, in *Are You There God? It's Me, Margaret*, ch 1]

(2) We must—we must—we must increase our bust!
   ▸ [Margaret, Nancy, Gretchen, Janie, in *Are You There God? It's Me, Margaret*, ch 7]

(3) I've been looking for you God. I looked in temple. I looked in church. And today, I looked for

you when I wanted to confess. But you weren't there. . . . Why do I only feel you when I'm alone?

▸ [Margaret, in *Are You There God? It's Me, Margaret*, ch 19]

(4) Andrew Marcus wanted freckles. . . . If he had freckles like Nicky, his mother would never know if his neck was dirty. So he wouldn't have to wash.

▸ [in *Freckle Juice*]

(5) Sharon's secret recipe for Freckle Juice:

One glass makes an average amount of freckles. To get like Nicky Lane drink two glasses.

Mix up all these things together—stir well and drink fast.

Grape juice, vinegar, mustard, mayonnaise, juice from one lemon, pepper and salt, ketchup, olive oil, and a speck of onion

P. S. The faster you drink it the faster you get F.R.E.C.K.L.E.S.

▸ [in *Freckle Juice*]

(6) I felt . . . scared about what school would be like here. Maybe all the kids would hate me. Maybe I'd hate them. Maybe we'd hate each other. Maybe I'd get a dumb teacher.

▸ [Peter, in *Superfudge*, ch 6]

(7) I'm really into violence. . . . I think hockey's a great game. It's a lot bloodier than football, and there are more team fights.

▸ [Jimmy Fargo, in *Superfudge*, ch 11]

❧ Bond, Michael

(1) WANTED ON VOYAGE

▸ [on Paddington's suitcase, in *A Bear Called Paddington*, ch 1]

(2) Please look after this bear. Thank you.

▸ [label around Paddington's neck, in *A Bear Called Paddington*, ch 1]

(3) Bears is sixpence extra. . . . Sticky bears is ninepence!

▸ [taxi driver, in *A Bear Called Paddington*, ch 1]

(4) I was brought up in Darkest Peru. By my Aunt Lucy. She's the one that lives in a home for retired bears in Lima.

▸ [Paddington, in *A Bear Called Paddington*, ch 2]

(5) Bears always land on their feet.

▸ [Mrs. Bird, in *A Bear Called Paddington*, ch 7]

❧ Bornstein, Ruth

(1) One day a bunny said, Good-by, I'm going to be an Indian.

▸ [in *Indian Bunny*]

(2) Little Gorilla was BIG!

And everybody came and everybody sang "Happy birthday Little Gorilla!"

And everybody still loved him.

▸ [in *Little Gorilla*]

❧ Borton, Elizabeth. *See* Treviño, Elizabeth Borton de

❧ Boston, Lucy Maria

(1) Snippet snappet
Shapen yew
Devil's image
Take on you.
Evil grow,
Evil be,
Green Noah
Demon Tree.
▸ [the curse of Green Noah, in *The Children of Green Knowe* "Alexander's Story"]

❧ Brandenberg, Aliki. *See* Aliki

❧ Bragg, Mabel Caroline. *See* Piper, Watty

❧ Bright, Robert

(1) Every night at the same time [Georgie] gave the loose board on the stairs a little creak. And the parlor door a little squeak. And then Mr. and Mrs. Whittaker knew it was time to go to bed.
▸ [in *Georgie*]

❧ Brink, Carol Ryrie

(1) What a lot has happened since last year.... How far I've come! I'm the same girl and yet not the same. I wonder if it's always like that? Folks keep growing from one person into another all their lives, and life is just a lot of everyday adventures. Well, whatever life is, I like it.
▸ [Caddie, in *Caddie Woodlawn*, ch 24]

❧ Brittain, Bill

(1) Here in Coven Tree we're no strangers to magic. I'm not talking about the rabbit-from-the-hat or coin-up-the-sleeve variety, either. I mean *real* magic.
▸ [in *The Wish Giver*, ch 1]

❧ Brooke, L. Leslie

(1) Johnny Crow
Would dig and sow
Till he made a little garden
And the Lion
Had a green and yellow Tie on
In Johnny Crow's garden.
▸ [in *Johnny Crow's Garden*]

❧ Brooks, Bruce

(1) How do you think you *feel* when you dead? Pretty bad, I reckon—near as low as you can get. Think about it. No more

breathing fresh air. No more eating salted cashews. No more sweating.

▶ [Dooley, in *Everywhere*, ch 1]

(2) Every person has a kind of animal they got their soul mixed up with way back when the world was made.

▶ [Dooley, in *Everywhere*, ch 1]

(3) All you get by giving stuff up is The Big Nothing.

▶ [Rex, in *Vanishing*, ch 15]

❧ Brown, Margaret Wise

(1) In the great green room
There was a telephone
And a red balloon
And a picture of—
The cow jumping over the moon

▶ [in *Goodnight Moon*]

(2) And a quiet old lady who was whispering "hush"

▶ [in *Goodnight Moon*]

(3) Goodnight stars
Goodnight air
Goodnight noises everywhere

▶ [in *Goodnight Moon*]

(4) There was a little fur family
warm as toast
smaller than most
in little fur coats
and they lived in a warm
wooden tree.

▶ [in *Little Fur Family*]

(5) Sleep, sleep, my little fur child,
Out of the windiness,
Out of the wild.
Sleep warm in your fur
All night long,
In your little fur family.
This is a song.

▶ [in *Little Fur Family*]

(6) Could Muffin hear that?

▶ [in *The Noisy Book*]

(7) Once there was a bunny who wanted to run away. So he said to his mother, "I am running away." "If you run away," said his mother, "I will run after you. For you are my little bunny."

▶ [in *The Runaway Bunny*]

(8) Born at sea in the teeth of a gale, the sailor was a dog. Scuppers was his name.

▶ [in *The Sailor Dog*]

❧ Brunhoff, Jean de

(1) In the great forest a little elephant is born. His name is Babar.

▶ [in *The Story of Babar, the Little Elephant*]

(2) BABAR THEN BUYS HIMSELF:
a shirt with a collar and tie, a suit of a becoming shade of green, then a handsome derby hat, and also shoes with spats.

▶ [in *The Story of Babar, the Little Elephant*]

❧ Burgess, Gelett

(1) *Are you a Goop, or are you Not?*
For, although it's Fun to See
them,
It is TERRIBLE to Be them.

▸ [in *Goops and How to Be Them*]

(2) Table Manners—1
The Goops they lick their fingers,
And the Goops they lick their
knives,
They spill their broth on the
tablecloth—
Oh, they lead disgusting lives!
The Goops they talk while eating,
And loud and fast they chew;
And that is why I'm glad that I
Am not a Goop—are you?

▸ [in *Goops and How to Be Them*]

❧ Burnett, Frances Hodgson

(1) I should rather not be an earl.
None of the boys are earls. Can't
I *not* be one?

▸ [Cedric, Lord Fauntleroy, in *Little Lord Fauntleroy*, ch 2]

(2) She [his mother] said that perhaps it was not so easy to be
rich; that if anyone had so many
things always, one might sometimes forget that everyone else
was not so fortunate.

▸ [Cedric, in *Little Lord Fauntleroy*, ch 9]

(3) [Cedric] was always lovable because he was simple and loving.
To be so is like being born a king.

▸ [in *Little Lord Fauntleroy*, ch 15]

(4) Once on a dark winter's day,
when the yellow fog hung so
thick and heavy in the streets of
London that the lamps were
lighted and the shop windows
blazed with gas as they do at
night, an odd-looking little girl
sat in a cab with her father and
was driven rather slowly through
the big thoroughfares.

▸ [in *The Little Princess*, ch 1]

(5) Miss Minchin, Select Seminary
for Young Ladies

▸ [in *The Little Princess*, ch 1; also
in *Sara Crewe*]

(6) But then I dare say soldiers—
even brave ones—don't really
like going into battle.

▸ [Sara, in *The Little Princess*, ch 1]

(7) What I believe about dolls . . . is
that they can do things they will
not let us know about. Perhaps,
really, Emily can read and talk
and walk, but she will only do it
when people are out of the room.
That is her secret. You see, if
people knew that dolls could do
things, they would make them
work.

▸ [Sara, in *The Little Princess*, ch 2]

(8) Never did she find anything so
difficult as to keep herself from
losing her temper when she was
suddenly disturbed while ab-
sorbed in a book. . . . "It makes
me feel as if someone had hit
me," Sara told Ermengarde.

▸ [in *The Little Princess*, ch 6]

(9) How it is that animals understand things I do not know, but

it is certain that they do understand. Perhaps there is a language which is not made up of words and everything in the world understands it. Perhaps there is a soul hidden in everything and it can always speak, without even making a sound, to another soul.

▶ [in *The Little Princess*, ch 9]

(10) He's [Colin's] been spoiled till salt won't save him.

▶ [Martha, in *The Secret Garden*, ch 18]

(11) Magic is in everything, only we have not sense enough to get hold of it and make it do things for us—like electricity and horses and steam.

▶ [Colin, in *The Secret Garden*, ch 23]

(12) When Mary found this garden it looked quite dead. . . . Then something began pushing things up out of the soil and making things out of nothing. One day things weren't there and another they were. I had never watched things before and it made me feel very curious. Scientific people are always curious and I am going to be scientific. I keep saying to myself. "What is it? What is it?" It's something. It can't be nothing! I don't know its name so I call it Magic.

▶ [Colin, in *The Secret Garden*, ch 23]

(13) The sun is shining—the sun is shining. That is the Magic. The flowers are growing—the roots are stirring. That is the Magic.

Being alive is the Magic—being strong is the Magic. The Magic is in me—the Magic is in me. It is in me—it is in me. It's in every one of us.

▶ [Colin, in *The Secret Garden*, ch 23]

(14) To let a sad thought or a bad one get into your mind is as dangerous as letting a scarlet fever germ get into your body. If you let it stay there after it has got in you may never get over it as long as you live.

▶ [in *The Secret Garden*, ch 27]

(15) With his head up in the air and his eyes full of laughter walked as strongly and steadily as any boy in Yorkshire—Master Colin.

▶ [in *The Secret Garden*, ch 27]

▌ Burton, Virginia Lee

(1) Everyone and everything was stopped . . .
but . . . .
KATY
    The city of Geoppolis was covered with a thick blanket of snow.

▶ [in *Katy and the Big Snow*]

(2) She [the Little House] couldn't be sold for gold or silver, so she just stayed there and waited.

▶ [in *The Little House*]

(3) That Little House looks just like the Little House my grandmother lived in when she was a little girl, only *that* Little House

was way out in the country on a hill covered with daisies and apple trees growing around.

▶ [great-great-granddaughter, in *The Little House*]

(4) Mike Mulligan had a steam shovel, a beautiful red steam shovel. Her name was Mary Anne. Mike Mulligan was very proud of Mary Anne. He always said that she could dig as much in a day as a hundred men could dig in a week, but he had never been quite sure that this was true.

▶ [in *Mike Mulligan and His Steam Shovel*]

(5) We've dug so fast and we've dug so well that we've quite forgotten to leave a way out!

▶ [Mike Mulligan, in *Mike Mulligan and His Steam Shovel*]

(6) Let her be the furnace for the new town hall and let Mike Mulligan be the janitor.

▶ [little boy, in *Mike Mulligan and His Steam Shovel*]

◣ Butterworth, Oliver

(1) But you know how it is when you're doing something that's your own idea. You just can't back down and let people say I told you so.

▶ [in *The Enormous Egg*, ch 1]

(2) We always wear bathrobes when our dinosaurs hatch.

▶ [Pop, in *The Enormous Egg*, ch 5]

(3) I guess [people] don't get excited about a thing until somebody starts taking it away from them. Then they wake up and fight for it. It's like fishing, isn't it? Sometimes you don't get a bite until you start to take in the line.

▶ [Dr. Ziemer, in *The Enormous Egg*, ch 16]

◣ Byars, Betsy

(1) When I type a title page, I hold it and I look at it and I think, I just need four thousand sentences to go with this and I'll have a book!

▶ [in *The Moon and I*, ch 5]

(2) The words *author* and *authority* go hand in hand.

▶ [in *The Moon and I*, ch 6]

(3) Writing is like anything—baseball playing, piano playing, sewing, hammering nails. The more you work on it, the better you get. But it seems to take a longer time to get better at writing than hammering nails.

▶ [in *The Moon and I*, ch 16]

(4) The real reason I had wanted to grow up, the main reason I had been willing to even consider becoming an adult, was so I could have as many pets as I wanted.

▶ [in *The Moon and I*, ch 17]

(5) I think how you look is the most important thing in the world. If you *look* cute, you *are* cute; if you *look* smart, you *are* smart,

and if you don't look like anything, then you aren't anything.

▶ [Sara, in *The Summer of the Swans*, ch 5]

▌Caldecott, Randolph

(1) . . . and they all fell to playing the game of catch-as-catch-can, till the gunpowder ran out at the heels of their boots.

▶ [in "The Great Panjandrum Himself," in *The Panjandrum Picture Book*]

▌Carle, Eric

(1) The spider didn't answer. She was very busy spinning her web.

▶ [in *The Very Busy Spider*]

(2) Pop!—out of the egg came a tiny and very hungry caterpillar.

▶ [in *The Very Hungry Caterpillar*]

(3) But he was still hungry.

▶ [in *The Very Hungry Caterpillar*]

▌Carroll, Lewis [pseud. of Charles Lutwidge Dodgson]

(1) Down the Rabbit-Hole

▶ [chapter title, in *Alice's Adventures in Wonderland*, ch 1]

(2) "And what is the use of a book," thought Alice, "without pictures or conversations?"

▶ [in *Alice's Adventures in Wonderland*, ch 1]

(3) If you drink much from a bottle marked "poison," it is almost certain to disagree with you, sooner or later.

▶ [in *Alice's Adventures in Wonderland*, ch 1]

(4) Curiouser and curiouser!

▶ [Alice, in *Alice's Adventures in Wonderland*, ch 2]

(5) One side will make you grow taller, and the other side will make you grow shorter.

▶ [the caterpillar, in *Alice's Adventures in Wonderland*, ch 5]

(6) "Would you tell me, please, which way I ought to go from here?"

"That depends a good deal on where you want to get to," said the Cat.

"I don't much care where—" said Alice.

"Then it doesn't much matter which way you go," said the Cat.

▶ [in *Alice's Adventures in Wonderland*, ch 6]

(7) A dog growls when it's angry, and wags its tail when it's pleased. Now I growl when I'm pleased, and wag my tail when I'm angry. Therefore I'm mad.

▶ [Cheshire Cat, in *Alice's Adventures in Wonderland*, ch 6]

(8) This time [the Cheshire Cat] vanished quite slowly, beginning with the end of the tail, and ending with the grin, which

remained some time after the rest of it had gone.

> ▶ [in *Alice's Adventures in Wonderland*, ch 6]

(9) "I've often seen a cat without a grin," thought Alice; "but a grin without a cat!"

> ▶ [in *Alice's Adventures in Wonderland*, ch 6]

(10) Why is a raven like a writing desk?

> ▶ [the Mad Hatter, in *Alice's Adventures in Wonderland*, ch 7]

(11) "Then you should say what you mean," the March Hare went on.

"I do," Alice hastily replied; "at least—at least I mean what I say—that's the same thing, you know."

"Not the same thing a bit!" said the Hatter. "Why, you might just as well say that 'I see what I eat' is the same thing as 'I eat what I see'!"

> ▶ [in *Alice's Adventures in Wonderland*, ch 7]

(12) Twinkle, twinkle, little bat!
How I wonder what you're at!
Up above the world you fly,
Like a tea-tray in the sky.

> ▶ [the Mad Hatter, in *Alice's Adventures in Wonderland*, ch 7]

(13) "I've had nothing yet," Alice replied in an offended tone: "so I can't take more."

"You mean you can't take *less*," said the Hatter: "it's very easy to take *more* than nothing."

> ▶ [in *Alice's Adventures in Wonderland*, ch 7]

(14) Off with her head!
Off with their heads!

> ▶ [the Queen of Hearts, in *Alice's Adventures in Wonderland*, ch 8]

(15) [The croquet-ground] was all ridges and furrows; the croquet balls were live hedgehogs, and the mallets live flamingoes.

> ▶ [in *Alice's Adventures in Wonderland*, ch 8]

(16) "That's the reason they're called lessons," the Gryphon remarked: "because they lessen from day to day."

> ▶ [in *Alice's Adventures in Wonderland*, ch 9]

(17) "Will you walk a little faster?"
said a whiting to a snail.
"There's a porpoise close
behind us, and he's treading
on my tail."

> ▶ [in the Mock Turtle's song, in *Alice's Adventures in Wonderland*, ch 10]

(18) Will you, won't you, will you, won't you, will you join the dance?

> ▶ [in the Mock Turtle's song, in *Alice's Adventures in Wonderland*, ch 10]

(19) Then turn not pale, beloved snail, but come and join the dance.

> ▶ [in the Mock Turtle's song, in *Alice's Adventures in Wonderland*, ch 10]

(20) 'Tis the voice of the Lobster: I
heard him declare
"You have baked me too
brown, I must sugar my hair."

> ▶ [in *Alice's Adventures in Wonderland*, ch 10]

(21) Begin at the beginning, . . . and go on till you come to the end: then stop.

 ▶ [the King of Hearts, in *Alice's Adventures in Wonderland*, ch 12]

(22) Sentence first—verdict afterwards.

 ▶ [the Queen of Hearts, in *Alice's Adventures in Wonderland*, ch 12]

(23) 'Twas brillig, and the slithy toves
Did gyre and gimble in the wabe:
All mimsy were the borogoves,
And the mome raths outgrabe.

 ▶ [in "Jabberwocky," in *Through the Looking-Glass*, ch 1]

(24) Now, *here,* you see, it takes all the running *you* can do, to keep in the same place. If you want to get somewhere else, you must run at least twice as fast as that.

 ▶ [the Red Queen, in *Through the Looking-Glass*, ch 2]

(25) "What's the use of their having names," the Gnat said, "if they won't answer to them?"

 "No use to *them*," said Alice; "but it's useful to the people that name them, I suppose."

 ▶ [in *Through the Looking-Glass*, ch 3]

(26) If it was so, it might be; and if it were so, it would be; but as it isn't, it ain't. That's logic.

 ▶ [Tweedledee, in *Through the Looking-Glass*, ch 4]

(27) "The time has come," the Walrus said, "To talk of many things:
Of shoes—and ships—and sealing-wax—
Of cabbages—and kings"

 ▶ [in "The Walrus and the Carpenter," recited by Tweedledee, in *Through the Looking-Glass*, ch 4]

(28) You're only a sort of a thing in his [Red King's] dream!

 ▶ [Tweedledee, in *Through the Looking-Glass*, ch 4]

(29) The rule is, jam to-morrow and jam yesterday—but never jam *to-day*.

 ▶ [the White Queen, in *Through the Looking-Glass*, ch 5]

(30) It's a poor sort of memory that only works backwards.

 ▶ [the White Queen, in *Through the Looking-Glass*, ch 5]

(31) "I can't believe *that!*" said Alice.

 "Can't you?" the Queen said in a pitying tone. "Try again: draw a long breath, and shut your eyes."

 Alice laughed. "There's no use trying," she said: "one *can't* believe impossible things."

 "I daresay you haven't had much practice," said the Queen. "When I was your age, I always did it for half-an-hour a day. Why, sometimes I've believed as many as six impossible things before breakfast."

 ▶ [in *Through the Looking-Glass*, ch 5]

(32) They gave it me—for an unbirthday present.

 ▶ [Humpty Dumpty, in *Through the Looking-Glass*, ch 6]

(33) When I use a word, . . . it means just what I choose it to mean—neither more nor less.

 ▶ [Humpty Dumpty, in *Through the Looking-Glass*, ch 6]

(34) "The question is," said Alice, "whether you *can* make words mean so many different things."

"The question is," said Humpty Dumpty, "which is to be master—that's all."

▶ [in *Through the Looking-Glass*, ch 6]

(35) It's as large as life, and twice as natural!

▶ [Haigha, in *Through the Looking-Glass*, ch 7]

❧ Christiansen, C. B.

(1) On a journey without a suitcase, where do you carry your most precious belongings?

▶ [Bitte, in *I See the Moon*, ch 6]

❧ Ciardi, John

(1) My dear, let me tell you about the shark.
Though his eyes are bright, his thought is dark. . . .
He has only one but he thinks it a lot.
And the thought he thinks but can never complete
Is his long dark thought of something to eat.

▶ [in "The Shark," in *Fast & Slow*]

(2) Whatever way a thing is done
Is wrong, as I hope you know.
For that is the rule of One times One.
It's the way things always go.

▶ [in "Rules," in *Someone Could Win a Polar Bear*]

(3) . . . the ancient rule of Two times Two,
Which is: *First, do it over.*

▶ [in "Rules," in *Someone Could Win a Polar Bear*]

(4) *Don't be right till it's time to be.*
That is the rule of Four times Four.

▶ [in "Rules," in *Someone Could Win a Polar Bear*]

(5) You'll have to learn sometime, my dear,
That what is true may not be clear
While what is clear may not be true
And you'll be wiser when you do.

▶ [in "The Lesson," in *Someone Could Win a Polar Bear*]

(6) To a river most things are the same.

▶ [in "About Rivers and Toes," in *Someone Could Win a Polar Bear*]

(7) For centuries he [the buffalo] ran and ran
Across the golden plain.
He ran so fast that he began
Not to come back again.

▶ [in "The Buffalo," in *Someone Could Win a Polar Bear*]

❧ Cleary, Beverly

(1) Beatrice Quimby's biggest problem was her little sister Ramona.

▶ [in *Beezus and Ramona*, ch 1]

(2) Probably nobody else in the whole world had a little sister who had spoiled two birthday cakes on the same day.

▸ [in *Beezus and Ramona*, ch 6]

(3) Ha-ha, Ramona, this is one of those times when I don't have to love you.

▸ [Beezus, in *Beezus and Ramona*, ch 6]

(4) It's not really his truck he is in love with. He loves the feel of power when he is sitting high in his cab controlling a mighty machine. He loves the excitement of never knowing where his next trip will take him. He loves the mountains and the desert sunrises and the sight of orange trees heavy with oranges and the smell of fresh-mown alfalfa.

▸ [Leigh's mother, in *Dear Mr. Henshaw*, Jan. 30]

(5) When school started in September, girls discovered that boys, awful in the sixth grade, had become terrible in the seventh grade.

▸ [in *A Girl from Yamhill*, "The Platoon System"]

(6) All my life, Mother had told me to use my imagination, but I had never expected to be asked, or even allowed, to use it in school.

▸ [in *A Girl from Yamhill*, "The Platoon System"]

(7) [Ralph] picked up his tail, took a deep breath, bent low over the handlebars, flattened his ears, and sped down the straightaway as fast as the motorcycle would go. He could feel his whiskers swept back by the force of his speed. It was glorious!

▸ [in *The Mouse and the Motorcycle*, ch 5]

(8) Grown-ups often forget that no child likes to be ordered to be nice to another child.

▸ [in *Ramona Quimby, Age 8*, ch 2]

(9) Ramona . . . took a firm hold on her egg, waited until everyone at her table was watching, and *whack*—she found herself with a handful of crumbled shell and something cool and slimy running down her face.

. . . Ramona needed a moment to realize what had happened. Her egg was raw. Her mother had not boiled her egg at all.

▸ [in *Ramona Quimby, Age 8*, ch 3]

(10) Deep down inside, [Ramona] felt she herself was nice all the time, but sometimes on the outside her niceness sort of—well, curdled. Then people did not understand how nice she really was. Maybe other people curdled too.

▸ [in *Ramona Quimby, Age 8*, ch 9]

(11) [Ramona] was a member of a nice sticking-together family, and she was old enough to be depended upon, so she could ignore—or at least try to ignore—a lot of things. . . . Ramona could get along.

▸ [in *Ramona Quimby, Age 8*, ch 9]

(12) Henry Huggins' dog Ribsy was a plain ordinary city dog, the kind of dog that strangers usually called Mutt or Pooch.
  ▶ [in *Ribsy*, ch 1, first line]

(13) Where would the world be without nagging mothers? Everything would go to pieces.
  ▶ [Leigh's mother, in *Strider*, June 6]

(14) Today I discovered two kinds of people go to high school: those who wear new clothes to show off on the first day, and those who wear their oldest clothes to show they think school is unimportant.
  ▶ [in *Strider*, Sept. 12]

(15) Doing what is expected of me without complaining is a sign of maturity.
  ▶ [in *Strider*, Sept. 24]

(16) Problem solving, and I don't mean algebra, seems to be my life's work. Maybe it's everyone's life's work.
  ▶ [in *Strider*, March 2]

\ Cleaver, Vera and Bill

(1) Charity is seldom of real service to those upon whom it is bestowed and those who receive it are always looked upon with suspicion, every need and want scrutinized.
  ▶ [Roy Luther, in *Where the Lilies Bloom*, ch 1]

(2) You don't thank people who set you in bondage and hold you there year after wretched year. . . . Do something. Do anything. But don't just stand there and let people beat on you and then thank them for doing it.
  ▶ [in *Where the Lilies Bloom*, ch 1]

(3) Freedom—the wondrous glory in it and its awful anxiety.
  ▶ [in *Where the Lilies Bloom*, ch 4]

(4) Spring is a wondrous necessity.
  ▶ [Mary Call, in *Where the Lilies Bloom*, ch 15]

\ Coatsworth, Elizabeth

(1) The great Buddha, the Buddha whom he had painted reclining with hands folded upon his breast, had stretched out an arm in blessing, and under the holy hand knelt the figure of a tiny cat, with pretty white head bowed in happy adoration.
  ▶ [in *The Cat Who Went to Heaven*]

\ Coerr, Eleanor

(1) Don't you remember that old story about the crane? It's supposed to live for a thousand years. If a sick person folds one thousand paper cranes, the gods will grant her wish and make her healthy again.
  ▶ [Chizuko, in *Sadako and the Thousand Paper Cranes*, ch 5]

▌Cohen, Barbara

(1) Molly's mother *is* a pilgrim. She's a modern pilgrim. She came here, just like the Pilgrims long ago, so she could worship God in her own way, in peace and freedom.
   ▶ [Molly's teacher, Miss Stickley, in *Molly's Pilgrim*]

(2) I decided it takes all kinds of Pilgrims to make a Thanksgiving.
   ▶ [Molly, in *Molly's Pilgrim*]

▌Cohen, Miriam

(1) "I waited all my life," said Jim. "Now I can read."
   ▶ [in *When Will I Read?*]

▌Cole, Brock

(1) We all hate what we create.
   ▶ [Celine, in *Celine*, ch 1]

(2) I must be in love. . . . In love, or possessed by cartoon characters.
   ▶ [Celine, in *Celine*, ch 3]

(3) I could do that, but I wouldn't.
   ▶ [Jake, looking at modern art, in *Celine*, ch 11]

▌Cole, Joanna

(1) Our class really has bad luck. This year, we got Ms. Frizzle, the strangest teacher in school.
   ▶ [in *The Magic School Bus at the Waterworks*]

(2) After all, with a teacher like Ms. Frizzle, *anything* can happen.
   ▶ [in *The Magic School Bus at the Waterworks*]

▌Collier, James Lincoln and Christopher

(1) In my house *I* will decide what constitutes treason.
   ▶ [Mr. Meeker, in *My Brother Sam Is Dead*, ch 1]

(2) You may know principle, Sam, but I know war.
   ▶ [Mr. Meeker, in *My Brother Sam Is Dead*, ch 1]

(3) What kept confusing me about it was that the argument [about war] didn't have two sides the way an argument should, but about six sides.
   ▶ [Timmy, in *My Brother Sam Is Dead*, ch 2]

(4) What's the use of principles if you have to be dead to keep them?
   ▶ [Mr. Meeker, in *My Brother Sam Is Dead*, ch 2]

(5) Well they can stop dying. . . . I don't need anybody's death.
   ▶ [Mother, when told people are dying for her sake, in *My Brother Sam Is Dead*, ch 11]

(6) And now I go to enjoy the freedom war has brought me.
   ▶ [Mr. Meeker, when dying, in *My Brother Sam Is Dead*, ch 12]

(7) In war the dead pay the debts for the living.

  ▸ [Mr. Meeker, in *My Brother Sam Is Dead*, ch 12]

(8) Hunger is a pretty terrible thing. It's like going around all day with a nail in your shoe.

  ▸ [Timmy, in *My Brother Sam Is Dead*, ch 12]

(9) I keep thinking that there might have been another way, beside war, to achieve the same end [a prosperous United States].

  ▸ [Timmy, in *My Brother Sam Is Dead*, epilogue]

❚ Collodi, Carlo [pseud. of Carlo Lorenzini]

(1) Once upon a time there was a piece of wood.

  ▸ [in *The Adventures of Pinocchio*, ch 1]

(2) "I promise you," said the puppet, sobbing, "that for the future I will be good."

  "All boys," replied Geppetto, "when they are bent upon obtaining something, say the same thing."

  ▸ [in *The Adventures of Pinocchio*, ch 7]

(3) Don't trust, my boy, to those who promise to make you rich in a day. Usually they are either mad or rogues!

  ▸ [Talking-Cricket, in *The Adventures of Pinocchio*, ch 13]

(4) I would rather die than drink that bitter medicine!

  ▸ [Pinocchio, in *The Adventures of Pinocchio*, ch 17]

(5) He had scarcely told the lie when his nose, which was already long, grew at once two fingers longer.

  ▸ [in *The Adventures of Pinocchio*, ch 17]

(6) If you are really dying of hunger, eat two fine slices of your pride, and be careful not to get an indigestion.

  ▸ [charcoal man, when Pinocchio declines to work for food, in *The Adventures of Pinocchio*, ch 24]

(7) Let me tell you that every man, whether he is born rich or poor, is obliged to do something in this world—to occupy himself, to work. Woe to those who lead slothful lives. Sloth is a dreadful illness and must be cured at once, in childhood. If not, when we are old it can never be cured.

  ▸ [Blue Fairy, in *The Adventures of Pinocchio*, ch 25]

(8) In that delightful land [of the Boobies] nobody ever studies. On Thursday there is never school; and every week consists of six Thursdays and one Sunday. Only think, the autumn holidays begin on the first of January and finish on the last day of December.

  ▸ [Candlewick, in *The Adventures of Pinocchio*, ch 30]

(9) It is written in the decrees of wisdom that all boys who are lazy, and who take dislike to books, to schools, and to masters,

and who pass their time in amusement, games, and diversions, must end sooner or later by becoming transformed into so many little donkeys.

▶ [Marmot, in *The Adventures of Pinocchio*, ch 32]

(10) [Pinocchio] discovered that he was no longer a wooden puppet, but that he had become instead a boy, like all other boys.

▶ [in *The Adventures of Pinocchio*, ch 36]

❧ Conly, Jane Leslie

(1) School was the most important thing that had ever happened to Timothy. . . . When trouble did come along—for surely everyone must anticipate at least a small amount of misfortune—he would be able to reason his way out of it.

▶ [in *Racso and the Rats of NIMH*, "Emergency!"]

(2) Your father had strong convictions and he followed them. That takes courage.

▶ [Nicodemus, in *Racso and the Rats of NIMH*, "Nicodemus"]

❧ Conly, Robert Leslie. *See* O'Brien, Robert C.

❧ Cooney, Barbara

(1) "I am going to be an artist," [Hattie] said.

"Just like Opa," said Mama, smiling.

"No," said Hattie. "Just like me."

▶ [in *Hattie and the Wild Waves*]

(2) The Lupine Lady lives in a small house overlooking the sea.

▶ [in *Miss Rumphius*]

(3) When I grow up, I too will go to faraway places, and when I grow old, I too will live beside the sea.

▶ [Alice Rumphius, in *Miss Rumphius*]

(4) But there is a third thing you must do. . . . You must do something to make the world more beautiful

▶ [grandfather, in *Miss Rumphius*]

(5) All that summer, Miss Rumphius, her pockets full of seeds, wandered over fields and headlands, sowing lupines. . . . Now some people called her That Crazy Old Lady.

▶ [in *Miss Rumphius*]

❧ Cooper, Susan

(1) The Walker is abroad. . . . And this night will be bad, and tomorrow will be beyond imagining.

▶ [Farmer Dawson, in *The Dark Is Rising*, part 1]

(2) Any great gift or power or talent is a burden. . . . But there is nothing to be done. If you were born with the gift, then you must serve it, and nothing in

this world or out of it may stand in the way of that service, because that is why you were born and that is the Law.

▸ [Merriman Lyon, in *The Dark Is Rising*, part 1]

(3) For the Dark, the Dark is rising. The Walker is abroad, the Rider is riding; they have woken, the Dark is rising. And the last of the Circle is come to claim his own, and the circles must now all be joined. The white horse must go to the Hunter, and the river take the valley; there must be fire on the mountain, fire under the stone, fire over the sea. Fire to burn away the Dark, for the Dark, the Dark is rising!

▸ [Merriman Lyon, in *The Dark Is Rising*, part 1]

(4) When the Dark comes rising,
      six shall turn it back,
Three from the circle, three
      from the track;
Wood, bronze, iron; water, fire,
      stone;
Five will return, and one go
      alone.

Iron for the birthday, bronze
      carried long;
Wood from the burning, stone
      out of song;
Fire in the candle-ring, water
      from the thaw;
Six Signs the circle, and the
      grail gone before.

Fire on the mountain shall find
      the harp of gold
Played to wake the Sleepers,
      oldest of the old;
Power from the green witch,
      lost beneath the sea;
All shall find the light at last,
      silver on the tree.

▸ [in *The Dark Is Rising*, throughout]

(5) Everything that matters is outside Time. And comes from there and can go there. . . . I mean the part of all of us, and of all the things we think and believe, that has nothing to do with yesterday or today or tomorrow because it belongs at a different kind of level. Yesterday is still there, on that level. Tomorrow is there too. You can visit either of them. And all Gods are there, and all the things they have ever stood for. And . . . the opposite, too.

▸ [Will Stanton, in *The Dark Is Rising*, part 2]

❧ Craik, Dinah Maria Mulock

(1) There was once a little Brownie who lived—where do you think he lived?—in a coal cellar.

▸ [in *The Adventures of a Brownie*, ch 1]

(2) He [Prince Dolor] learned how to take advice before attempting to give it, to obey before he could righteously command.

▸ [in *The Little Lame Prince*, ch 10]

▌ Crampton, Gertrude

(1) I won't sail in a bathtub. . . . A tub is no place for a red-painted tugboat. I was meant for bigger things.
   ▶ [Scuffy, in "Scuffy the Tugboat and His Adventures Down the River," in *Family Treasury of Little Golden Books*]

(2) Far, far to the west of every-where is the village of Lower Trainswitch. All the baby loco-motives go there to learn to be big locomotives.
   ▶ [in "Tootle," in *Family Treasury of Little Golden Books*]

(3) Of all the things that are taught in the Lower Trainswitch School for Locomotives, the most impor-tant is, of course, Staying on the Rails No Matter What.
   ▶ [in "Tootle," in *Family Treasury of Little Golden Books*]

▌ Creech, Sharon

(1) Life is a bowl of spaghetti . . . every now and then you get a meatball.
   ▶ [in *Chasing Redbird*, ch 1]

(2) It wasn't that I was stupid. . . . It was just that there didn't seem to be a lot to say that someone wasn't already saying.
   ▶ [Zinnia, in *Chasing Redbird*, ch 2]

(3) . . . skinny as six o'clock
   ▶ [Aunt Jessie, in *Chasing Redbird*, ch 4]

(4) My father says I lean on broken reeds and will get a face full of swamp mud one day.
   ▶ [in *Walk Two Moons*, ch 2]

(5) I prayed to trees. This was easier than praying directly to God. There was nearly always a tree nearby.
   ▶ [Sal, in *Walk Two Moons*, ch 2]

(6) If people expect you to be brave, sometimes you pretend that you are, even when you are frightened down to your very bones.
   ▶ [in *Walk Two Moons*, ch 3]

(7) Everybody is just walking along concerned with his own problems, his own life, his own worries. And we're all expecting other people to tune into our own agenda. "Look at my worry. Worry with me. Step into my life. Care about my problems. Care about me."
   ▶ [Gram, in *Walk Two Moons*, ch 12]

(8) In the course of a lifetime, what does it matter?
   ▶ [in *Walk Two Moons*, ch 17]

▌ Cresswell, Helen

(1) You're immortal if your name gets put on cups and shields.
   ▶ [Jack, in *Ordinary Jack*, ch 1]

(2) Most of the [Bagthorpe] family had second Strings to their Bows, and some had three or even four.
   ▶ [in *Ordinary Jack*, ch 1]

(3)   The only good reason for swimming, so far as I can see, is to escape drowning.

▶ [Uncle Parker, in *Ordinary Jack*, ch 1]

(4)   It's your own opinion of yourself that matters, not other people's.

▶ [Uncle Parker, in *Ordinary Jack*, ch 12]

(5)   Rosie, in retrospect, became overweeningly proud that her Birthday Party had been the greatest and best Bagthorpian Party of all times.

▶ [in *Ordinary Jack*, epilogue]

❧ Crews, Donald

(1)   A train runs across this track.

▶ [in *Freight Train*]

❧ Crowe, Robert L.

(1)   A long time ago monsters and people made a deal. . . . Monsters don't scare people—and people don't scare monsters.

▶ [father monster, in *Clyde Monster*]

❧ Curtis, Jamie Lee

(1)   When I was little, I didn't understand time-outs. Now I do, but I don't like them.

▶ [in *When I Was Little: A Four-Year-Old's Memoir of Her Youth*]

(2)   When I was little, I didn't know who I was. Now I do!

▶ [in *When I Was Little: a Four-Year-Old's Memoir of Her Youth*]

❧ Cushman, Karen

(1)   That gold you claimed is lying in the fields around here must be hidden by all the lizards, dead leaves, and mule droppings.

▶ [Lucy, in *The Ballad of Lucy Whipple*, ch 1]

(2)   Grampop always said Prairie was like him—just tickled the ground and it laughed beans.

▶ [in *The Ballad of Lucy Whipple*, ch 1]

(3)   There are more important things than being safe, daughter.

▶ [Pa, in *The Ballad of Lucy Whipple*, ch 4]

(4)   Seems to me God made a big mistake when He failed to put handles on watermelons.

▶ [Lucy, in *The Ballad of Lucy Whipple*, ch 12]

(5)   Minds, like diapers, need occasional changing.

▶ [Mama, in *The Ballad of Lucy Whipple*, ch 17]

(6)   I am bit by fleas and plagued by family. That is all there is to say.

▶ [Catherine, in *Catherine Called Birdy*, Sept. 12]

(7) Remember, Little Bird, in the world to come, you will not be asked "Why were you not George?" or "Why were you not Perkin?" but "Why were you not Catherine?"

▶ [Jewish woman, in *Catherine Called Birdy*, Oct. 4]

(8) I was wondering . . . if the world needs a few rotten people to make the sweetest mix. This would explain the problem of God allowing evil in the world.

▶ [Catherine, in *Catherine Called Birdy*, Oct. 26]

(9) Marriage . . . seems to me to be but spinning, bearing children, and weeping.

▶ [Catherine, in *Catherine Called Birdy*, July 15]

(10) If you spit in the air, it will fall on your face.

▶ [mother, in *Catherine Called Birdy*, July 15]

(11) I think sometimes that people are like onions. On the outside smooth and whole and simple but inside ring upon ring, complex and deep.

▶ [Catherine, in *Catherine Called Birdy*, Sept. 12, 2nd year]

(12) I know what I want. A full belly, a contented heart, and a place in this world.

▶ [Alyce, in *The Midwife's Apprentice*, ch 12]

(13) Just because you don't know everything don't mean you know nothing.

▶ [Will Russet, in *The Midwife's Apprentice*, ch 13]

◣ Dahl, Roald

(1) The witching hour . . . was a special moment in the middle of the night when every child and every grown-up was in a deep deep sleep, and all the dark things came out from hiding and had the world to themselves.

▶ [in *The BFG*, ch 1]

(2) Just because I is a giant, you think I is a man-gobbling cannybull.

▶ [The BFG, in *The BFG*, ch 5]

(3) "Oh, but the bean *is* a vegetable," Sophie said.

"Not the *human* bean," the Giant said. "The human bean has two legs and a vegetable has no legs at all."

▶ [in *The BFG*, ch 5]

(4) I is the only nice and jumbly giant in Giant country! I is the BIG FRIENDLY GIANT! I is the BFG.

▶ [The BFG, in *The BFG*, ch 5]

(5) I cannot be right all the time. Quite often I is left instead of right.

▶ [The BFG, in *The BFG*, ch 6]

(6) The loss of an arm, he [Dahl's father] used to say, caused him only one serious inconvenience. He found it impossible to cut the top off a boiled egg.

▶ [in *Boy: Tales of Childhood*, ch 1]

(7) All grown-ups appear as giants to small children. But Headmasters (and policemen) are the biggest giants of all and acquire a marvellously exaggerated stature.

▶ [in *Boy: Tales of Childhood*, ch 5]

(8) I began to realize how simple life could be if one had a regular routine to follow with fixed hours and a fixed salary and very little original thinking to do.

The life of a writer is absolute hell compared with the life of a businessman. The writer has to force himself to work.

▶ [in *Boy: Tales of Childhood*, ch 25]

(9) There are five children in this book:
Augustus Gloop
A greedy boy
Veruca Salt
A girl who is spoiled by her parents
Violet Beauregarde
A girl who chews gum all day long
Mike Teavee
A boy who does nothing but watch television
and
Charlie Bucket
The hero

▶ [in *Charlie and the Chocolate Factory*, Introduction]

(10) Dear friends, we surely all agree
There's almost nothing worse to see
Than some repulsive little bum
Who's always chewing chewing gum.
(It's very near as bad as those
Who sit around and pick their nose.)

▶ [Oompa-Loompa song, in *Charlie and the Chocolate Factory*, ch 21]

(11) Do you *know* what breakfast cereal is made of? It's made of those little curly wooden shavings you find in pencil sharpeners!

▶ [Willy Wonka, in *Charlie and the Chocolate Factory*, ch 27]

(12) It [television] rots the senses in the head!
It kills imagination dead!
It clogs and clutters up the mind!
It makes a child so dull and blind
He can no longer understand
A fantasy, a fairyland!
His brain becomes as soft as cheese!
He cannot think—he only sees!

▶ [Oompa-Loompa song, in *Charlie and the Chocolate Factory*, ch 27]

(13) Most of the really exciting things we do in our lives scare us to death.

▶ [in *Danny the Champion of the World*, ch 7]

(14) The sense of loneliness was overwhelming, the silence was as deep as death, and the only sounds were the ones I made myself. . . . Even the silence was listening.

▶ [in *Danny the Champion of the World*, ch 8]

(15) A MESSAGE To Children Who Have Read This Book

When **you** grow up and have children of your own, do **please** remember something **important.**

A STODGY parent is *no fun at all!* What a child *wants*—and DESERVES—is a parent who is SPARKY!

▸ [in *Danny the Champion of the World*, epilogue]

(16) Boggis and Bunce and Bean
One fat, one short, one lean.
These horrible crooks
So different in looks
Were nonetheless equally mean.

▸ [in *Fantastic Mr. Fox*]

(17) Then, one day, James's mother and father went to London to do some shopping, and there a terrible thing happened. Both of them suddenly got eaten up (in full daylight, mind you, and on a crowded street) by an enormous angry rhinoceros which had escaped from the London Zoo.

▸ [in *James and the Giant Peach*, ch 1]

(18) I put the magic finger on them all!
▸ [in *The Magic Finger*]

(19) And now *we* are going to allow each other to shoot you.
▸ [ducks, in *The Magic Finger*]

(20) It's a funny thing about mothers and fathers. Even when their own child is the most disgusting little blister you could ever imagine, they still think that he or she is wonderful.
▸ [in *Matilda*, ch 1]

(21) Never do anything by halves if you want to get away with it. Be outrageous. Go the whole hog. Make sure everything you do is so completely crazy it's unbelievable.
▸ [Matilda, in *Matilda*, ch 11]

(22) One child a week is fifty-two a year,
Squish them and squiggle them and make them disappear.
That is the motto of all witches
▸ [in *The Witches*, Introduction]

(23) It doesn't matter who you are or what you look like so long as somebody loves you.
▸ [in *The Witches*, ch 20]

❧ Dalgliesh, Alice

(1) Keep up your courage, Sarah Noble. Keep up your courage.
▸ [Sarah, to herself, in *The Courage of Sarah Noble*, throughout]

(2) To be afraid and to be brave is the best kind of courage of all.
▸ [John Noble, Sarah's father, in *The Courage of Sarah Noble*, ch 7]

(3) Friends have ways of speaking without words.
▸ [in *The Courage of Sarah Noble*, ch 8]

❧ De Angeli, Marguerite

(1) Thou hast only to follow the wall far enough and there will be a door in it.
▸ [Brother Luke, in *The Door in the Wall*]

(2) We can only do the best we can with what we have. That, after all, is the measure of success: what we do with what we have.

▶ [Brother Luke, in *The Door in the Wall*]

❧ de Brunhoff, Jean. *See* Brunhoff, Jean de

❧ DeFelice, Cynthia

(1) If a man's going to keep animals to work for him and feed him, he's got an obligation to treat them right. A man who mistreats a poor, dumb beast is no better than a beast himself.

▶ [Pa, in *Weasel*, ch 7]

(2) The difference between savages and civilized men was that civilized men buried their dead.

▶ [in *Weasel*, ch 8]

❧ DeJong, Meindert

(1) That's the trouble with being twins—if you don't know something, you don't know it double.

▶ [Pier, in *The Wheel on the School*, ch 1]

(2) Fathers always come through when it's possible.

▶ [teacher, in *The Wheel on the School*, ch 12]

❧ de la Mare, Walter

(1) My aged friend Miss Wilkinson,
Whose mother was a Lambe,
Saw Wordsworth once, and
    Coleridge, too,
One morning in her pram.

▶ [in "The Bards," in *The Complete Poems of Walter de la Mare*]

(2) Some one came knocking
At my wee, small door.

▶ [in "Some One, "in *The Complete Poems of Walter de la Mare*]

(3) So I know not who came
    knocking,
At all, at all, at all.

▶ [in "Some One," in *The Complete Poems of Walter de la Mare*]

(4) What ever Miss T. eats
Turns into Miss T.

▶ [in "Miss T.," in *The Complete Poems of Walter de la Mare*]

(5) I know a little cupboard,
With a teenytiny key,
And there's a jar of Lollipops
For me, me, me.

▶ [in "The Cupboard," in *The Complete Poems of Walter de la Mare*]

(6) And when I'm very good, my
    dear,
As good as good can be,
There's Banbury cakes, and
    Lollipops,
For me, me, me.

▶ [in "The Cupboard," in *The Complete Poems of Walter de la Mare*]

❧ Demi [Hitz, Demi]

(1) Where you got your seeds from, I do not know. For the seeds I gave you had all been cooked. So it was impossible for any of them to grow. I admire Ping's great courage to appear before me with the empty truth, and now I reward him with my entire kingdom and make him Emperor of all the land!

▶ [Emperor, in *The Empty Pot*]

❧ dePaola, Tomie

(1) Perhaps that was a kiss from Nana Upstairs.

▶ [Mother, about a falling star, in *Nana Upstairs and Nana Downstairs*]

(2) Now you are both Nana Upstairs.

▶ [Tommy, in *Nana Upstairs and Nana Downstairs*]

(3) In a town in Calabria, a long time ago, there lived an old lady everyone called Strega Nona, which meant "Grandma Witch."

▶ [in *Strega Nona: An Old Tale Retold*]

(4) [Strega Nona] could cure a headache, with oil and water and a hairpin. She made special potions for the girls who wanted husbands. And she was very good at getting rid of warts.

▶ [in *Strega Nona: An Old Tale Retold*]

(5) Bubble, bubble, pasta pot.
Boil me some pasta, nice and hot.
I'm hungry and it's time to sup.
Boil enough pasta to fill me up.

▶ [in *Strega Nona: An Old Tale Retold*]

(6) All right, Anthony, you wanted pasta from my magic pasta pot, and I want to sleep in my little bed tonight. So start eating.

▶ [Strega Nona, in *Strega Nona: An Old Tale Retold*]

❧ DeRegniers, Beatrice Schenk

(1) Soft paws.
Sharp claws.
Thick fur.
Loud purr.

▶ [in *It Does Not Say Meow and Other Animal Riddles*]

(2) It's glad when you're glad,
Sad when you're sad,
Has a head you can pat,
But it's not a cat.
(It does *not* say *me-ow*.)

▶ [in *It Does Not Say Meow and Other Animal Riddles*]

(3) The King and Queen
Invited me
To come to their house
On Saturday for tea.

▶ [in *May I Bring a Friend?*]

(4) Any friend of our friend
Is welcome here.

▶ [King and Queen, in *May I Bring a Friend?*]

(5) So I brought my friend.
▶ [in *May I Bring a Friend?*]

(6) So that is why . . .
The King and Queen
And I and all
My friends were seen
On Saturday at half past two
Having tea at the City Zoo.
▶ [in *May I Bring a Friend?*]

(7) Poke,
once our Only—
now no longer lonely—
Cat.
▶ [in *So Many Cats!*]

❚ de Treviño, Elizabeth Borton. *See* Treviño, Elizabeth Borton de

❚ Devlin, Wende and Harry

(1) Boil a cauldron,
Make a brew,
What kind of berries
Make pancakes blue?
▶ [in *Old Black Witch*]

(2) Snakes and snacks
And gophers' knees!
If you think they are bad,
Then just taste these!
▶ [in *Old Black Witch*]

❚ Dodgson, Charles Lutwidge. *See* Carroll, Lewis

❚ DuBois, William Pene. *See* Pene DuBois, William

❚ Duvoisin, Roger

(1) Don't we all need something that makes us feel important? For Crocus it's his teeth.
▶ [Bertha the toothless duck, in *Crocus*]

(2) I do not like a cow who wants to be different. It's a good-for-nothing cow if you ask me.
▶ [Clover the cow, in *Jasmine*]

(3) Jasmine who did not mind NOT being like everyone else.
▶ [in *Jasmine*]

(4) Ah, where one does not take the same left and right turn every day; where the world is green and blue; where the owls sing and bears steal ice cream.
▶ [milkman, when asked where he went, in *The Missing Milkman*]

(5) Now I understand. It was not enough to carry wisdom under my wing. I must put it in my mind and in my heart. And to do that I must learn to read.
▶ [Petunia, in *Petunia*]

❚ Eastman, P. D.

(1) A mother bird sat on her egg.
▶ [in *Are You My Mother?*]

(2) "Oh, you are not my mother," said the baby bird. "You are a Snort. I have to get out of here!"

▶ [in *Are You My Mother?*]

(3) "You are not a kitten. You are not a hen. You are not a dog. You are not a cow. You are not a boat, not a plane, or a Snort! You are a bird, and you are my mother!"

▶ [in *Are You My Mother?*]

❙ Eckert, Allan W.

(1) A man has a right to be judged by how he acts, not by how someone may have *told* you he acts.

▶ [William MacDonald, in *Incident at Hawk's Hill*, ch 1]

❙ Edmonds, Walter D.

(1) He [Great-Grandfather Dygert] bought it [the Spanish gun] in Bergen op Zoom to bring to the wild America.

▶ [Edward, in *The Matchlock Gun*, ch 1]

(2) Teunis, riding in with half a dozen militiamen, found them so: Gertrude still unconscious, Trudy asleep, and Edward sitting up with the gun across his knees, the bell mouth pointing at the three dead Indian bodies.

▶ [in *The Matchlock Gun*, ch 10]

❙ Egielski, Richard

(1) Hey, you with the wings! Freeze!

▶ [pills, in *Buz*]

❙ Ehrlich, Amy

(1) Zeek Silver Moon was born in the twilight of a summer night. When he left off crying and fell asleep in his mother's arms, all the birds down by the harbor began to sing.

▶ [in *Zeek Silver Moon*]

(2) Welcome to the coming spirit
Welcome for joy
Welcome to the coming spirit
It's Zeek. It's a boy.

▶ [in *Zeek Silver Moon*]

❙ Emberley, Barbara

(1) Drummer Hoff fired it off.

▶ [in *Drummer Hoff*]

❙ Estes, Eleanor

(1) A hundred dresses . . . all lined up in the closet.

▶ [Wanda, in *The Hundred Dresses*, ch 2]

(2) After a long, long time, [Maddie] reached an important conclusion. She was never going to stand by and say nothing again. If she

ever heard anybody picking on someone because they were funny looking or because they had strange names, she'd speak up.

▶ [in *The Hundred Dresses*, ch 6]

⬛ Ets, Marie Hall

(1) And just to show that he can sweep without a broom, Wind scatters the leaves all about again.

▶ [in *Gilberto and the Wind*]

⬛ Exupery, Antoine de Saint. *See* Saint-Exupery, Antoine de

⬛ Fatio, Louise

(1) I suppose this must be the way people behave when they are not at the zoo.

▶ [lion, after people run away from him, in *The Happy Lion*]

⬛ Feiffer, Jules

(1) The word Jimmy heard most about his father was "overworked." The way his mother said it, "overworked" sounded important, even a little mysterious, something that perhaps Jimmy should grow up to be.

▶ [in *The Man in the Ceiling*, ch 1]

(2) What else does a father do with a son but talk baseball?

▶ [in *The Man in the Ceiling*, ch 2]

(3) Every "failure" is a piece of future luck. Because it brings you closer to being ready. To fail, fail some more, and fail again and double-fail, triple- and quadruple-fail. Fail so badly that nobody thinks you'll ever do anything else.

▶ [Uncle Lester, in *The Man in the Ceiling*, ch 17]

(4) Failure is the ugly duckling.

▶ [Uncle Lester, in *The Man in the Ceiling*, ch 17]

(5) Failure was only good if you treated it as if it weren't failure but normal. If you treated it as if it didn't prove what a jerk, what a loser you were. . . . Failure only worked if you went on.

▶ [in *The Man in the Ceiling*, ch 17]

⬛ Field, Eugene

(1) But up in that tree sits a chocolate cat,
And a gingerbread dog prowls below—

▶ [in "The Sugar-Plum Tree," in *Poems of Childhood*]

(2) And the sugar-plums tumble, of course, to the ground—
Hurrah for that chocolate cat!

▶ [in "The Sugar-Plum Tree," in *Poems of Childhood*]

(3) Wynken, Blynken, and Nod
   one night
   Sailed off in a wooden shoe—
   Sailed on a river of crystal light,
   Into a sea of dew.

   ▶ [in "Wynken, Blynken, and Nod," in *Poems of Childhood*]

(4) Wynken and Blynken are two
   little eyes,
   And Nod is a little head,
   And the wooden ship they
   sailed the skies
   Is a wee one's trundle bed.

   ▶ [in "Wynken, Blynken, and Nod," in *Poems of Childhood*]

(5) The little toy dog is covered
   with dust,
   But sturdy and stanch he stands;
   And the little toy soldier is red
   with rust,
   And his musket moulds in his
   hands.

   ▶ [in "Little Boy Blue," in *Poems of Childhood*]

(6) And they wonder, as waiting
   the long years through
   In the dust of that little chair,
   What has become of our Little
   Boy Blue,
   Since he kissed them and put
   them there.

   ▶ [in "Little Boy Blue," in *Poems of Childhood*]

(7) The Rock-a-By Lady from
   Hushaby street
   Comes stealing; comes
   creeping;

   ▶ [in "The Rock-a-By Lady," in *Poems of Childhood*]

(8) The gingham dog and the
   calico cat
   Side by side on the table sat;
   'Twas half-past twelve, and
   (what do you think!)
   Nor one nor t'other had slept a
   wink!

   ▶ [in "The Duel," in *Poems of Childhood*]

(9) But the truth about the cat and
   pup
   Is this: they ate each other up!

   ▶ [in "The Duel," in *Poems of Childhood*]

(10) Father calls me William, sister
   calls me Will,
   Mother calls me Willie, but the
   fellers call me Bill!

   ▶ [in "Jest 'Fore Christmas," in *Poems of Childhood*]

(11) But jest 'fore Christmas I'm as
   good as I kin be!

   ▶ [in "Jest 'Fore Christmas," in *Poems of Childhood*]

(12) I pity him who has a beard
   But has no little girl to pull it!

   ▶ [in "Beard and Baby," in *Poems of Childhood*]

(13) Before you went to selling clothes
   and I to peddling rimes—

   ▶ [in "Our Whippings," in *Poems of Childhood*]

(14) Mother's whippings didn't hurt,
   but father's! oh, my!

   ▶ [in "Our Whippings," in *Poems of Childhood*]

(15)   I'll see you in the woodshed after supper all alone!

▶ [father, in "Our Whippings," in *Poems of Childhood*]

❧ Field, Rachel

(1)   Still, infirmities are one thing, and claws are another, as I have reason to know.

▶ [in *Hitty Her First Hundred Years*, ch 1]

(2)   It is rather lonely to be a god for days on end.

▶ [in *Hitty Her First Hundred Years*, ch 7]

(3)   True worth counts for little. . . . It is a hard world for those of us who are not able to keep our complexions.

▶ [in *Hitty Her First Hundred Years*, ch 10]

(4)   Something told the wild geese
It was time to go.
Though the fields lay golden
Something whispered,—"Snow."

▶ [in "Something Told the Wild Geese," in *Poems*]

(5)   Summer sun was on their wings,
Winter in their cry.

▶ [in "Something Told the Wild Geese," in *Poems*]

(6)   If once you have slept on an island
You'll never be quite the same.

▶ [in "If Once You Have Slept on an Island," in *Poems*]

❧ Fisher, Dorothy Canfield

(1)   It was possible that what stirred inside her head at that moment was her brain, waking up. She was nine years old, and she was in the third-A grade at school, but that was the first time she had ever had a whole thought of her very own. . . . Somebody had always been explaining things to Elizabeth Ann so carefully that she had never found out a single thing for herself before.

▶ [in *Understood Betsy*, "Betsy Holds the Reins"]

(2)   [Betsy] weighed out the salt needed on the scales, and was very much surprised to find that there really is such a thing as an ounce. She had never met it before outside the pages of her arithmetic book and didn't know it lived anywhere else.

▶ [in *Understood Betsy*, "A Short Morning"]

(3)   The matter was that never before had [Betsy] known what she was doing in school. She had always thought she was there to pass from one grade to another, and she was ever so startled to get a glimpse of the fact that she was there to learn how to use her mind, so she could take care of herself when she came to be grown up.

▶ [in *Understood Betsy*, "What Grade Is Betsy?"]

(4) I thought they [examinations] were sort of fun. . . . Like taking a dare, don't you know. Somebody stumps you to jump off the hitching post, and you do it to show 'em. I always used to think examinations were like that. Somebody stumps you to spell "pneumonia," and you do it to show 'em.

▶ [Cousin Ann, in *Understood Betsy*, "Elizabeth Ann Fails an Examination"]

(5) There was, of course, no reason on earth why they should giggle, which is, of course, the reason why they did. If you've ever been a little girl you know about that.

▶ [in *Understood Betsy*, "Betsy Starts a Sewing Society"]

(6) It was a very important conversation, when Betsy's fate hung on the curl of an eyelash and the flicker of a voice, as fates often do.

▶ [in *Understood Betsy*, "Understood Aunt Frances"]

❚ Fitzgerald, John D.

(1) After all, there is nothing as tolerant and understanding as a kid you can whip.

▶ [in *The Great Brain*, ch 1]

❚ Fitzhugh, Louise

(1) It won't do you a bit of good to know everything if you don't do anything with it.

▶ [Ole Golly, in *Harriet the Spy*, ch 2]

(2) Good manners are very important, particularly in the morning.

▶ [Ole Golly, in *Harriet the Spy*, ch 2]

(3) When people don't do anything they don't think anything, and when they don't think anything there's nothing to think about them.

▶ [Harriet, quoting Ole Golly, in *Harriet the Spy*, ch 3]

(4) [Harriet] never minded admitting she didn't know something. So what, she thought; I could always learn.

▶ [in *Harriet the Spy*, ch 3]

(5) [Harriet] hated math. She hated math with every bone in her body. She spent so much time hating it that she never had time to do it.

▶ [in *Harriet the Spy*, ch 7]

(6) When somebody goes away there's things you want to tell them. When somebody dies maybe that's the worst thing. You want to tell them things that happen after.

▶ [Harriet, in *Harriet the Spy*, ch 8]

(7) [Ole Golly] always said that people who try to control people and change people's habits are the ones that make all the trouble. If you don't like somebody, walk away, she said, but don't try and make them like you.

▶ [Harriet, in *Harriet the Spy*, ch 12]

(8) [Harriet] managed to convince her mother that she was just about to come down with a terrible cold, the type of cold that could be nipped in the bud by only one little day home from school.

▶ [in *Harriet the Spy*, ch 16]

(9) There is no sight so ugly as the human face in anger.

▶ [Mrs. Hansen, in *The Long Secret*, ch 2]

(10) I do feel that, like the Good Book says, we should honor our father and mother, but I, personally, think we should honor our friends too.

▶ [Jessie Mae, in *The Long Secret*, ch 7]

(11) Ain't the book what's sacred. . . . It's what's *in* the book that's sacred.

▶ [Mama Jenkins, in *The Long Secret*, ch 11]

(12) Never laugh at anyone's religion, because whether you take it seriously or not, they do. And more than that, people who think enough to even *have* a religion should be respected at least for the thinking.

▶ [Mr. Welsch, in *The Long Secret*, ch 12]

(13) [Fanatics] tend to think the end justifies the means. . . . How *can* it? When there never *are* any ends . . . everything goes on and on . . . so it remains that we are all *means*.

▶ [Mr. Welsch, in *The Long Secret*, ch 12]

(14) I guess . . . that people made up God to make themselves feel better. After all, when you think about space, I mean *all that space* out there, it is pretty ghastly.

▶ [Janie, in *The Long Secret*, ch 13]

(15) Religion is a tool, Jessie, just like a tractor or a shovel or a pitchfork. It is a tool to get through life with. And if it works, it is a good tool. And if it don't work, it is a bad tool.

▶ [The Preacher, in *The Long Secret*, ch 21]

(16) It is important to be a lady, but not if you lose everything else, not if you lose yourself in the process.

▶ [Mrs. Hansen, in *The Long Secret*, ch 24]

(17) If you are ever in real trouble . . . remember . . . there must be some way out of it and there must be humor in it somewhere.

▶ [Mr. Roche, in *Sport*, ch 18]

❧ Flack, Marjorie

(1) Each day as Angus grew older he grew longer but not much higher. Scottie dogs grow that way.

▶ [in *Angus and the Cat*]

(2) And Angus knew and the CAT knew that Angus knew that— Angus was GLAD the cat came back.

▶ [in *Angus and the Cat*]

(3) There, directly in front of him, were two white DUCKS. They were marching forward, one-foot-up and one-foot-down. Quack! Quack! Quackety! Quack!!!

▶ [in *Angus and the Ducks*]

(4) For exactly THREE minutes by the clock, Angus was NOT curious about anything at all.

▶ [in *Angus and the Ducks*]

(5) Danny gave his mother a Big Birthday Bear hug.

▶ [in *Ask Mr. Bear*]

(6) Their home was a boat with two wise eyes on the Yangtze River.

▶ [in *The Story about Ping*]

(7) Ping was always careful, very, very careful not to be the last, because the last duck to cross over the bridge always got a spank on the back.

▶ [in *The Story about Ping*]

❧ Fleischman, Paul

(1) Break now, waves, and split your ribs on the rocks! Let the spray fly up, let the waters foam! Fishes—swim! Snails—crawl! Sea gulls—dive for your dinners in the sea!

▶ [Aaron, in *The Half-a-Moon Inn*]

❧ Fleischman, Sid

(1) I guess there's nothing thicker and wetter than a ground-hugging California tule fog. Aunt Etta

was always saying not to stand in one too long. You'd grow webbed feet.

▶ [in *The Ghost on Saturday Night*]

(2) The young prince was known here and there (and just about everywhere else) as Prince Brat. Not even black cats would cross his path.

▶ [in *The Whipping Boy*]

❧ Fleming, Ian

(1) Most motorcars are conglomerations (this is a long word for "bundles") of steel and wire and rubber and plastic, and electricity and oil and gasoline and water, and the toffee papers you pushed down the back seat last Sunday.

▶ [in *Chitty Chitty Bang Bang*, ch 1]

❧ Forbes, Esther

(1) Nobody can make a monkey out of anyone who isn't a monkey to start with.

▶ [Miss Bessie, in *Johnny Tremain*, ch 7]

(2) There's a time for the casting of silver and a time for the casting of cannon. If that's not in the Bible, it should be.

▶ [Paul Revere, in *Johnny Tremain*, ch 8]

(3) We give all we have, lives, property, safety, skills . . . we

fight, we die, for a simple thing. Only that a man can stand up.

▸ [James Otis, in *Johnny Tremain*, ch 8]

(4) [Age sixteen] is a boy in time of peace and a man in time of war.

▸ [Johnny Tremain, in *Johnny Tremain*, ch 11]

❧ Forbes, Kathryn [pseud. of Kathryn McLean]

(1) You must laugh, Daughter. Unless you . . . cripple something inside of you. Something that makes you lift your head after you have made a mistake. Something that makes you go on—with—with pride, Katrin. . . . [W]ith the shame and the sorrow there must also be the saving laughter.

▸ [Mama, in *Mama's Bank Account*, ch 11]

❧ Fox, Mem

(1) Once upon a time, there lived a pirate named Boris von der Borch. . . . But when his parrot died, he cried and cried. All pirates cry. And so do I.

▸ [in *Tough Boris*]

❧ Fox, Paula

(1) There are days at sea when all you want is to be on a path that has no end, a path you can run straight ahead on till your breath gives out.

▸ [Benjamin Stout, in *The Slave Dancer*, "The Moonlight"]

(2) I wondered if there was something about a ship that makes men glide from one state of mind to another as effortlessly as the ship cuts through water.

▸ [in *The Slave Dancer*, "The Moonlight"]

(3) Why do you have to like everything? . . . I mean, . . . can't you just be interested in things? And forget about liking?

▸ [Gran, in *Western Wind*, ch 1]

(4) I tend to believe in demons. Other explanations for such behavior seem wanting.

▸ [Gran, discussing people who would abandon an animal on a barren islet, in *Western Wind*, ch 2]

(5) Life is all getting used to what you're not used to.

▸ [Gran, in *Western Wind*, ch 2]

(6) You can do anything with words . . . except eat them. . . . You can't take them back either. They sit there like big damp frogs.

▸ [Aaron, in *Western Wind*, ch 5]

(7) I've come to think your soul should be stolen, all of it used up by the time you leave the world.

  ▶ [Gran, in *Western Wind*, ch 7]

(8) Gran had said you can't pursue happiness. It can strike in the middle of trouble, and it can disappear for no apparent reason, even when you think you ought to be happy.

  ▶ [in *Western Wind*, ch 10]

❚ Frasier, Debra

(1) While you waited in darkness,
tiny knees curled to chin,
the Earth and her creatures
with the Sun and the Moon
all moved in their places,
each ready to greet you
the very first moment
of the very first day you arrived.

  ▶ [in *On the Day You Were Born*]

❚ Freeman, Don

(1) You must be a friend. I've always wanted a friend.

  ▶ [Corduroy, in *Corduroy*]

(2) I've always wanted a purple pocket with my name tucked inside.

  ▶ [Corduroy, in *A Pocket for Corduroy*]

❚ Fritz, Jean

(1) Ann felt it was the strength from her own body that was making the vines so stout and healthy and turning the pumpkins golden. She felt her own hard work going down into the ground and making the potatoes grow.

  ▶ [in *The Cabin Faced West*, ch 6]

(2) Deep in my heart I knew that goodness didn't come natural to me. If I had to choose, I would rather be clever, but I didn't understand why anyone had to choose.

  ▶ [in *Homesick: My Own Story*, ch 2]

(3) Good! That's all anyone can think about. Good! I haven't even thought about being good. I haven't tried to be good. I don't care about being good. I have just been *me*. Doesn't anyone ever look at *me?*

  ▶ [in *Homesick: My Own Story*, ch 3]

❚ Gackenbach, Dick

(1) I knew there was something terrible down in the cellar. I just knew, because the cellar was dark and damp and it smelled.

  ▶ [in *Harry and the Terrible Whatzit*]

(2) A double-headed, three-clawed, six-toed, long-horned Whatzit.
> ▸ [in *Harry and the Terrible Whatzit*]

(3) I am your best friend. Not a banana.
> ▸ [Poppy, in *Poppy the Panda*]

❧ Gag, Wanda

(1) Cats here, cats there,
Cats and kittens everywhere.
Hundreds of cats,
Thousands of cats,
Millions and billions and trillions of cats.
> ▸ [in *Millions of Cats*]

❧ Gage, Wilson [pseud. of Mary Q. Steele]

(1) She picked up some big ripe peaches and threw them high in the air. They came down—SQUASH! She took them into the kitchen and made a squash pie.
> ▸ [in *Squash Pie*]

❧ Gardiner, John Reynolds

(1) If your teacher don't know—you ask me. If I don't know—you ask the library. If the library don't know—then you've got yourself a good question!
> ▸ [Grandfather, in *Stone Fox*, ch 3]

(2) Anyone crosses this line—I shoot.
> ▸ [Stone Fox, in *Stone Fox.*, ch 10]

❧ Gates, Doris

(1) The offer had been proffered not out of pity but out of friendship. And something told her [Janey] that you could accept from a friend. Perhaps there were times when you had to. This was undoubtedly one of them.
> ▸ [in *Blue Willow*, ch 3]

(2) You know, an adventure is just something that comes along that's unexpected and you don't know for sure how it will turn out. Sometimes there may be danger mixed up in it. And it doesn't matter whether it happened a thousand years ago or right this minute. It's still an adventure. Every day that comes along is an adventure to us, and may be dangerous because we don't know for sure what it's going to bring. Perhaps I'm wrong, but I've got a hunch that it takes just about as much courage to live like that without losing your grip on things as ever it took to buckle on armor and go out to fight some fellow who had a grudge against you.
> ▸ [Mr. Larkin, in *Blue Willow*, ch 5]

(3) He'll [Mr. Larkin] just have to do the best he can and take his chances with the rest. I guess that's the way all life is, mostly.
> ▸ [Mrs. Larkin, in *Blue Willow*, ch 6]

▌ Geisel, Theodor Seuss. *See* Seuss, Dr. *and* LeSeig, Theo

▌ George, Jean Craighead

(1) Change your ways when fear seizes, for it usually means you are doing something wrong.
   ▶ [Kapugen, and Julie (Miyax), in *Julie of the Wolves*, part 1]

(2) Amaroq, wolf, my friend,
   You are my adopted father.
   My feet shall run because of you.
   My heart shall beat because of you.
   And I shall love because of you.
   ▶ [Julie (Miyax), in *Julie of the Wolves*, part 1]

(3) I am on my mountain in a tree home that people have passed without ever knowing I am here.
   ▶ [Sam, in *My Side of the Mountain*, ch 1, first line]

(4) Fortunately, the sun has a wonderfully glorious habit of rising every morning.
   ▶ [in *My Side of the Mountain*, ch 2]

▌ Gerrard, Roy

(1) Yet the truth that I had learned was that triumph must be earned, And that fortune often smiles on those who dare.
   ▶ [in *Wagons West!*]

▌ Giff, Patricia Reilly

(1) I told her that saying goodbye didn't matter, not a bit. What mattered were all the days you were together before that, all the things you remembered.
   ▶ [in *Lily's Crossing*, ch 26]

▌ Ginsburg, Mirra

(1) Can you guess what happens to a mushroom when it rains? It grows!
   ▶ [in *Mushroom in the Rain*]

▌ Gipson, Fred

(1) We called him Old Yeller. The name had sort of a double meaning. One part meant that his short hair was a dingy yellow, a color we called "yeller" in those days. The other meant that when he opened his head, the sound he let out came closer to being a yell than a bark.
   ▶ [in *Old Yeller*, ch 1, first line]

(2) What I mean is, things like that happen. They may seem cruel and unfair, but that's how life is a part of the time. But that isn't the only way life is. A part of the time, it's mighty good. And a man can't afford to waste all the good part, worrying about the bad parts. That makes it all bad.
   ▶ [Papa, in *Old Yeller*, ch 16]

◣ Godden, Rumer

(1) It is an anxious, sometimes a dangerous thing to be a doll. Dolls cannot choose; they can only be chosen; they cannot "do"; they can only be done by; children who do not understand this often do wrong things, and then the dolls are hurt and abused and lost; and when this happens dolls cannot speak, nor do anything except be hurt and abused and lost.
▶ [in *The Dolls' House*, ch 1]

◣ Graham, Margaret Bloy

(1) Helen was too fast for him. She had eight legs and moved like lightning.
▶ [in *Be Nice to Spiders*]

◣ Grahame, Kenneth

(1) Book-learning often came in useful at a pinch, in spite of what their neighbors said.
▶ [in *The Reluctant Dragon*]

(2) Rules always come right if you wait quietly.
▶ [Boy, in *The Reluctant Dragon*]

(3) The specially nice thing about a banquet is that it comes when something's over, and there's nothing more to worry about, and tomorrow seems a long way off.
▶ [in *The Reluctant Dragon*]

(4) After all, the best part of a holiday is perhaps not so much to be resting yourself, as to see all the other fellows busy working.
▶ [in *The Wind in the Willows*, ch 1]

(5) Never in his life had he seen a river before—this sleek, sinuous, full-bodied animal, chasing and chuckling, gripping things with a gurgle and leaving them with a laugh, to fling itself on fresh playmates that shook themselves free, and were caught and held again.
▶ [in *The Wind in the Willows*, ch 1]

(6) There is nothing—absolutely nothing—half so much worth doing as simply messing about in boats.
▶ [Water Rat, in *The Wind in the Willows*, ch 1]

(7) All along the backwater,
Through the rushes tall,
Ducks are a-dabbling,
Up tails all!
▶ [Ducks' Ditty, in *The Wind in the Willows*, ch 2]

(8) Who ever heard of a door-mat *telling* one anything? They simply don't do it. They are not that sort at all. Door-mats know their place.
▶ [Mole, in *The Wind in the Willows*, ch 3]

(9) Once well underground, you know exactly where you are. Nothing can happen to you, and nothing can get at you. You're entirely your own master, and you don't have to consult anybody

or mind what they say. Things go on all the same overhead, and you let 'em, and don't bother about 'em. When you want to, up you go, and there the things are, waiting for you.

▶ [Mole, in *The Wind in the Willows*, ch 4]

(10) People come—they stay for a while, they flourish, they build—and they go. It is their way. But we [animals] remain.

▶ [Badger, in *The Wind in the Willows*, ch 4]

(11) Villagers all this frosty tide,
Let your doors swing open wide,
Though wind may follow, and
  snow beside,
Yet draw us in by your fire to
  bide;
Joy shall be yours in the morning!

Here we stand in the cold and
  the sleet,
Blowing fingers and stamping
  feet,
Come from far away you to
  greet—
You by the fire and we in the
  street—
Bidding you joy in the morning!

▶ [Carol sung by the field-mice, in *The Wind in the Willows*, ch 5]

(12) The motor car went Poop-poop-
  poop,
As it raced along the road.
Who was it steered it into a
  pond?
Ingenious Mr. Toad!

▶ [Toad's song, in *The Wind in the Willows*, ch 10]

(13) Indeed, much that he [Toad] related belonged more properly to the category of what-might-have-happened-had-I-only-thought-of-it-in-time-instead-of-ten-minutes-afterwards. Those are always the best and the raciest adventures; and why should they not be truly ours, as much as the somewhat inadequate things that really come off?

▶ [in *The Wind in the Willows*, ch 11]

▌Gramatky, Hardie

(1) But what he couldn't create in sound, Little Toot made up for in smoke.

▶ [in *Little Toot*]

(2) And it is said he [Little Toot] can haul as big a load as his father can . . . that is, when Big Toot hasn't a very big load to haul.

▶ [in *Little Toot*]

▌Gray, Elizabeth Janet

(1) It's a pity there's nothing in this world that's *all* good . . . but then nothing is all bad either.

▶ [Roger, in *Adam of the Road*, ch 3]

(2) A road's a kind of holy thing. . . . That's why it's a good work to keep a road in repair, like giving alms to the poor or tending

the sick. It's open to the sun and wind and rain. It brings all kinds of people and all parts of England together. And it's home to a minstrel, even though he may happen to be sleeping in a castle.

▶ [Roger, in *Adam of the Road*, ch 4]

(3) For the first time in his life he [Adam] had played the part of an oyster. He had taken the bit of grit that was scratching him and made something of it that was comfortable to him and pleasing to someone outside.

▶ [in *Adam of the Road*, ch 5]

❚ Gray, Libba Moore

(1) I smiled so big I thought my smile would ride off my face.

▶ [in *Little Lil and the Swing-Singing Sax*]

(2) . . . moving slow and moving weary and sighing like a slow-leaking tire.

▶ [in *Little Lil and the Swing-Singing Sax*]

(3) Bless the world
it feels like
a tip-tapping
song-singing
finger-snapping
kind of day.
Let's celebrate!

▶ [in *My Mama Had a Dancing Heart*]

(4) I'm a grassy grassy
garter snake
a sassy sassy
flashy flashy
tail twisting
tail turning
tail snapping
green snake
hiss a hiss
a hiss a hiss

▶ [in *Small Green Snake*]

❚ Greene, Bette

(1) But leaders don't usually spring forth to impose their will upon a helpless people. They, like department stores, are in business to give people what they think they want.

▶ [Anton, in *Summer of My German Soldier*, ch 12]

(2) There is more nobility in building a chicken coop than in destroying a cathedral.

▶ [Anton, in *Summer of My German Soldier*, ch 12]

(3) Does a person have to ask for credentials before they give food to a hungry man? Are you responsible because you give nourishment to a bad man?

▶ [Grandmother, in *Summer of My German Soldier*, ch 18]

(4) Don't have to spend my money on sadness. Plenty of that to be had for free.

▶ [Mr. Grimes, in *Summer of My German Soldier*, ch 19]

(5) When I goes shoppin' and I sees the label stamped, "Irregular" or "Seconds," then I knows I won't have to pay so much for it. But you've got yourself some irregular seconds folks, and you've been paying more'n top dollar for them.

▶ [Ruth, in *Summer of My German Soldier*, ch 20]

❘ Greene, Constance C.

(1) To expect people to be perfect just because they're adults and/or parents is unrealistic.

▶ [in *Beat the Turtle Drum*, May]

(2) There's a difference between wet and dry tears. Wet ones are cried by babies and little kids who've skinned their knees. Dry ones are done by people who have so much misery inside them it's like a desert. No oasis.

▶ [in *Beat the Turtle Drum*, July]

❘ Grifalconi, Ann

(1) We live together peacefully here—Because each one has a place to be apart, and a time to be together.

▶ [in *The Village of Round and Square Houses*]

❘ Hadithi, Mwenye [pseud. of Bruce Hobson]

(1) And now and then he [Hippo] floats to the top and opens his huge mouth ever so wide and says: "Look, Ngai! No fishes!"

▶ [in *Hot Hippo*]

❘ Hale, Lucretia P.

(1) The lady from Philadelphia

▶ [in *The Peterkin Papers,* throughout]

(2) It was a sad blow to the Peterkin family when they found Solomon John had nothing to say in the book which he tried once to write.

"I think it must happen often," said Elizabeth Eliza; "for everybody does not write a book, and this must be the reason."

▶ [in *The Peterkin Papers,* ch 5]

(3) It is a good thing to learn, . . . not to get up any earlier than is necessary.

▶ [Mr. Peterkin, in *The Peterkin Papers,* ch 11]

(4) It is well, in prosperity, to be brought up as though you were living in adversity; then, if you have to go back to adversity, it is all the same.

On the other hand, it might be as well, in adversity, to act as though you were living in prosperity; otherwise, you would seem to lose the prosperity either way.

▶ [Elizabeth Eliza, in *The Last of the Peterkins*, ch 2]

(5) I suppose there really is not as much danger about these uncommon things as there is in the small things, because they don't happen so often, and because you are more afraid of them.

I never saw it counted up, but I conclude that more children tumble into mud-puddles than into the ocean or Niagara Falls, for instance.

▶ [Elizabeth Eliza, in *The Last of the Peterkins*, ch 2]

❧ Hale, Sara Josepha

(1) Mary had a little lamb
Its fleece was white as snow
And everywhere that Mary went
The lamb was sure to go.

▶ [in *Mary Had a Little Lamb*]

❧ Hamilton, Virginia

(1) Move slowly. Think fast. . . . Keep in mind what's behind and look closely at what's in front.

▶ [Thomas, in *The House of Dies Drear*, ch 4]

(2) Darkness has a way of falling down on you around here. It doesn't give you time to wander home, as it will in the South.

▶ [Mr. Small, in *The House of Dies Drear*, ch 5]

(3) When hoot owl screeching,
westward flies,
Gauge the sun . . .
Look to Dies,
And run.

▶ [Pluto, in *The House of Dies Drear*, ch 7]

(4) Come, my winged bird, my glory, nightbird! Come, all ye demons three who walk with me forever. Come parade awhile with Pluto, who has missed ye so!

▶ [Pluto, in *The House of Dies Drear*, ch 18]

(5) The same thing day after day is enemy to a growing boy.

▶ [Banina, in *M. C. Higgins, the Great,* ch 7]

(6) Real fine lettuce that June, coming in green and fresh. And her papa, Jason Mills, standing looking at those pretty green leaves. Saying, "But when do they make a head of lettuce?" And Uncle Jimmy pausing and finally saying, "Late at night, city boy, late at night!"

▶ [in *Willie Bea and the Time the Martians Landed,* ch 1]

(7) Corn be high as heaven, . . . and me, I'm on my way.

▶ [Grand, in *Willie Bea and the Time the Martians Landed,* ch 2]

(8) Do you know what it is like to swim at night? . . . It is being in something that is all movement, that you cannot see, and it ceases to be wet. You must be

very calm or you will not find your way out of it.

▶ [Zeely, in *Zeely,* ch 15]

\ Harris, Joel Chandler

(1) [Brer Rabbit] hauls off and hits the Tar Baby. BIP! And his fist was stuck to the side of the Tar Baby's face.

▶ [in "Brer Rabbit and the Tar Baby," in *The Tales of Uncle Remus: The Adventures of Brer Rabbit,* adapted by Julius Lester]

(2) Don't throw me in that briar patch!

▶ [Brer Rabbit, in "Brer Rabbit and the Tar Baby," in *The Tales of Uncle Remus: The Adventures of Brer Rabbit,* adapted by Julius Lester]

(3) Po' Brer Fox. If it wasn't for bad luck, he wouldn't have no luck at all.

▶ [in "Brer Rabbit Gets Even," in *The Tales of Uncle Remus: The Adventures of Brer Rabbit,* adapted by Julius Lester]

(4) Brer Rabbit asked [Brer Fox] how he had made out hunting.

I caught a handful of common sense, Brer Rabbit.

If I'd knowed that was what you was hunting for, I'd have loaned you some of mine.

▶ [in "Brer Fox and Brer Rabbit Go Hunting," in *The Tales of Uncle Remus: The Adventures of Brer Rabbit,* adapted by Julius Lester]

(5) Of course, that was cheating, and the creatures had begun to cheat, and then the folks took it up, and it kept appearing. It's mighty catching.

▶ [in "Brer Rabbit Finds His Match," in *Jump! The Adventures of Brer Rabbit,* adapted by Van Dyke Parks]

\ Hedderwick, Mairi

(1) A whole hillside to eat and she wants *that* blade of grass!

▶ [Grannie Island, about her sheep Alecina, in *Katie Morag and the Two Grandmothers*]

\ Henkes, Kevin

(1) She did not think her name was absolutely perfect. She thought it was absolutely dreadful.

▶ [in *Chrysanthemum*]

(2) "There is no Jessica," said Ruthie's parents. But there was.

▶ [in *Jessica*]

(3) Lilly spent more time than usual in the uncooperative chair.

▶ [in *Julius, Baby of the World*]

(4) You will live to regret that bump under your dress.

▶ [Lilly, to pregnant woman, in *Julius, Baby of the World*]

(5) Today was a difficult day. Tomorrow will be better.

▶ [note from Mr. Slinger, in *Lilly's Purple Plastic Purse*]

(6) Haven't you heard of the blanket fairy?

▶ [Mrs. Tweezers, in *Owen*]

(7) At dinner, Sheila Rae made believe that the cherries in her fruit cocktail were the eyes of a dead bear, and she ate five of them.

▶ [in *Sheila Rae, the Brave*]

(8) So they played house and Wendell made the rules. He was the father, the mother, and the five children. Sophie was the dog.

▶ [in *A Weekend with Wendell*]

❙ Henry, Marguerite

(1) When Allah created the horse, he said to the wind, "I will that a creature proceed from thee. Condense thyself." And the wind condensed itself, and the result was the horse.

▶ [Achmet, in *King of the Wind*, ch 2]

(2) Yer know, the best thing about havin' fourteen head of children is ye're bound to get one or two good grandchildren outen the lot.

▶ [Grandpa, in *Misty of Chincoteague*, ch 4]

(3) Facts are fine, fer as they go, . . . but they're like water bugs skittering atop the water. Legends, now—they go deep down and bring up the heart of a story.

▶ [Grandpa, in *Misty of Chincoteague*, ch 4]

❙ Hesse, Karen

(1) How supremely heaven playing piano can be.

▶ [Billie Jo, in *Out of the Dust*, January 1934]

(2) The way I see it, hard times aren't only
about money,
or drought,
or dust.
Hard times are about losing spirit,
and hope,
and what happens when dreams dry up.

▶ [Billie Jo, in *Out of the Dust*, December 1935]

❙ Hill, Elizabeth Starr

(1) Maybe what you need is to leave your corner for a while. . . . Maybe you need to step out now, and help somebody else.

▶ [Evan's mother, in *Evan's Corner*]

❙ Hite, Sid

(1) There is an old saying that beauty is in the eye of the beholder. It is a true saying, but beauty also lives in the heart of its holder.

▶ [in *Answer My Prayer*, ch 1]

(2) Even an angel can dance no faster than the music plays.

▶ [in *Answer My Prayer*, ch 15]

❚ Hitz, Demi. *See* Demi

❚ Hoban, Russell

(1) Being careful is not as much fun as being friends. Do you want to be careful or do you want to be friends?

    ▶ [Frances, in *A Bargain for Frances*]

(2) Sisters that are much too small to throw or catch or bat a ball Are really not much good at all, Except for crying.

    ▶ [Frances, in *Best Friends for Frances*]

(3) When the wasps and the bumble-bees have a party, nobody comes that can't buzz.

    ▶ [Frances, in *Best Friends for Frances*] [also quoted in *A Baby Sister for Frances*]

(4) Alice is somebody that nobody can see. And that is why she does not have a birthday. So I am singing Happy Thursday to her.

    ▶ [Frances, in *A Birthday for Frances*]

(5) Your birthday is always the one that is not now.

    ▶ [Frances, in *A Birthday for Frances*]

(6) Chomps Bars are nice to get. Chomps Bars taste better yet When they're someone else's.

    ▶ [Frances, in *A Birthday for Frances*]

(7) I do not like the way you slide, I do not like your soft inside, I do not like you lots of ways, And I could do for many days Without eggs.

    ▶ [Frances, in *Bread and Jam for Frances*] [also in *Egg Thoughts and Other Frances Songs*]

(8) Jam on biscuits, jam on toast Jam is the thing that I like most. Jam is sticky, jam is sweet, Jam is tasty, jam's a treat— Raspberry, strawberry, gooseberry, I'm very FOND . . . OF . . . JAM!

    ▶ [Frances, in *Bread and Jam for Frances*]

(9) But she liked to practice with a string bean when she could.

    ▶ [in *Bread and Jam for Frances*]

(10) Albert made the sandwich, the pickle, the egg, and the milk come out even.

    ▶ [in *Bread and Jam for Frances*]

(11) Jam in the morning, jam at noon, Bread and jam by the light of the moon. Jam . . . is . . . very . . . nice.

    ▶ [Frances, in *Bread and Jam for Frances*]

(12) Jam for snacks and jam for meals, I know how a jam jar feels— FULL . . . OF . . . JAM!

    ▶ [Frances, in *Bread and Jam for Frances*]

(13) What I am Is tired of jam.

    ▶ [Frances, in *Bread and Jam for Frances*]

(14) "Between his table manners and his electric guitar that boy will destroy the world," said Mother.

"Maybe the world will get him first," said Emma.

▶ [in *Dinner at Alberta's*]

(15) All the sandwich cookies sweet
In their frilly paper neat,
They are gone this afternoon,
They have left you, Lorna Doone.

▶ [in "Lorna Doone Last Cookie Song (I Shared It with Gloria)," in *Egg Thoughts and Other Frances Songs*]

(16) Lorna Doone, Lorna Doone,
You were last but you weren't wasted.
Lorna Doone, Lorna Doone,
We'll remember how you tasted.

▶ [in "Lorna Doone Last Cookie Song (I Shared It with Gloria)," in *Egg Thoughts and Other Frances Songs*]

(17) Still, I guess I would have missed her,
Gloria my little sister.

▶ [in "Gloria, My Little Sister," in *Egg Thoughts and Other Frances Songs*]

(18) Summer goes, summer goes,
Like the sand between my toes
When the waves go out.

▶ [in "Summer Goes," in *Egg Thoughts and Other Frances Songs*]

(19) Summer took, summer took,
All the lessons in my book,
Blew them far away.

▶ [in "Summer Goes," in *Egg Thoughts and Other Frances Songs*]

(20) Homework sits on top of Sunday, squashing Sunday flat.
Homework has the smell of Monday, homework's very fat.

▶ [in "Homework," in *Egg Thoughts and Other Frances Songs*]

(21) All roads, whether long or short, are hard.

▶ [Frog, in *The Mouse and His Child*, ch 2]

(22) A territory is your place.... It's where everything smells right.... You feel all safe and strong there. It's the place where, when you fight, you win.

▶ [shrew drummer boy, in *The Mouse and His Child*, ch 3]

(23) Now we walk ... and behind us an enemy walks faster. That's life.

▶ [father mouse and Euterpe, in *The Mouse and His Child*, ch 4]

(24) Why into Here often equals There, and so one moves about.

▶ [Muskrat, in *The Mouse and His Child*, ch 5]

(25) There's nothing on the other side of nothing but us.

▶ [mouse's child, in *The Mouse and His Child*, ch 6]

(26) I don't suppose anyone ever is completely self-winding. That's what friends are for.

▶ [Frog, in *The Mouse and His Child*, ch 10]

❧ Hoberman, Mary Ann

(1) A glove is a house for a hand,
   a hand.
   A stocking's a house for a knee.
   A shoe or a boot is a house for
   a foot.
   And a house is a house for me!
   ▸ [in *A House Is a House for Me*]

(2) A box is a house for a teabag.
   A teapot's a house for some tea.
   If you pour me a cup and I
   drink it all up,
   Then the teahouse will turn
   into me!
   ▸ [in *A House Is a House for Me*]

❧ Hobson, Bruce. *See* Hadithi, Mwenye

❧ Hoff, Syd

(1) It's good to take an hour or two
   off after a hundred million years.
   ▸ [dinosaur, in *Danny and the Dinosaur*]

❧ Hoffman, Mary

(1) Raj said, "You can't be Peter—
   that's a boy's name." "You can't
   be Peter Pan," whispered Natalie.
   "He isn't black."
   ▸ [in *Amazing Grace*]

❧ Holman, Felice

(1) Aremis Slake, at the age of thirteen, took his fear and misfortune and hid them underground. The thing is, he had to go with them.
   ▸ [*Slake's Limbo*, epigraph]

(2) This is the year . . . *this* is the year the leaves *will* stay on the trees.
   ▸ [Slake, in *Slake's Limbo*, ch 1]

(3) Slake did not know exactly where he was going, but the general direction was up.
   ▸ [*Slake's Limbo*, ch 15, last line]

❧ Howe, Deborah and James

(1) Allow me to introduce myself. My name is Harold. I come to writing purely by chance. My full-time occupation is dog.
   ▸ [Harold, in *Bunnicula: A Rabbit-Tale of Mystery*, Editor's Note]

(2) I don't know if you've ever watched a cat try to decide where to sit, but it involves a lot of circling around, sitting, getting up again, circling some more, thinking about it, lying down, standing up, bathing a paw or tail and . . . circling!
   ▸ [Harold, in *Bunnicula: A Rabbit-Tale of Mystery*, ch 4]

❧ Hunt, Irene

(1) I don't know if anybody ever "wins" a war, Jeth. I think that the beginnin's of this war [Civil War] has been fanned by hate till it's a blaze now; and a blaze kin destroy him that makes it and him that the fire was set to hurt.

▶ [Bill Creighton, in *Across Five Aprils,* ch 3]

(2) This war is a beast with long claws.

▶ [Matthew Creighton, in *Across Five Aprils,* ch 6]

(3) You know, Aunt Cordelia, there will come a time when I'll eat berries like these some morning, fresh, dewy berries like these, and I'll think, "What's the matter? These are not like the ones I ate with so much pleasure long ago." And then I'll tell myself, "Of course not, for where is the sunny kitchen overlooking the woods, and where is the beautiful room upstairs where you awakened that morning, where is the aunt who quoted from one of Shakespeare's sonnets and above all, where is the sixteen-year-old girl who had just experienced a miracle?" It will never be the same, Aunt Cordelia; I'll never eat raspberries like these again.

▶ [Julie, in *Up a Road Slowly,* ch 9]

(4) Firelight does for an old room like this what wisdom does for an old face. . . . It softens the grimmer aspects and compensates for the drained color.

▶ [Cordelia, in *Up a Road Slowly,* ch 11]

(5) I've seen some very unlovely old faces that belonged with very well-stocked brains. These were the ones that lacked the other elements of wisdom—kindness, compassion, a sense of humor.

▶ [Cordelia, in *Up a Road Slowly,* ch 11]

❧ Hurd, Edith Thacher

(1) I have to dig a hole just for myself.
I have to dig a hole that's all my own.

▶ [Joe, in *Dinosaur My Darling*]

❧ Hurwitz, Johanna

(1) DeDe was the only girl in the class with a large, black moustache.

▶ [in *Aldo Applesauce,* ch 2]

❧ Hutchins, Pat

(1) "No one makes cookies like Grandma," said Ma as the doorbell rang.

▶ [in *The Doorbell Rang*]

❧ Irving, Washington

(1) Headless Horseman of Sleepy Hollow

▶ [in *The Legend of Sleepy Hollow*]

(2) He who wins a thousand common hearts is therefore entitled to some renown; but he who keeps undisputed sway over the heart of a coquette, is indeed a hero.

▶ [in *The Legend of Sleepy Hollow*]

(3) A curtain lecture is worth all the sermons in the world for teaching the virtues of patience and long-suffering. A termagant wife may, therefore, in some respects, be considered a tolerable blessing, and if so, Rip Van Winkle was thrice blessed.

▶ [in *Rip Van Winkle*]

(4) A sharp tongue is the only edged tool that grows keener with constant use.

▶ [in *Rip Van Winkle*]

(5) I was myself last night, but I fell asleep on the mountain, and they've changed my gun, and everything's changed, I'm changed, and I can't tell what's my name, or who I am.

▶ [Rip Van Winkle, in *Rip Van Winkle*]

(6) Even to this day, they [old Dutch inhabitants] never hear a thunderstorm of a summer afternoon about the Kaatskill, but they say Hendrick Hudson and his crew are at their game of ninepins; and it is a common wish of all henpecked husbands in the neighborhood, when life hangs heavy on their hands, that they might have a quieting draught out of Rip Van Winkle's flagon.

▶ [*Rip Van Winkle*]

❚ Jackson, Kathryn

(1) Once there was a tawny, scrawny, hungry lion who never could get enough to eat. He chased monkeys on Mondays—kangaroos on Tuesday—zebras on Wednesday —bears on Thursday—camels on Friday—and on Saturday, elephants!

▶ [in "Tawny Scrawny Lion," in *Family Treasury of Little Golden Books*]

(2) Then he [lion] sat down in the soft grass, looking fat as butter, sleek as satin, and jolly as all get out, all ready for another good big supper of carrot stew.

▶ [in "Tawny Scrawny Lion," in *Family Treasury of Little Golden Books*]

❚ Jackson, Kathryn and Byron

(1) I don't know what kind of animal I am. I live all alone in the jungle. I dance and I kick—and I call myself Sooki.

▶ [little elephant, in "The Saggy Baggy Elephant," in *Family Treasury of Little Golden Books*]

❚ Jeter, Jacky

(1) Even a very special cat likes cream.

▶ [in *The Cat and the Fiddler*]

▟ Johnson, Crockett [pseud. of David Leisk]

(1) There wasn't any moon, and Harold needed a moon for a walk in the moonlight.
  ▶ [in *Harold and the Purple Crayon*]

(2) He [Harold] remembered where his bedroom window was, when there was a moon. It was always right around the moon.
  ▶ [in *Harold and the Purple Crayon*]

(3) One moonlit evening, mainly to prove to himself he could do it, Harold went for a walk on a tightrope.
  ▶ [in *Harold's Circus*]

▟ Jones, Diana Wynne

(1) A place is less real if it is seen from outside, or only seen in memory; and also . . . if a person settles in a place and calls that place Home, then it becomes very real indeed.
  ▶ [Uquar (Prometheus), in *The Homeward Bounders*, ch 14]

(2) Hope is the forward-looking part of memory.
  ▶ [Uquar (Prometheus), in *The Homeward Bounders*, ch 14]

▟ Joosse, Barbara M.

(1) What if I turned into a polar bear, and I was the meanest bear you ever saw and I had sharp, shiny teeth, and I chased you into your tent and you cried?
    Then I would be very surprised and very scared. But still, inside the bear, you would be you, and I would love you.
  ▶ [in *Mama, Do You Love Me?*]

▟ Joyce, William

(1) Now this is an egg a frog could get attached to.
  ▶ [Bently, in *Bently & Egg*]

(2) Oh, special egg, oh, roundy egg, Oh, splendid, artful Bently egg, I painted you with feelings too Mysterious to say to you.
  ▶ [Bently, in *Bently & Egg*]

(3) Your father never goes out in his pajamas unless he has a smashing idea.
  ▶ [Mrs. Lazardo, in *Dinosaur Bob and His Adventures with the Family Lazardo*]

▟ Juster, Norton

(1) Expectations is the place you must always go to before you get to where you're going. Of course, some people never go beyond Expectations.
  ▶ [Whether Man, in *The Phantom Tollbooth*, ch 2]

(2) People who don't pay attention often get stuck in the Doldrums.
  ▶ [Lethargarian, in *The Phantom Tollbooth*, ch 2]

(3) For always remember that while it is wrong to use too few [words], it is often far worse to use too many.

▶ [Faintly Macabre, in *The Phantom Tollbooth,* ch 5]

(4) Being lost is never a matter of not knowing where you are; it's a matter of not knowing where you aren't.

▶ [Alec Bings, in *The Phantom Tollbooth,* ch 10]

(5) It's much harder to tell whether you *are* lost than whether you *were* lost, for, on many occasions, where you're going is exactly where you are. On the other hand, you often find that where you've been is not at all where you should have gone, and, since it's much more difficult to find your way back from someplace you've never left, I suggest you go there immediately and then decide.

▶ [ordinary man, in *The Phantom Tollbooth,* ch 10]

(6) As long as the answer is right, who cares if the question is wrong?

▶ [Dodecahedron, in *The Phantom Tollbooth,* ch 14]

(7) You'll find . . . that the only thing you can do easily is be wrong, and that's hardly worth the effort.

▶ [Mathemagician, in *The Phantom Tollbooth,* ch 16]

(8) If you only do the easy and useless jobs, you'll never have to worry about the important ones which are so difficult. You just won't have the time.

▶ [Terrible Trivium, in *The Phantom Tollbooth,* ch 17]

(9) You must never feel badly about making mistakes . . . as long as you take the trouble to learn from them. For you often learn more by being wrong for the right reasons than you do by being right for the wrong reasons.

▶ [Pure Reason, in *The Phantom Tollbooth,* ch 18]

(10) So many things are possible just as long as you don't know they're impossible.

▶ [Mathemagician, in *The Phantom Tollbooth,* ch 19]

▌Keith, Harold

(1) It was a soldier's job to starve to death, take the guff from the officers, march all night, and be shot to pieces in the daytime without ever opening his mouth in protest.

▶ [in *Rifles for Watie,* ch 12]

(2) Treat evahbody like a gennelman, but let the ivory handle of your revolver allus be in sight.

▶ [Heifer, in *Rifles for Watie,* ch 21]

▌Kellogg, Steven

(1) He just moved in down the street. He doesn't bark, he has no fur, he has no hoofs, he smells like us, he doesn't eat much, he doesn't

shed, his name is Ralph, and he says he'll be my friend. Can I keep him?

▶ [Arnold, in *Can I Keep Him?*]

(2) Here we can all *feel* like kings. . . . And that is the most important part of being king, as everyone knows.

▶ [Jenny, in *The Island of the Skog*]

(3) Heroes, let your voices ring,
To our island home we sing.
Shelter us from stormy seas.
Keep our kitchens stuffed with
cheese.
Save our pelts from lice and
fleas.
Save our pelts from fleas and
lice.
Shout it once! Shout it twice!
Friends forever! Skog and mice!

▶ [anthem, in *The Island of the Skog*]

❚ Kelly, Eric P.

(1) Ancient oath of the Krakow Trumpeter
I swear on my honor as a Pole, as a servant of the King of the Polish people, that I will faithfully and unto death, if there be need, sound upon the trumpet the Heynal in honor of Our Lady each hour in the tower of the church which bears Her Name.

▶ [in *The Trumpeter of Krakow*]

❚ Kerr, M. E. [pseud. of Marijane Meaker]

(1) Birds look free, but they're not, you know. They're very restricted. They're prisoners, really, of their own territory. They can't move easily from one territory to another.

▶ [Mr. Trenker, in *Gentlehands,* ch 3]

(2) Obstacles are challenges for winners, and excuses for losers.

▶ [Mr. Trenker, in *Gentlehands,* ch 3]

(3) You can become anything you want to be. . . . It's a matter of authority. Whatever a man's confidence, that's his capacity.

▶ [Mr. Trenker, in *Gentlehands,* ch 13]

(4) Once you know something is wrong, you're responsible, whether you see it, or hear about it, and most particularly when you're a part of it.

▶ [Mr. Trenker, in *Gentlehands,* ch 14]

❚ Kimmel, Eric A.

(1) Isn't this a strange moss-covered rock!

▶ [magic words in *Anansi and the Moss-Covered Rock*]

(2) Stupid, am I? Why do you say that? I'm not the one who talks to melons!

▶ [Anansi, inside the melon, in *Anansi and the Talking Melon*]

(3) We bananas should have warned you. Talking melons are nothing but trouble.

> ▶ [Anansi, in *Anansi and the Talking Melon*]

❧ Kindl, Patrice

(1) Your own story always seems unique, your own miseries unlike the miseries suffered by anyone else on the planet. It is hard to recognize your own particular predicament as the common fate of millions.

> ▶ [Anna, in *The Woman in the Wall*, ch 6]

(2) I will be my own house. I will build myself a house out of my own flesh and bones where my frightened child-self can find shelter. After all, isn't that one of the things women do? We are houses for our children, until they are strong enough to breathe and walk alone. Someday I may carry a baby inside me, shielding it from harm within the stronghold of my body. So surely I must be able to give myself shelter now.

> ▶ [Anna, in *The Woman in the Wall*, ch 18]

❧ King-Smith, Dick

(1) People only eat stupid animals. Like sheep and cows and ducks and chickens. They don't eat clever ones like dogs.

> ▶ [Fly, in *Babe the Gallant Pig*, ch 2]

(2) Pigs enjoy eating, and they also enjoy lying around most of the day thinking about eating again.

> ▶ [in *Babe the Gallant Pig*, ch 8]

(3) I may be ewe, I may be ram,
I may be mutton, may be lamb,
But on the hoof or on the hook,
I bain't so stupid as I look.

> ▶ [sheep's password, in *Babe the Gallant Pig*, ch 10]

(4) I'd much rather be your pet than your breakfast.

> ▶ [Drusilla, in *Martin's Mice*, ch 3]

(5) A mouse a day . . . keeps the vet away.

> ▶ [Dulcie Maude, in *Martin's Mice*, ch 5]

❧ Kipling, Rudyard

(1) The Law of the Jungle

> ▶ [in "Mowgli's Brothers," in *The Jungle Book*]

(2) Man-eaters become mangy, and lose their teeth.

> ▶ [in "Mowgli's Brothers," in *The Jungle Book*]

(3) Each dog barks in his own yard!

> ▶ [Shere Khan, in "Mowgli's Brothers," in *The Jungle Book*]

(4) Nag, come up and dance with death!

> ▶ [Rikki-Tikki-Tavi, in "Rikki-Tikki-Tavi," in *The Jungle Book*]

(5) The motto of all the mongoose family is, "Run and find out."
  ▶ [in "Rikki-Tikki-Tavi," in *The Jungle Book*]

(6) And when didst *thou* see the elephants dance?
  ▶ [drivers' saying, in "Toomai of the Elephants," in *The Jungle Book*]

(7) You can work it out by Fractions or by simple Rule of Three,
But the way of Tweedle-dum is not the way of Tweedle-dee.
You can twist it, you can turn it, you can plait it till you drop,
But the way of Pilly-Winky's *not* the way of Winkie-Pop!
  ▶ [in "Servants of the Queen," in *The Jungle Book*]

(8) I know just enough to be uncomfortable, and not enough to go on in spite of it.
  ▶ [Two Tails, the elephant, in "Servants of the Queen," in *The Jungle Book*]

(9) And for that reason [that in Afghanistan you obey your own wills], . . . your Amir whom you do not obey must come here and take orders from our Viceroy.
  ▶ [officer, in "Servants of the Queen," in *The Jungle Book*]

(10) In a cave in the Jungle sat Fear, and . . . he had no hair, and went upon his hind legs.
  ▶ [in "How Fear Came," in *The Second Jungle Book*]

(11) Only when there is one great Fear over all, as there is now, can we of the Jungle lay aside our little fears, and meet together in one place as we do now.
  ▶ [Hathi, in "How Fear Came," in *The Second Jungle Book*]

(12) New land means new quarrels.
  ▶ [the Mugger, in "The Undertakers," in *The Second Jungle Book*]

(13) If we listened to the howling of every jackal the business of the town would stop.
  ▶ [the Adjutant, in "The Undertakers," in *The Second Jungle Book*]

(14) To delight in ornaments is to end with a rope for necklace.
  ▶ [the Mugger, in "The Undertakers," in *The Second Jungle Book*]

(15) He who trusts a woman will walk on duckweed in a pool.
  ▶ [the Mugger, in "The Undertakers," in *The Second Jungle Book*]

(16) When tomorrow comes we will kill tomorrow.
  ▶ [Mowgli, in "Red Dog," in *The Second Jungle Book*]

(17) Having cast the skin . . . we may not creep into it afresh. It is the law.
  ▶ [Kaa, in "The Spring Running," in *The Second Jungle Book*]

(18) O my Best Beloved
  ▶ [in *Just So Stories,* throughout]

(19) And from that day to this, the Camel always wears a humph (we call it a "hump" now, not to hurt his feelings); but he has never yet caught up with the three days that he missed at the beginning of the world, and he

has never yet learned how to behave.

> ▶ [in "How the Camel Got His Hump," in *Just So Stories*]

(20) There came to the beach from the altogether Uninhabited Interior one Rhinoceros with a horn on his nose, two piggy eyes, and few manners.

> ▶ [in "How the Rhinoceros Got His Skin," in *Just So Stories*]

(21) In those days the Rhinoceros's skin fitted him quite tight. There were no wrinkles in it anywhere.

> ▶ [in "How the Rhinoceros Got His Skin," in *Just So Stories*]

(22) He [the Rhinoceros] had no manners then, and he has no manners now, and he never will have any manners.

> ▶ [in "How the Rhinoceros Got His Skin," in *Just So Stories*]

(23) From that day to this every rhinoceros has great folds in his skin and a very bad temper, all on account of the cake crumbs inside.

> ▶ [in "How the Rhinoceros Got His Skin," in *Just So Stories*]

(24) But there was one Elephant—a new Elephant—an Elephant's Child—who was full of 'satiable curiosity.

> ▶ [in "The Elephant's Child," in *Just So Stories*]

(25) I got a new one [nose] from the Crocodile on the banks of the great gray-green, greasy Lim-popo river. . . . I asked him what he had for dinner, and he gave me this to keep.

> ▶ [in "The Elephant's Child," in *Just So Stories*]

(26) I keep six honest serving men
(They taught me all I knew);
Their names are What and Why and When
And How and Where and Who.

> ▶ [in *Just So Stories*]

(27) Roll down—roll down to Rio—
Roll really down to Rio!
Oh, I'd love to roll to Rio
Someday before I'm old!

> ▶ [in *Just So Stories*]

(28) But the wildest of all the wild animals was the Cat. He walked by himself, and all places were alike to him.

> ▶ [in "The Cat That Walked by Himself," in *Just So Stories*]

(29) His name is not Wild Dog anymore, but First Friend, because he will be our friend for always and always and always.

> ▶ [Woman, in "The Cat That Walked by Himself," in *Just So Stories*]

(30) I am not a friend, and I am not a servant. I am the Cat who walks by himself.

> ▶ [Cat, in "The Cat That Walked by Himself," in *Just So Stories*]

(31) From that day to this, Best Beloved, three proper Men out of five will always throw things at

a Cat whenever they meet him, and all proper Dogs will chase him up a tree.

> ▶ [in "The Cat That Walked by Himself," in *Just So Stories*]

(32) [The Cat] goes out . . . waving his wild tail, and walking by his wild lone.

> ▶ [in "The Cat That Walked by Himself," in *Just So Stories*]

(33) Suleiman-bin-Daoud . . . very seldom showed off, and when he did he was sorry for it.

> ▶ [in "The Butterfly That Stamped," in *Just So Stories*]

(34) [Suleiman-bin-Daoud] didn't really want nine hundred and ninety-nine wives, but in those days everybody married ever so many wives, and of course the King had to marry ever so many more just to show that he was the King.

> ▶ [in "The Butterfly That Stamped," in *Just So Stories*]

(35) If it pleases my husband to believe that I believe he can make Suleiman-bin-Daoud's Palace disappear by stamping his foot, I'm sure *I* don't care.

> ▶ [Butterfly's Wife, in "The Butterfly That Stamped," in *Just So Stories*]

❧ Knight, Eric

(1) Joe Carraclough solved his problem as hundreds of thousands of boys solve their problems the world over. He ran home to tell his mother.

> ▶ [in *Lassie Come-Home,* "I Never Want Another Dog"]

(2) And sometimes, when a chap don't have much, Joe, he clings to being honest harder than ever—because that's all he does have left. At least, he stays honest. And there's a funny thing about honesty; there's no two ways about it. There's only one way about it. Honest is honest.

> ▶ [Sam Carraclough, in *Lassie Come-Home,* "Nothing Left but Honesty"]

(3) For five years I've sworn I'd have that dog. And now I've got her. . . . But I had to buy the man to get her.

> ▶ [Duke of Rudling, in *Lassie Come-Home,* "Journey's End"]

❧ Knutson, Kimberley

(1) smucky mush
smacky mush
squooshy slooshy muddigush

> ▶ [in *Muddigush*]

❧ Konigsburg, E. L.

(1) Johnathan Richter's mother hadn't let him go [to New York City] for fear he'd get separated from the group . . . she was certain that he would "come home lost."

> ▶ [in *From the Mixed-up Files of Mrs. Basil E. Frankweiler,* ch 1]

(2) Jamie liked perspiration, a little bit of it, and complications.

> ▶ [in *From the Mixed-up Files of Mrs. Basil E. Frankweiler,* ch 3]

(3) Rich people have only penny wishes.

> ▶ [Claudia, in *From the Mixed-up Files of Mrs. Basil E. Frankweiler,* ch 5]

(4) I guess homesickness is like sucking your thumb. It's what happens when you're not very sure of yourself.

> ▶ [Jamie, in *From the Mixed-up Files of Mrs. Basil E. Frankweiler,* ch 5]

(5) Five minutes of planning are worth fifteen minutes of just looking.

> ▶ [Claudia, in *From the Mixed-up Files of Mrs. Basil E. Frankweiler,* ch 9]

(6) When the stakes are high, I never cheat. I consider myself too important to do that.

> ▶ [Mrs. Frankweiler, in *From the Mixed-up Files of Mrs. Basil E. Frankweiler,* ch 9]

(7) I think you should learn, of course, and some days you must learn a great deal. But you should also have days when you allow what is already in you to swell up inside of you until it touches everything. And you can feel it inside you. If you never take time out to let that happen, then you just accumulate facts, and they begin to rattle around inside of you. You can make noises with them, but

never really feel anything with them. It's hollow.

> ▶ [Mrs. Frankweiler, in *From the Mixed-up Files of Mrs. Basil E. Frankweiler,* ch 9]

(8) After a time having a secret is no fun. And although you don't want others to know what the secret is, you want them to at least know you have one.

> ▶ [Mrs. Frankweiler, in *From the Mixed-up Files of Mrs. Basil E. Frankweiler,* ch 10]

(9) Biding one's time is a very different thing from patience.

> ▶ [in *A Proud Taste for Scarlet and Miniver,* "Inside Heaven"]

(10) I know what I ought to be. I have always known what I ought to be.

> ▶ [Eleanor, in *A Proud Taste for Scarlet and Miniver,* "Inside Heaven"]

(11) In Heaven lawyers are as hard to find as bank presidents.

> ▶ [Abbot Suger, in *A Proud Taste for Scarlet and Miniver,* "Inside Heaven"]

(12) Any man with responsibilities in government is bound for Hell at least for a little while.

> ▶ [Abbot Suger, in *A Proud Taste for Scarlet and Miniver,* "Inside Heaven"]

(13) Indecisiveness wears a person out.

> ▶ [in *A Proud Taste for Scarlet and Miniver,* "Abbot Suger's Tale," ch 2]

(14) True simplicity is elegant.

> ▸ [Eleanor, in *A Proud Taste for Scarlet and Miniver,* "Abbot Suger's Tale," ch 6]

(15) Self-righteous people never looked beyond themselves for the reasons that things happen.

> ▸ [in *A Proud Taste for Scarlet and Miniver,* "Matilda-Empress's Tale," ch 1]

(16) If a man paid homage to someone who was magnificent, he thought better of himself than if he paid homage to someone who was simple.

> ▸ [in *A Proud Taste for Scarlet and Miniver,* "Matilda-Empress's Tale," ch 6]

(17) I shall weave my tale but not embroider it.

> ▸ [William the Marshal, in *A Proud Taste for Scarlet and Miniver,* "Back in Heaven," part 2]

(18) Every job in the world has some built-in boredom. No man can stay excited about something every minute he is doing it. Routine is as necessary to life as water is to beer; it is the base that holds the flavors and spices together.

> ▸ [Henry II, in *A Proud Taste for Scarlet and Miniver,* "William the Marshal's Tale," ch 3]

(19) Being king is a business. . . . It is a lot of privilege, but you pay heavily for that privilege. A king is not a free man.

> ▸ [Henry II, in *A Proud Taste for Scarlet and Miniver,* "William the Marshal's Tale," ch 7]

(20) A pussy cat does not tell a lion not to roar.

> ▸ [Richard the Lion Heart, to his brother Henry, in *A Proud Taste for Scarlet and Miniver,* "William the Marshal's Tale," ch 7]

(21) He cost me much. . . . Would that he could cost me more.

> ▸ [Henry II, after his son Henry's death, in *A Proud Taste for Scarlet and Miniver,* "William the Marshal's Tale," ch 7]

(22) It is always the incidental inconvenience that upsets the common man.

> ▸ [Eleanor, in *A Proud Taste for Scarlet and Miniver,* "William the Marshal's Tale," ch 11]

(23) English is a strong language. It has a great assortment of four-lettered words.

> ▸ [Eleanor, in *A Proud Taste for Scarlet and Miniver,* "William the Marshal's Tale," ch 11]

(24) To drink life from only the good is to taste only half of it.

> ▸ [Eleanor, in *A Proud Taste for Scarlet and Miniver,* "Eleanor of Aquitaine's Own Tale," ch 3]

(25) The ballpoint pen has been the biggest single factor in the decline of Western Civilization. It makes the written word cheap, fast, and totally without character.

> ▸ [Tillie Nachman, in *The View from Saturday,* ch 1]

(26) Whenever someone makes out a guest list, the people not on it become officially uninvited, and that makes them the enemies of

the invited. Guest lists are just a way of choosing sides.

▶ [Ethan Potter, in *The View from Saturday*, ch 3]

(27) Let us say that I am as American as pizza pie. I did not originate here, but I am here to stay.

▶ [Julian Singh, in *The View from Saturday*, ch 3]

(28) Chops . . . is to magic what doing scales is to a chanteuse. Without it you cannot be a magician, with it alone you cannot be an artist.

▶ [Julian Singh, in *The View from Saturday*, ch 3]

(29) It often takes more courage to be a passenger than a driver.

▶ [Mr. Singh, in *The View from Saturday*, ch 10]

(30) Can you know excellence if you've never seen it? Can you know good if you have only seen bad?

▶ [Mr. Singh, in *The View from Saturday*, ch 11]

❱ Krasilovsky, Phyllis

(1) Hendrika! I thought you were home in the pasture eating grass, not here [in the marketplace] eating hats!

▶ [Mr. Hofstra, in *The Cow Who Fell in the Canal*]

❱ Kraus, Robert

(1) A watched bloomer doesn't bloom.

▶ [Leo's mother, in *Leo the Late Bloomer*]

(2) Then one day, in his own good time, Leo bloomed!

▶ [in *Leo the Late Bloomer*]

❱ Krauss, Ruth

(1) I'm afraid it won't come up.

▶ [mother and father, in *The Carrot Seed*]

(2) And then, one day, a carrot came up just as the little boy had known it would.

▶ [in *The Carrot Seed*]

(3) Dogs are to kiss people

▶ [in *A Hole Is to Dig*]

(4) A lap is so you don't get crumbs on the floor

▶ [in *A Hole Is to Dig*]

(5) The sun is so it can be a great day

▶ [in *A Hole Is to Dig*]

❱ Krumgold, Joseph

(1) Whenever something grows and you keep it from growing anymore, that's a sin. And if it's a life, living, and you let it die, that's a sin.

▶ [Grandpa, in *And Now Miguel*, ch 5]

(2) It's a law. A universal, natural law. You only get when you give. It's a law like gravity.

▶ [Gabriel, in *And Now Miguel*, ch 13]

(3) Losing's just a number on a scoreboard.

▶ [Mr. Rusch, in *Onion John*, ch 1]

(4) No one's private rights ought to get invaded even if it's with kindness.

▶ [Ernie Miller, in *Onion John*, ch 15]

(5) A good many lies, there's at least two sides to them and you can take a point of view. But this was a flat lie. You couldn't get around it.

▶ [Andy, in *Onion John*, ch 16]

❭ Kuskin, Karla

(1) They are the members of the Philharmonic Orchestra, and their job is to play. Beautifully.

▶ [in *The Philharmonic Gets Dressed*]

(2) Rabbits don't like rabbit stew. I don't blame them much, do you?

▶ [in *Something Sleeping in the Hall*]

(3) A bear went walking
down the street
and everyone that bear did meet
that bear did greet
and eat.
How sweet.

▶ [in *Something Sleeping in the Hall*]

(4) Nothing tastes as good as toes.

▶ [dragon, in *Something Sleeping in the Hall*]

❭ Lasker, Joe

(1) I love lentil soup. But *this* lentil soup is not like my mother's lentil soup.

▶ [Matt, in *Lentil Soup*]

❭ Lawson, Robert

(1) There is enough for all.

▶ [motto on the fountain, in *Rabbit Hill*, ch 12]

❭ Leaf, Munro

(1) He liked to sit just quietly and smell the flowers.

▶ [in *The Story of Ferdinand*]

(2) She was an understanding mother, even though she was a cow.

▶ [in *The Story of Ferdinand*]

(3) Well, if you were a bumble bee and a bull sat on you what would you do?

▶ [in *The Story of Ferdinand*]

(4) They called him Ferdinand the Fierce and all the Banderilleros were afraid of him and the Pica-dores were afraid of him and the Matador was scared stiff.

▶ [in *The Story of Ferdinand*]

⚊ Lear, Edward

(1) There was an Old Man who
     said, "Hush!
     I perceive a young bird in this
     bush!"
     When they said, "Is it small?"
     he replied, "Not at all,
     It is four times as big as the bush!"
     ▶ [in "The Book of Nonsense," in
     The Complete Nonsense Book]

(2) There was an old man with a
     beard,
     Who said, "It is just as I feared!—
     Two Owls and a Hen, four
     larks and a Wren,
     Have all built their nests in my
     beard."
     ▶ [in "The Book of Nonsense," in
     The Complete Nonsense Book]

(3) The Pobble who has no toes
     Had once as many as we.
     ▶ [in "The Pobble Who Has No
     Toes," in "Laughable Lyrics," in
     The Complete Nonsense Book]

(4) And his Aunt Jobiska made
     him drink
     Lavender water tinged with pink;
     For she said, "The World in
     general knows
     There's nothing so good for a
     Pobble's toes!"
     ▶ [in "The Pobble Who Has No
     Toes," in "Laughable Lyrics," in
     The Complete Nonsense Book]

(5) Nobody knew; and nobody
     knows
     How the Pobble was robbed of
     his twice five toes!
     ▶ [in "The Pobble Who Has No
     Toes," in "Laughable Lyrics," in
     The Complete Nonsense Book]

(6) It's a fact the whole world
     knows,
     That Pobbles are happier
     without their toes.
     ▶ [Aunt Jobiska, in "The Pobble
     Who Has No Toes," in "Laugh-
     able Lyrics," in *The Complete
     Nonsense Book*]

(7) A was once an apple-pie,
     Pidy,
     Widy,
     Tidy,
     Pidy,
     Nice insidy,
     Apple-pie!
     ▶ [in "Nonsense Alphabets," in *The
     Complete Nonsense Book*]

(8) The Owl and the Pussy-Cat
     went to sea
     In a beautiful pea-green boat:
     ▶ [in "The Owl and the Pussy-Cat,"
     in "Nonsense Songs and Stories,"
     in *The Complete Nonsense Book*]

(9) They sailed away for a year
     and a day,
     To the land where the bong-
     tree grows;
     And there in a wood a Piggy-
     wig stood
     With a ring at the end of his
     nose
     ▶ [in "The Owl and the Pussy-Cat,"
     in "Nonsense Songs and Stories,"
     in *The Complete Nonsense Book*]

(10) And hand in hand, on the edge
     of the sand
     They danced by the light of the
     moon.
     ▶ [in "The Owl and the Pussy-Cat,"
     in "Nonsense Songs and Stories,"
     in *The Complete Nonsense Book*]

(11) Far and few, far and few,
Are the lands where the
    Jumblies live:
Their heads are green, and
    their hands are blue;
And they went to sea in a sieve.

▸ [in "The Jumblies," in *Nonsense Songs and Stories*]

▸ [Also found in: "The Dong with a Luminous Nose," in "Laughable Lyrics," in *The Complete Nonsense Book*]

❚ Le Guin, Ursula K.

(1) All I know is the dark, the night underground. And that's all there really is. That's all there is to know, in the end. The silence, and the dark. . . . I know one thing—the one true thing!

▸ [Tenar/Arha, in *The Tombs of Atuan*, "The Great Treasure"]

(2) Alone, no one wins freedom.

▸ [Ged, in *The Tombs of Atuan*, "The Anger out of the Dark"]

(3) Freedom is a heavy load, a great and strange burden for the spirit to undertake. It is not easy. It is not a gift given, but a choice made, and the choice may be a hard one. The road goes upward towards the light; but the laden traveler may never reach the end of it.

▸ [in *The Tombs of Atuan*, "Voyage"]

(4) To hear, one must be silent.

▸ [Ogion, in *A Wizard of Earthsea*, ch 2]

(5) But you must not change one thing, one pebble, one grain of sand, until you know what good and evil will follow on that act. The world is in balance, in Equilibrium.

▸ [Master Hand, in *A Wizard of Earthsea*, ch 3]

(6) To light a candle is to cast a shadow.

▸ [Master Hand, in *A Wizard of Earthsea*, ch 3]

(7) And the truth is that as a man's real power grows and his knowledge widens, ever the way he can follow grows narrower: until at last he chooses nothing, but does only and wholly what he *must* do.

▸ [The Summoner, in *A Wizard of Earthsea*, ch 4]

(8) A man would know the end he goes to, but he cannot know it if he does not turn, and return to his beginning, and hold that beginning in his being. If he would not be a stick whirled and whelmed in the stream, he must be the stream itself, all of it, from its spring to its sinking in the sea.

▸ [Ogion, in *A Wizard of Earthsea*, ch 7]

❚ Leisk, David. *See* Johnson, Crockett

❚ L'Engle, Madeleine

(1) It was a dark and stormy night.

▸ [in *A Wrinkle in Time*, ch 1, first line]

(2) There *is* such a thing as a tesseract.
  ▶ [Mrs. Whatsit, in *A Wrinkle in Time*, ch 1]

(3) But of course we can't take any credit for our talents. It's how we use them that counts.
  ▶ [Mrs. Whatsit, in *A Wrinkle in Time*, ch 5]

(4) So I simply pushed the atoms aside and we walked through the space between them.
  ▶ [Charles Wallace, in *A Wrinkle in Time*, ch 8]

(5) Like and equal are two entirely different things.
  ▶ [Lucy, in *A Wrinkle in Time*, ch 9]

(6) You mean you're comparing our lives to a sonnet? A strict form, but freedom within it?
    Yes. . . . You're given the form, but you have to write the sonnet yourself. What you say is completely up to you.
  ▶ [Calvin and Mrs. Whatsit, in *A Wrinkle in Time*, ch 12]

❧ Leodhas, Sorche Nic. *See* Nic Leodhas, Sorche

❧ LeSieg, Theo [pseud. of Theodor Seuss Geisel]

(1) I wish that I had duck feet.
    And I can tell you why.
    You can splash around in duck feet.
    You don't have to keep them dry.
  ▶ [in *I Wish That I Had Duck Feet*]

(2) It all began with that shoe on the wall.
  ▶ [in *Wacky Wednesday*]

❧ Levine, Gail Carson

(1) I said I didn't want to be king if people threw tomatoes at me. I said it seemed a thankless task. . . . It is a thankless task, but tomatoes are the least of it.
  ▶ [Prince Char, in *Ella Enchanted*, ch 24]

❧ Levy, Elizabeth

(1) Gwen stood outside the circle, tap, tap, tapping on her braces. Gwen always tapped her braces whenever she thought something queer was going on.
  ▶ [in *Something Queer at the Ball Park: A Mystery*]

(2) This isn't a game. It's real. It's baseball.
  ▶ [Jill, in *Something Queer at the Ball Park: A Mystery*]

❧ Lewin, Hugh

(1) I don't think there's anything quite so nice as being a flamingo flying off into the sunset.
  ▶ [Jafta, in *Jafta*]

❧ Lewis, C. S.

(1) It's she [the White Witch] that makes it always winter. Always winter and never Christmas; think of that!

▸ [Mr. Tumnus, in *The Lion, the Witch, and the Wardrobe,* ch 2]

(2) Wrong will be right, when
    Aslan comes in sight,
At the sound of his roar,
    sorrows will be no more,
When he bares his teeth,
    winter meets its death,
And when he shakes his mane,
    we shall have spring again.
▸ [Mr. Beaver, in *The Lion, the Witch, and the Wardrobe,* ch 8]

(3) When Adam's flesh and Adam's
    bone
Sits at Cair Paravel in throne,
The evil time will be over and
    done.
▸ [Mr. Beaver, in *The Lion, the Witch, and the Wardrobe,* ch 8]

(4) Battles are ugly when women
    fight.
▸ [Father Christmas, in *The Lion, the Witch, and the Wardrobe,* ch 10]

(5) And, whatever happens, never
    forget to wipe your sword.
▸ [Aslan, in *The Lion, the Witch, and the Wardrobe,* ch 12]

(6) If you've been up all night and
    cried till you have no more tears
    left in you—you will know that
    there comes in the end a sort of
    quietness. You feel as if nothing
    was ever going to happen again.
▸ [in *The Lion, the Witch, and the Wardrobe,* ch 15]

(7) When a willing victim who had
    committed no treachery was killed
    in a traitor's stead, the Table

would crack and Death itself
would start working backwards.
▸ [Aslan, in *The Lion, the Witch, and the Wardrobe,* ch 15]

(8) The worst of sleeping out of doors
    is that you wake up so dreadfully
    early.
▸ [in *Prince Caspian,* ch 3]

❧ Lexau, Joan M. *See* Nodset, Joan L.

❧ Lindgren, Astrid

(1) [Pippi's] hair, the color of a
    carrot, was braided in two tight
    braids that stuck straight out.
    Her nose was the shape of a
    very small potato and was dotted
    all over with freckles.
▸ [in *Pippi Longstocking,* ch 1]

(2) My name is Pippilotta Delicatessa
    Windowshade   Mackrelmint
    Efraim's Daughter Longstocking,
    daughter of Efraim Longstocking,
    formerly the Terror of the Sea,
    now a cannibal king.
▸ [Pippi, in *Pippi Longstocking,* ch 4]

❧ Lindgren, Barbro

(1) Mama loved her baby Ben,
    her small and precious child,
    but he always disobeyed her,
    he was reckless, loud and wild.
▸ [in *The Wild Baby*]

(2) Of course, he's since run off again.

> ▶ [in *The Wild Baby*]

◣ Lionni, Leo

(1) Why don't we stay together? We will still change color wherever we go, but you and I will always be alike.

> ▶ [one chameleon to another, in *A Color of His Own*]

(2) Frogs are frogs and fish is fish and that's that!

> ▶ [tadpole, in *Fish Is Fish*]

(3) I gather sun rays for the cold dark winter days.

> ▶ [Frederick, in *Frederick*]

(4) I gather colors. For winter is gray.

> ▶ [Frederick, in *Frederick*]

(5) I am gathering words. For the winter days are long and many, and we'll run out of things to say.

> ▶ [Frederick, in *Frederick*]

(6) Who scatters snowflakes?
Who melts the ice?
Who spoils the weather? Who makes it nice?
Who grows the four-leaf clovers in June?
Who dims the daylight? Who lights the moon?

Four little field mice who live in the sky.
Four little field mice . . . like you and like I.

One is the Springmouse who turns on the showers.
Then comes the Summer who paints in the flowers.
The Fallmouse is next with walnuts and wheat.
And Winter is last . . . with little cold feet.

Aren't we lucky the seasons are four?
Think of a year with one less . . . or one more!

> ▶ [Frederick, in *Frederick*]

(7) "But Frederick," they said, "you are a poet!"

> ▶ [in *Frederick*]

(8) Only one of them was as black as a mussel shell. His name was Swimmy.

> ▶ [in *Swimmy*]

(9) . . . an eel whose tail was almost too far away to remember.

> ▶ [in *Swimmy*]

(10) We are going to swim all together like the biggest fish in the sea!

> ▶ [Swimmy, in *Swimmy*]

(11) And when they had learned to swim like one giant fish, [Swimmy] said, "I'll be the eye."

> ▶ [in *Swimmy*]

◣ Lisle, Janet Taylor

(1) But, even without being believed, magic can begin to change things. It moves invisibly, through the air, dissolving the usual ways

of seeing, allowing new ways to creep in, secretly, quietly, like a stray cat sliding through bushes.

▶ [*Afternoon of the Elves,* ch 1]

(2) It isn't where you look for elves so much as how you look. . . . Go slowly and quietly, and look deep.

▶ [Sara-Kate, in *Afternoon of the Elves,* ch 6]

❧ Lobel, Arnold

(1) There was a vague pig from Glens Falls
Who had lost all his windows and walls.
While in search of his floor
He misplaced his front door,
That forgetful, vague pig from Glens Falls.

▶ [in *The Book of Pigericks*]

(2) There was a young pig from Schenectady
Who cried, "What is wrong with my neck today?"

▶ [in *The Book of Pigericks*]

(3) So great was his speed
That his legs took the lead,
As they left him behind in East Flushing.

▶ [in *The Book of Pigericks*]

(4) Without a doubt, there is such a thing as too much order.

▶ [in *Fables*]

(5) It is the high and mighty who have the longest distance to fall.

▶ [in *Fables*]

(6) Advice from friends is like the weather. Some of it is good; some of it is bad.

▶ [in *Fables*]

(7) Wishes, on their way to coming true, will not be rushed.

▶ [in *Fables*]

(8) Winter may be beautiful, but bed is much better.

▶ [Toad, in *Frog and Toad All Year,* "Down the Hill"]

(9) I was very happy. I had found the corner that spring was just around.

▶ [Frog, in *Frog and Toad All Year,* "The Corner"]

(10) What you see is the clear warm light of April.

▶ [Frog, in *Frog and Toad Are Friends,* "Spring"]

(11) Come back again and wake me up at about half past May.

▶ [Toad, in *Frog and Toad Are Friends,* "Spring"]

(12) That is not my button. That button is black. My button was white.

▶ [Toad, in *Frog and Toad Are Friends,* "A Lost Button"]

(13) The whole world is covered with buttons, and not one of them is mine!

▶ [Toad, in *Frog and Toad Are Friends,* "A Lost Button"]

(14) "Now seeds," said Toad, "start growing."

▶ [in *Frog and Toad Together,* "The Garden"]

(15) These poor seeds are afraid to grow!
  ▶ [Frog, in *Frog and Toad Together,* "The Garden"]

(16) These must be the most frightened seeds in the whole world!
  ▶ [Toad, in *Frog and Toad Together,* "The Garden"]

(17) MORNING IS TOPS
  ▶ [beetles' sign, in *Grasshopper on the Road,* "The Club"]

(18) When does the clover sparkle with dew? . . . When is the sunshine yellow and new?
  ▶ [Beetles, in *Grasshopper on the Road,* "The Club"]

(19) My bathtub is in the living room! My bed is in the kitchen!
  ▶ [worm, in *Grasshopper on the Road,* "A New House"]

(20) I will sweep until the whole world is clean, clean, clean!
  ▶ [housefly, in *Grasshopper on the Road,* "The Sweeper"]

(21) Mouse soup must be mixed with stories to make it taste really good.
  ▶ [mouse, in *Mouse Soup*]

(22) [Owl] began to think of things that were sad. . . . Books that cannot be read . . . because some of the pages have been torn out. . . . Mornings nobody saw because everybody was sleeping.
  ▶ [in *Owl at Home,* "Tear-Water Tea"]

(23) It tastes a little bit salty, but tearwater tea is always good.

  ▶ [Owl, in *Owl at Home,* "TearWater Tea"]

(24) Then he [Small Pig] sits down and sinks down into the good soft mud.
  ▶ [in *Small Pig*]

(25) Every new day deserves a good, loud trumpet.
  ▶ [Uncle Elephant, in *Uncle Elephant,* "Uncle Elephant Trumpets the Dawn"]

❱ Lofting, Hugh

(1) Animals don't always speak with their mouths. . . . They talk with their ears, with their feet, with their tails—with everything. Sometimes they don't *want* to make a sound. . . . Dogs nearly always use their noses for asking questions.
  ▶ [Polynesia, in *The Story of Doctor Dolittle,* ch 2]

(2) And if you don't help the other animals now, the lions may find themselves left all alone when *they* are in trouble. That often happens to proud people.
  ▶ [Doctor Dolittle, in *The Story of Doctor Dolittle,* ch 8]

(3) This, Doctor, . . . is the pushmi-pullyu—the rarest animal of the African jungles, the only two-headed beast in the world!
  ▶ [Chee-Chee, in *The Story of Doctor Dolittle,* ch 10]

❚ Lord, Bette Bao

(1) In our national pastime, each player is a member of a team, but when he comes to bat, he stands alone. One man. Many opportunities. For no matter how far behind, how late in the game, he, by himself, can make a difference. He can change what has been. He can make it a new ball game.

▶ [Mrs. Rappaport, in *In the Year of the Boar and Jackie Robinson,* June]

❚ Lord, John Vernon

(1) One hot summer in Itching Down
Four million wasps flew into town.

▶ [in *The Giant Jam Sandwich*]

(2) What became of the sandwich? Well,
In Itching Down they like to tell
How the birds flew off with it in their beaks
And had a feast for a hundred weeks.

▶ [in *The Giant Jam Sandwich*]

❚ Lorenzini, Carlo. *See* Collodi, Carlo

❚ Lothrop, Harriet Mulford. *See* Sidney, Margaret

❚ Lovelace, Maud Hart

(1) But the nicest present [Betsy] received was not the usual kind of present. It was the present of a friend. It was Tacy.

▶ [in *Betsy-Tacy,* ch 2]

❚ Lowrey, Janette Sebring

(1) Five little puppies dug a hole under the fence and went for a walk in the wide, wide world.

▶ [in "The Poky Little Puppy," in *Family Treasury of Little Golden Books*]

(2) Now where in the world is that poky little puppy?

▶ [puppies, in "The Poky Little Puppy," in *Family Treasury of Little Golden Books*]

❚ Lowry, Lois

(1) Warts, you know . . . have a kind of magic to them. They come and go without any reason at all, rather like elves.

▶ [Myron Krupnik, in *Anastasia Krupnik,* ch 1]

(2) I don't hate grandmother. . . . But I hate it that she's so old.

▶ [Anastasia, in *Anastasia Krupnik,* ch 6]

(3)   Memory is the happiness of being alone.

> ▶ [Anastasia, interpreting Wordsworth's poem "I Wandered Lonely as a Cloud," in *Anastasia Krupnik,* ch 7]

(4)   Papa, do you remember what you heard the boy say to the soldier? That all of Denmark would be the king's bodyguard? . . . Well, . . . now I think that all of Denmark must be bodyguard for the Jews, as well.

> ▶ [Annemarie, in *Number the Stars,* ch 3]

▌Lyon, George Ella

(1)   I work for *you* . . . for the tilling of your minds and the fruit of your ever-growing souls.

> ▶ [Mr. Aden, Mandy's teacher, in *Borrowed Children,* ch 3]

(2)   A baby is a very heavy thing, any mother will tell you.

> ▶ [Mandy, in *Borrowed Children,* ch 8]

(3)   Different people have different centers.

> ▶ [Aunt Laura, in *Borrowed Children,* ch 13]

(4)   You can't replace a tree anyway. Like people, you don't know how big they were till they're gone.

> ▶ [Omie, Mandy's grandmother, in *Borrowed Children,* ch 18]

(5)   They're [children are] every one borrowed.

> ▶ [Omie, Mandy's grandmother, in *Borrowed Children,* ch 24]

(6)   Good-bye is always hello to something else. Good-bye/hello, good-bye/hello, like the sound of a rocking chair.

> ▶ [Mandy, in *Borrowed Children,* ch 27]

▌MacDonald, Betty

(1)   I love all children but it distresses me when I see a child who has a disease like Selfishness or Answerbackism or Won't-Put-Away-Toys-itis and his parents don't do a thing to cure him.

> ▶ [Mrs. Piggle-Wiggle, in *Mrs. Piggle-Wiggle,* ch 4]

(2)   The Radish Cure is just what Patsy needs. . . . When she has about half an inch of rich black dirt all over her . . . scatter radish seeds on her arms and head. . . . When the little radish plants have three leaves you may begin pulling the largest ones.

> ▶ [Mrs. Piggle-Wiggle, in *Mrs. Piggle-Wiggle,* ch 5]

▌MacDonald, George

(1)   Sometimes beautiful things grow bad by doing bad, and it takes some time for their badness to spoil their beauty. So little boys may be mistaken if they go after things because they are beautiful.

> ▶ [North Wind, in *At the Back of the North Wind,* ch 1]

(2) The most foolish thing is to fight for no good, and to please nobody.
  ▶ [in *At the Back of the North Wind,* ch 1]

(3) Poverty will not make a man worthless—he may be worth a great deal more when he is poor than he was when he was rich; but dishonesty goes very far indeed to make a man of no value.
  ▶ [in *At the Back of the North Wind,* ch 12]

(4) It is a strange thing how the pain of seeing the suffering of those we love will sometimes make us add to their suffering by being cross with them.
  ▶ [in *At the Back of the North Wind,* ch 32]

(5) It's only loving a thing that can make it yours.
  ▶ [Joseph, paraphrasing Diamond, in *At the Back of the North Wind,* ch 33]

(6) The people who think lies, and do lies, are very likely to dream lies.
  ▶ [North Wind, in *At the Back of the North Wind,* ch 37]

(7) People are so ready to think themselves changed when it is only their mood that is changed!
  ▶ [in *The Lost Princess,* ch 4]

(8) Some foolish people think they take another's part when they take the part he takes.
  ▶ [in *The Lost Princess,* ch 7]

(9) To do one's duty will make anyone conceited who only does it sometimes. Those who do it always would as soon think of being conceited of eating their dinner as of doing their duty. To be conceited of doing one's duty is, then, a sign of how little one does it, and how little one sees what a contemptible thing it is not to do it.
  ▶ [in *The Lost Princess,* ch 9]

(10) There is one road talk never finds, and that is the way into the talker's own hands and feet.
  ▶ [in *The Lost Princess,* ch 10]

(11) There is but one true way, however, to get out of any position we may be in, and that is to do the work of it so well that we grow fit for a better one.
  ▶ [in *The Lost Princess,* ch 12]

(12) Nobody can be a *real* princess . . . until she is a princess over herself—that is, until, when she finds herself unwilling to do the thing that is right, she makes herself do it.
  ▶ [Wise Woman, in *The Lost Princess,* ch 14]

▲ MacLachlan, Patricia

(1) This is Sophie. She is almost a year old and she is good.
  ▶ [note left with baby Sophie, in *Baby,* ch 3]

(2) Silence can change you, too.
  ▶ [Larkin, in *Baby,* ch 6]

(3) It doesn't get any better than excellent.

  ▶ [Rebel, in *Baby,* ch 8]

(4) All the world can be found in poetry. All you need to see and hear. All the moments, good and bad, joyous and sad.

  ▶ [Ms. Minifred, in *Baby,* ch 8]

(5) You should know that there are some things for which there are no answers, no matter how beautiful the words may be.

  ▶ [Byrd, in *Baby,* ch 9]

(6) Did you know that words have a life? They travel out into the air with the speed of sound, a small life of their own, before they disappear. Like the circles that a rock makes when it's tossed into the middle of the pond.

  ▶ [Papa, in *Baby,* ch 13]

(7) There are three things to remember about spring on the island. . . . One, it comes after winter. Two, it comes after winter. Three, it comes after winter and you think it's still winter.

  ▶ [old man Brick, in *Baby,* ch 14]

(8) Life is made up of circles. . . . Life is not a straight line. . . . And sometimes we circle back to a past time. But we are not the same. We are changed forever.

  ▶ [Ms. Minifred, in *Baby,* ch 14]

(9) There is no sea here. But the land rolls a little like the sea.

  ▶ [Sarah, in *Sarah, Plain and Tall,* ch 3]

(10) There are always things to miss. . . . No matter where you are.

  ▶ [Maggie, in *Sarah, Plain and Tall,* ch 7]

❧ Marshall, James

(1) But George never said "I told you so." Because that's not what friends are for.

  ▶ [in *George and Martha Encore,* "The Beach"]

(2) A cash reward or chocolate eclairs. . . . That must have been a difficult decision.

  ▶ [Eugene, in *Yummers Too: The Second Course*]

❧ Martin, Bill, Jr., and John Archambault

(1) A told B, and B told C, "I'll meet you at the top of the coconut tree."

  ▶ [in *Chicka Chicka Boom Boom*]

(2) Dark mountains are always around us. They have no beginnings and they have no endings. But we know they are there, Grandfather, when we suddenly feel afraid.

  ▶ [in *Knots on a Counting Rope*]

(3) Boy-Strength-of-Blue-Horses, you have raced darkness and won! You now can see with your heart, feel a part of all that

surrounds you. Your courage lights the way.

▶ [Grandfather, in *Knots on a Counting Rope*]

❧ Martin, Sarah Catherine

(1) Old Mother Hubbard
Went to the cupboard
To fetch her poor dog a bone;
But when she got there
The cupboard was bare
And so the poor dog had none.

▶ [in Baring-Gould, *The Annotated Mother Goose*]

❧ Mayer, Mercer

(1) Go away, Nightmare, or I'll shoot you.

▶ [in *There's a Nightmare in My Closet*]

(2) I suppose there's another nightmare in my closet, but my bed's not big enough for three.

▶ [in *There's a Nightmare in My Closet*]

❧ McCloskey, Robert

(1) Little Bear and Little Sal's mother and Little Sal and Little Bear's mother were all mixed up with each other among the blueberries on Blueberry Hill.

▶ [in *Blueberries for Sal*]

(2) Forty-two pounds of Edible Fungus
In the Wilderness a-growin'
Saved the Settlers from Starvation,
Helped the founding of the Nation.
Forty-two pounds of Edible Fungus
In the Wilderness a-growin'.

▶ [choral work for One Hundred Years of Centerburg Progress Week, in *Homer Price,* "Wheels of Progress"]

(3) Jack, Kack, Lack, Mack, Nack, Ouack, Pack, and Quack.

▶ [names of ducklings, in *Make Way for Ducklings*]

❧ McCully, Emily Arnold

(1) Once you start [walking the high wire], your feet are never happy again on the ground.

▶ [Bellini, in *Mirette on the High Wire*]

(2) Think only of the wire, and of crossing to the end.

▶ [Bellini, in *Mirette on the High Wire*]

❧ McGraw, Eloise

(1) It was Old Bess, the Wise Woman of the village, who first suspected that the baby at her daughter's house was a changeling.

▶ [in *The Moorchild*, ch 1, first line]

(2) Time runs different in the Mound.
  ▶ [The Prince of the Moorfolk, in *The Moorchild,* ch 3]

▌McKinley, Robin

(1) She [Harry Crewe] had always suffered from a vague restlessness, a longing for adventure that she told herself severely was the result of reading so many novels when she was a small child.
  ▶ [in *The Blue Sword,* ch 1]

(2) They [the old rulers of Damar] were sorcerers—or so the story goes. Magicians. They could call the lightning down on the heads of their enemies, that sort of thing—useful stuff for founding an empire.
  ▶ [Jack Dedham, in *The Blue Sword,* ch 1]

(3) Cigars should be like onions. . . . Either the whole company does, or the whole company does not.
  ▶ [Lady Amelia, in *The Blue Sword,* ch 2]

(4) It [malak] tasted as good as it smelled, which . . . gave it points over coffee.
  ▶ [in *The Blue Sword,* ch 4]

(5) It seems to me further that it is very odd that fate should lay so careful a trail and spend so little time preparing the one that must follow it.
  ▶ [Harry Crewe, in *The Blue Sword,* ch 13]

(6) Logic has little to do with government, and nothing at all to do with military administration.
  ▶ [Jack Dedham, in *The Blue Sword,* ch 13]

(7) Royalty isn't allowed to hide—at least not once it has declared itself.
  ▶ [King Arlbeth, in *The Hero and the Crown,* ch 11]

▌McLean, Kathryn. *See* Forbes, Kathryn

▌Meaker, Marijane. *See* Kerr, M. E.

▌Merrill, Jean

(1) I have always believed that we cannot have peace in the world until *all of us* understand how wars start.
  ▶ [in *The Pushcart War,* Introduction]

(2) The Pushcart War started on the afternoon of March 15, 1976, when a truck ran down a pushcart belonging to a flower peddler.
  ▶ [in *The Pushcart War,* ch 1, first line]

(3) The truck drivers had gotten together and figured out that in crowded traffic conditions, the only way to get where you wanted to go was to be *so* big that you didn't have to get out of the

way for anybody. This is known as the Large Object Theory of History.

▶ [in *The Pushcart War,* ch 4]

(4) I think that there are too many trucks and that the trucks are too big.

▶ [Wenda Gambling, in *The Pushcart War,* ch 6]

(5) It is better to have enemies you already know. It is easier to guess what they are going to do. Also, it is better to have enemies who have learned to be a little afraid of you.

▶ [Maxie Hammerman, in *The Pushcart War,* ch 26]

(6) That is what we fought the war for, so that there should always be a few pushcarts in the city of New York.

▶ [Maxie Hammerman, in *The Pushcart War,* ch 36]

❚ Milne, A. A.

(1) The more it snows
       (Tiddely pom),
The more it goes
       (Tiddely pom),
The more it goes
       (Tiddely pom),
On snowing.
And nobody knows
       (Tiddely pom),
How cold my toes
       (Tiddely pom),
How cold my toes
       (Tiddely pom),
Are growing.

▶ [Winnie-the-Pooh, in *The House at Pooh Corner,* ch 1]

(2) But whatever his [Tigger's] weight in pounds, shillings, and ounces,
He always seems bigger because of his bounces.

▶ [Winnie-the-Pooh, in *The House at Pooh Corner,* ch 2]

(3) It is the best way to write poetry, letting things come.

▶ [Winnie-the-Pooh, in *The House at Pooh Corner,* ch 2]

(4) So *that's* what Tiggers like!

▶ [Tigger, referring to Extract of Malt, in *The House at Pooh Corner,* ch 2]

(5) It was eleven o'clock. Which was Time-for-a-little-something.

▶ [in *The House at Pooh Corner,* ch 4]

(6) Tiggers can't climb downwards, because their tails get in the way, only upwards, and Tigger forgot about that when we started, and he's only just remembered.

▶ [Roo, in *The House at Pooh Corner,* ch 4]

(7) They're funny things, Accidents. You never have them till you're having them.

▶ [Eeyore, in *The House at Pooh Corner,* ch 4]

(8) He was the sort of Tigger who was always in front when you were showing him the way anywhere, and was generally out of sight when at last you came to the place and said proudly, "Here we are!"

▶ [in *The House at Pooh Corner,* ch 5]

(9) GON OUT
BACKSON
BISY
BACKSON.
C. R.

> ▶ [Christopher Robin's notice, in *The House at Pooh Corner,* ch 5]

(10) the Spotted or Herbaceous Backson

> ▶ [Owl, in *The House at Pooh Corner,* ch 5]

(11) Rabbit . . . never let things come to him, but always went and fetched them.

> ▶ [in *The House at Pooh Corner,* ch 5]

(12) Pooh was getting rather tired of that sand-pit, and suspected it of following them about, because whichever direction they started in, they always ended up at it, and each time, as it came through the mist at them, Rabbit said triumphantly, "Now I know where we are!" and Pooh said sadly, "So do I," and Piglet said nothing.

> ▶ [in *The House at Pooh Corner,* ch 7]

(13) But wherever they go, and whatever happens to them on the way, in that enchanted place on the top of the Forest, a little boy and his Bear will always be playing.

> ▶ [in *The House at Pooh Corner,* ch 10]

(14) King John was not a good man— He had his little ways.

> ▶ [in "King John's Christmas," in *Now We Are Six*]

(15) Wherever I am, there's always Pooh,
There's always Pooh and Me.

> ▶ [in "Us Two," in *Now We Are Six*]

(16) "I wasn't afraid," said Pooh, said he,
"I'm *never* afraid with you."

> ▶ [in "Us Two," in *Now We Are Six*]

(17) Christopher Robin
Had wheezles
And sneezles.

> ▶ [in "Sneezles," in *Now We Are Six*]

(18) They wondered
If wheezles
Could turn
Into measles,
If sneezles
Would turn
Into mumps.

> ▶ [in "Sneezles," in *Now We Are Six*]

(19) When I was One,
I had just begun.

> ▶ [in "The End," in *Now We Are Six*]

(20) So I think I'll be six now for ever and ever.

> ▶ [in "The End," in *Now We Are Six*]

(21) They're changing the guard at Buckingham Palace—
Christopher Robin went down with Alice.
Alice is marrying one of the guard.
"A soldier's life is terrible hard,"
Says Alice.

> ▶ [in "Buckingham Palace," in *When We Were Very Young*]

(22) James gave the huffle of a
        snail in danger
      And nobody heard him at all.

   ▶ [in "The Four Friends," in *When
      We Were Very Young*]

(23) James James
      Morrison Morrison
      Weatherby George Dupree
      Took great
      Care of his Mother,
      Though he was only three.
      James James
      Said to his Mother,
      "Mother," he said, said he:
      "You must never go down to
        the end of the town,
      if you don't go down with me."

   ▶ [in "Disobedience," in *When We
      Were Very Young*]

(24) *Has anybody seen my mouse?*
      I opened his box for half a minute,
      Just to make sure he was
        really in it,
      And I while I was looking, he
        jumped outside!

   ▶ [in "Missing," in *When We Were
      Very Young*]

(25) Nobody,
      My darling,
      Could call me
      A fussy man—
      BUT
      *I do like a little bit of butter to
      my bread!*

   ▶ [The King, in "The King's Break-
      fast," in *When We Were Very
      Young*]

(26) *Hush! Hush! Whisper who dares!
      Christopher Robin is saying
      his prayers.*

   ▶ [in "Vespers," in *When We Were
      Very Young*]

(27) Here is Edward Bear, coming
      downstairs now, bump, bump,
      bump, on the back of his head,
      behind Christopher Robin. It is,
      as far as he knows, the only way
      of coming downstairs, but some-
      times he feels that there really
      is another way, if only he could
      stop bumping for a moment and
      think of it.

   ▶ [in *Winnie-the-Pooh,* ch 1, first
      line]

(28) He's Winnie-ther-Pooh. Don't
      you know what *"ther"* means?

   ▶ [Christopher Robin, in *Winnie-
      the-Pooh,* ch 1]

(29) Once upon a time, a very long
      time ago now, about last Fri-
      day, Winnie-the-Pooh lived in
      a forest all by himself under the
      name of Sanders.
      *("What does 'under the name'
      mean?" asked Christopher Robin.
      "It means he had the name
      over the door in gold letters,
      and lived under it.")*

   ▶ [in *Winnie-the-Pooh,* ch 1]

(30) The only reason for making a
      buzzing-noise that *I* know of is
      because you're a bee. . . . And the
      only reason for being a bee that
      I know of is making honey. . . .
      And the only reason for making
      honey is so as *I* can eat it.

   ▶ [Winnie-the-Pooh, in *Winnie-
      the-Pooh,* ch 1]

(31) Isn't it funny
How a bear likes honey?
Buzz! Buzz! Buzz!
I wonder why he does?
▸ [Winnie-the-Pooh, in *Winnie-the-Pooh*, ch 1]

(32) Silly old Bear!
▸ [Christopher Robin, referring to Winnie-the-Pooh, in *Winnie-the-Pooh*, throughout]

(33) There must be somebody there, because somebody must have *said* "Nobody."
▸ [Winnie-the-Pooh, when Rabbit says Nobody is at home, in *Winnie-the-Pooh*, ch 2]

(34) Not very how. . . . I don't seem to have felt at all how for a long time.
▸ [Eeyore, in *Winnie-the-Pooh*, ch 4]

(35) I am a Bear of Very Little Brain, and long words Bother me.
▸ [Winnie-the-Pooh, in *Winnie-the-Pooh*, ch 4]

(36) And honey, I should say, right down to the bottom of the jar.
▸ [Winnie-the-Pooh, in *Winnie-the-Pooh*, ch 5]

(37) Help, help! . . . a Heffalump, a Horrible Heffalump!
▸ [Piglet, in *Winnie-the-Pooh*, ch 5]

(38) "Good morning, Pooh Bear," said Eeyore gloomily. "If it is a good morning," he said. "Which I doubt."
▸ [in *Winnie-the-Pooh*, ch 6]

(39) My spelling is wobbly. It's good spelling but it Wobbles, and the letters get in the wrong places.
▸ [Winnie-the-Pooh, in *Winnie-the-Pooh*, ch 6]

(40) In the Usual Way, if you know what I mean, Pooh.
▸ [Christopher Robin, explaining how Kanga and Roo came to the Forest, in *Winnie-the-Pooh*, ch 7]

(41) It is hard to be brave, . . . when you're only a Very Small Animal.
▸ [Piglet, in *Winnie-the-Pooh*, ch 7]

(42) Impossible without Me! *That* sort of Bear.
▸ [Winnie-the-Pooh, in *Winnie-the-Pooh*, ch 7]

(43) this   take
If is   shall   really to
   flying I   never   it.
▸ [Piglet, in Kanga's pocket, in *Winnie-the-Pooh*, ch 7]

(44) NORTH POLE
DISCOVERED BY POOH
POOH FOUND IT.
▸ [sign by Christopher Robin, in *Winnie-the-Pooh*, ch 8]

(45) Piglet told himself that never in all his life, and *he* was goodness knows *how* old—three, was it, or four?—never had he seen so much rain.
▸ [in *Winnie-the-Pooh*, ch 9]

(46) It's so much more friendly with two.
▸ [Piglet, in *Winnie-the-Pooh*, ch 9]

(47) Sometimes it's a Boat, and sometimes it's more of an Accident. It all depends. . . . On whether I'm on the top of it or underneath it.

▶ [Winnie-the-Pooh, in *Winnie-the-Pooh*, ch 9]

(48) 3 cheers for Pooh!
(For Who?)
For Pooh—
(Why what did he do?). . .
3 Cheers for Pooh!
(For Who?)
For Pooh—
3 Cheers for Bear!
(For where?)
For Bear—
3 Cheers for the wonderful Winnie-the-Pooh!
(Just tell me, somebody—
WHAT DID HE DO?)

▶ [Winnie-the-Pooh, in *Winnie-the-Pooh*, ch 10]

(49) This writing business. Pencils and what-not. Over-rated, if you ask me.

▶ [Eeyore, in *Winnie-the-Pooh*, ch 10]

(50) "When you wake up in the morning, Pooh," said Piglet at last, "what's the first thing you say to yourself?"

"What's for breakfast?" said Pooh. "What do *you* say, Piglet?"

"I say, I wonder what's going to happen exciting *today*?" said Piglet.

Pooh nodded thoughtfully.
"It's the same thing," he said.

▶ [in *Winnie-the-Pooh*, ch 10]

▌ Minarik, Else Holmelund

(1) For you are my little bear, and I know it.

▶ [Mother Bear, in *Little Bear*, "Little Bear Goes to the Moon"]

(2) You can't have that wish, my Little Bear.

▶ [Mother Bear, in *Little Bear*, "Little Bear's Wish"]

▌ Montgomery, Lucy Maud

(1) more scope for the imagination

▶ [Anne, in *Anne of Green Gables*, throughout]

(2) There is nothing more aggravating than a man who won't talk back—unless it is a woman who won't.

▶ [in *Anne of Green Gables*, ch 4]

(3) It's been my experience that you can nearly always enjoy things if you make up your mind firmly that you will. Of course, you must make it up *firmly*.

▶ [Anne, in *Anne of Green Gables*, ch 5]

(4) Saying one's prayers isn't exactly the same thing as praying.

▶ [Anne, in *Anne of Green Gables*, ch 10]

(5) Maples are such sociable trees. . . . They're always rustling and whispering to you.

▶ [Anne, in *Anne of Green Gables*, ch 15]

(6) All great things are wound up with all things little.

 ▶ [in *Anne of Green Gables,* ch 18]

(7) Ruby Gillis says when she grows up she's going to have ever so many beaus on the string and have them all crazy about her; but I think that would be too exciting. I'd rather have just one in his right mind.

 ▶ [Anne, in *Anne of Green Gables,* ch 18]

(8) That's the worst part of growing up. . . .The things you wanted so much when you were a child don't seem half so wonderful to you when you get them.

 ▶ [Anne, in *Anne of Green Gables,* ch 29]

❧ Moore, Clement Clark

(1) 'Twas the night before
  Christmas,
 when all through the house
 Not a creature was stirring,
 not even a mouse.

 ▶ [in *A Visit from St. Nicholas (The Night Before Christmas)*]

(2) visions of sugarplums
 danced in their heads

 ▶ [in *A Visit from St. Nicholas (The Night Before Christmas)*]

(3) Now, Dasher! Now, Dancer!
 Now, Prancer and Vixen!
 On, Comet! On, Cupid!
 On Donder and Blitzen!

 ▶ [in *A Visit from St. Nicholas (The Night Before Christmas)*]

❧ Morey, Walt

(1) I only know that sometimes something does happen between people and animals. There seems to be a bond that overcomes all fear, prejudice, everything objectionable. I suppose you might call it perfect love.

 ▶ [Ellen, in *Gentle Ben,* ch 2]

(2) Fear's the worst thing. It makes people take drastic action to protect themselves.

 ▶ [Karl, in *Gentle Ben,* ch 10]

(3) Now you can prove your love for Ben by turning him loose. Freedom is the greatest gift you can give him.

 ▶ [Ellen, in *Gentle Ben,* ch 10]

❧ Morris, Gerald

(1) If you want to know a king, see how he treats his defeated foes. All are gracious to their equals; one in a thousand is gracious to an enemy he has conquered.

 ▶ [Gawain, in *The Squire's Tale,* ch 2]

(2) I know that the greatest victory is not won with one's strength but is won over one's own weakness.

 ▶ [Sir Marhault, in *The Squire's Tale,* ch 6]

(3) There is no love that might not appear ridiculous to someone else. Are you so sure that you will never love foolishly?

 ▶ [Nimue, in *The Squire's Tale,* ch 9]

(4) Sometimes it is a compliment to be admired. Other times it is an insult.
  ▶ [Nimue, in *The Squire's Tale,* ch 10]

(5) To forgive the unforgivable is the breath of life in this world.
  ▶ [Lorie, in *The Squire's Tale,* ch 10]

❧ Mosel, Arlene

(1) Her second son she called Chang, which meant "little or nothing." But her first and honored son, she called Tikki tikki tembo-no sa rembo-chari bari ruchi-pip peri pembo, which meant "the most wonderful thing in the whole wide world!"
  ▶ [in *Tikki Tikki Tembo*]

(2) And from that day to this the Chinese have always thought it wise to give all their children little, short names instead of great long names.
  ▶ [in *Tikki Tikki Tembo*]

❧ Moss, Lloyd

(1) With mournful moan and silken tone,
Itself alone came ONE TROMBONE.
  ▶ [in *Zin! Zin! Zin! A Violin*]

❧ Munsch, Robert

(1) I'll love you forever,
I'll like you for always,
As long as I'm living
my baby you'll be.
  ▶ [in *Love You Forever*]

(2) Your clothes are really pretty and your hair is very neat. You look like a real prince, but you are a bum.
  ▶ [Princess Elizabeth, in *The Paper Bag Princess*]

❧ Murphy, Jill

(1) "Oh, NO!" said Mr. Bear, "I can't stand THIS."
  ▶ [in *Peace at Last*]

❧ Myers, Walter Dean

(1) If you're the baddest dude on the block you've got responsibilities. If you got the weight you got to take the freight.
  ▶ [in *Fast Sam, Cool Clyde, and Stuff,* ch 1]

(2) If crying was going to bring anybody back to life, then there wouldn't be any dead people.
  ▶ [Clyde's mother, in *Fast Sam, Cool Clyde, and Stuff,* ch 3]

(3) Not hurting his friend is more important to him than proving he's a man . . . and that makes

him a real *person*. And in my book that's better then being a real *man*. Because being a real man is biology and what I'm talking about is living like people.

▶ [Maria, in *Fast Sam, Cool Clyde, and Stuff*, ch 3]

(4) Sometimes things happen and even though the thing that happens is bad you don't mind so much because no one knows about it except you. It's like having on raggedy underwear. You don't really feel cool having it on, but you don't feel nearly as bad as if you knew somebody else knew.

▶ [in *Fast Sam, Cool Clyde, and Stuff*, ch 4]

◣ Napoli, Donna Jo

(1) Summer comes over the hill like a hairy blanket.

▶ [in *The Magic Circle,* ch 1, first line]

(2) Forgiveness is a little thing when love is there.

▶ [Gretel, in *The Magic Circle,* ch 9]

(3) I'm De Fawg Pin.

▶ [Pin, in *The Prince of the Pond,* ch 6]

(4) An animal fed comes back again and again. A man fed is no better.

▶ [Mother, in *Zel*, ch 8]

◣ Nash, Ogden

(1) the realio, trulio, cowardly dragon

▶ [in *Custard the Dragon*]

◣ Naylor, Phyllis Reynolds

(1) Life is like a dumpster. As soon as you get rid of one embarrassment, you pick up another.

▶ [Alice, in *The Agony of Alice,* ch 2]

(2) It's all right to have secrets, . . . as long as you don't have any secrets from yourself.

▶ [Mrs. Plotkin, in *The Agony of Alice,* ch 16]

(3) I also know that you can lie not only by what you say but what you don't say.

▶ [Marty, in *Shiloh,* ch 6]

(4) His truck's got to be perfect, to make up for all the ways Judd's not.

▶ [Marty, in *Shiloh,* ch 15]

(5) No matter what you decide to be, it's going to have its gringy moments.

▶ [Mrs. Morley, in *Witch's Sister,* ch 2]

◣ Nesbit, Edith

(1) It is very wise to let children choose exactly what they like, because they are very foolish and inexperienced, and sometimes they will choose a really instructive thing without meaning to.

▶ [in *Five Children and It,* ch 4]

(2) When Arden's lord still lacketh
       ten
     And may not see his nine again,
     Let Arden stand as Arden may
     On Arden Knoll at death of day.
     If he have skill to say the spell
     He shall find the treasure, and
       all be well!
     ▶ [in *The House of Arden*, "Arden's
       Lord"]

(3) One of the uses of poetry—one
     says it to oneself in distressing
     circumstances, . . . or when one
     has to wait at railway stations,
     or when one cannot get to sleep
     at night.
     ▶ [in *The House of Arden*, "The
       Key of the Parlor"]

❦ Ness, Evaline

(1) There's good MOONSHINE
     and bad MOONSHINE. . . . The
     important thing is to know the
     difference.
     ▶ [Sam's father, in *Sam, Bangs, &
       Moonshine*]

❦ Neville, Emily

(1) My father is always talking about
     how a dog can be very educa-
     tional for a boy. This is one reason
     I got a cat.
     ▶ [Dave, in *It's Like This, Cat*, ch
       1, first line]

❦ Nic Leodhas, Sorche [pseud. of Leclaire Alger]

(1) There's room galore.
     Och, come awa' in! There's
       room for one more,
     Always room for one more!
     ▶ [in *Always Room for One More*]

❦ Noble, Trinka Hakes

(1) "How was your class trip to the
     farm?"
         "Oh . . . boring . . . kind of
     dull . . . until the cow started
     crying."
     ▶ [in *The Day Jimmy's Boa Ate
       the Wash*]

❦ Nodset, Joan L. [pseud. of Joan M. Lexau]

(1) The farmer had a hat, an old
       brown hat.
     Oh, how he liked that old
       brown hat!
     ▶ [in *Who Took the Farmer's Hat?*]

❦ Norton, Mary

(1) Factories go on making safety
     pins, and every day people go on
     buying safety pins and yet, some-
     how, there never is a safety pin
     just when you want one.
     ▶ [Kate, in *The Borrowers*, ch 1]

(2) I been "seen."
> ▶ [Pod, in *The Borrowers,* ch 4]

(3) I don't think it's so clever to live on alone, for ever and ever, in a great, big, half-empty house; under the floor, with no one to talk to, no one to play with, nothing to see but dust and passages, no light but candlelight and firelight and what comes through the cracks.
> ▶ [Arrietty, in *The Borrowers,* ch 6]

(4) It shocked her [Arrietty] to be right. Parents were right, not children. Children could say anything, Arrietty knew, and enjoy saying it—knowing they were safe and wrong.
> ▶ [in *The Borrowers,* ch 6]

(5) Human beans are *for* Borrowers— like bread's for butter!
> ▶ [Arrietty, in *The Borrowers,* ch 10]

▌ Numeroff, Laura Joffe

(1) If you give a mouse a cookie, he's going to ask for a glass of milk.
> ▶ [in *If You Give a Mouse a Cookie*]

▌ O'Brien, Robert C. [pseud. of Robert Leslie Conly]

(1) All doors are hard to unlock until you find the key.
> ▶ [Mrs. Frisby, remembering her husband's words, in *Mrs. Frisby and the Rats of NIMH,* "Mr. Fitzgibbon's Plow"]

(2) That's what reading is: using symbols to suggest a picture or an idea.
> ▶ [Nicodemus, in *Mrs. Frisby and the Rats of NIMH,* "A Lesson in Reading"]

(3) We could not find any easy answer—because there was none. There was, however, a hard answer.
> ▶ [Nicodemus, in *Mrs. Frisby and the Rats of NIMH,* "Thorn Valley"]

(4) No. We haven't [got a civilization]. We're just living on the edge of somebody else's, like fleas on a dog's back. If the dog drowns, the fleas drown, too.
> ▶ [Nicodemus, in *Mrs. Frisby and the Rats of NIMH,* "Thorn Valley"]

▌ O'Dell, Scott

(1) Though his words sounded the same as before and meant nothing to me, they now seemed sweet. They were the sound of a human voice. There is no sound like this in all the world.
> ▶ [Karana, in *Island of the Blue Dolphins,* ch 28]

(2) Young men never think about death. That's why they make good soldiers.
> ▶ [Mr. Pennywell, in *Sarah Bishop,* ch 9]

(3) Fear is something that encourages people to harm thee. Fear causes hatred.
> ▶ [Isaac Morton, in *Sarah Bishop,* ch 32]

(4) We cannot live without God's love. And our own love, which we must share with Him and with each other.

▶ [Isaac Morton, in *Sarah Bishop*, ch 41]

(5) I hope that he [Tall Boy] does not kill another bear. If he does he will call himself Very Tall Boy and we will have much trouble with him.

▶ [Bright Morning's mother, in *Sing Down the Moon*, ch 3]

❧ O'Hara, Mary

(1) Here in her world of men, husband and sons, hired men, haying crew, horse buyers, to be the *Missus* meant to be that before which they could remove their hats, and bend their heads. In the cities a woman could turn into a driving machine, or harden herself to meet difficulties, but the Missus on a farm or ranch, though she might be milker of cows or trainer of horses, must be more and not less woman for all of that, or she would rob the men around her of something which was as sweet to them as the sugar in their coffee.

▶ [in *My Friend Flicka*, ch 2]

(2) There's a responsibility we have towards animals. . . . We use them. We shut them up, keep their natural food and water away from them; that means we have to feed and water them. Take their freedom away, rope them, harness them, that means we have to supply a different sort of safety for them. Once I've put a rope on a horse, or taken away its ability to take care of itself, then I've got to take care of it.

▶ [Rob McLaughlin, in *My Friend Flicka*, ch 4]

(3) He [Ken] wanted them all [colts], and until he chose, in a way, they were all his.

▶ [in *My Friend Flicka*, ch 13]

(4) If you find *love*—if a person or an animal finds love—it's the same as finding safety, isn't it? It's comfort and friendliness and help.

▶ [Nell McLaughlin, in *My Friend Flicka*, ch 27]

❧ O'Neill, Mary

(1) Time is purple
Just before night

▶ [in "What Is Purple?" in *Hailstones and Halibut Bones*]

(2) Black is beauty
In its deepest form,
The darkest cloud
In a thunderstorm.

▶ [in "What Is Black?" in *Hailstones and Halibut Bones*]

(3) Orange is music
Of the tango.

▶ [in "What Is Orange?" in *Hailstones and Halibut Bones*]

(4) Red is a show-off
No doubt about it.

> ▶ [in "What Is Red?" in *Hail-stones and Halibut Bones*]

❚ Oppenheim, Shulamith Levey

(1) And this is why I *think* the camel has the look it does. For while man knows only ninety-nine names for Allah, the camel knows the hundredth name, and he has never told.

> ▶ [in *The Hundredth Name*]

❚ Orr, Wendy

(1) Nobody tells you that real pain is more than something in your body, it's a black vortex that engulfs your mind, leaving you wondering if there's a border between life and death and which side you're on.

> ▶ [Anna, in *Peeling the Onion*, ch 2]

❚ Palmer, Helen [pseud. of Helen Geisel]

(1) When you feed a fish,
never feed him a lot.
So much and no more!
Never more than a spot,
or something may happen!
You never know what!

> ▶ [Mr. Carp, in *A Fish out of Water*]

❚ Park, Barbara

(1) Moving makes you feel all alone inside.

> ▶ [Howard, in *The Kid in the Red Jacket*, ch 1]

(2) Bounce right back! I'm not kidding. [Mom] really said that! She made me sound like a Nerf ball. Like she had a foam rubber son with no emotions at all!

> ▶ [Howard, in *The Kid in the Red Jacket*, ch 1]

(3) Even though sometimes you can control your anger, you can't control your sadness.

> ▶ [Howard, in *The Kid in the Red Jacket*, ch 1]

(4) Jails are for the really big mistakes that "I'm sorry" just doesn't cover.

> ▶ [Howard, in *The Kid in the Red Jacket*, ch 9]

(5) Just let me say right off the bat, it was a bike accident.

> ▶ [Phoebe, in *Mick Harte Was Here*, "Mick," first line]

(6) Tap Dancing on God's Piano

> ▶ [chapter title, in *Mick Harte Was Here*]

(7) But see, he's never going to be lost, Mom. I swear to God he's not. Because Zoe and I sort of figured out he's everywhere now. And if you're everywhere, then how can you be lost?

> ▶ [Phoebe, talking about her brother's death, in *Mick Harte Was Here*, "Dogs Can Laugh in Heaven"]

❧ Paterson, Katherine

(1) Even a prince may be a fool.

▶ [Leslie, in *Bridge to Terabithia*, ch 6]

(2) She [Leslie] had made him [Jess] leave his old self behind and come into her world, and then before he was really at home in it but too late to go back, she had left him stranded there alone— like an astronaut wandering about on the moon. Alone.

▶ [in *Bridge to Terabithia*, ch 12]

(3) It's like the smarter you are, the more things can scare you.

▶ [Jess, in *Bridge to Terabithia*, ch 13]

(4) Terabithia was like a castle where you came to be knighted. After you stayed for a while and grew strong you had to move on.

▶ [in *Bridge to Terabithia*, ch 13]

(5) It was up to [Jess] to pay back to the world in beauty and caring what Leslie had loaned him in vision and strength.

▶ [in *Bridge to Terabithia*, ch 13]

(6) You couldn't just slam your brain like a back door.

▶ [Vinnie, when told to close the door to unpleasantness, in *Flip-Flop Girl*, ch 3]

(7) A smart person like you oughta be able to think of a few regular words to stick in amongst the cusses.

(8) Sometimes . . . you gotta walk on your heel and favor your toe even if it makes your heel a little sore.

▶ [Maime Trotter, in *The Great Gilly Hopkins*, "Pow"]

(9) All that stuff about happy endings is lies. The only ending in this world is death. Now that might or might not be happy, but either way, you ain't ready to die, are you?

▶ [Maime Trotter, in *The Great Gilly Hopkins*, "Homecoming"]

(10) I had never caused my parents "a minute's worry." Didn't they know that worry proves you care? Didn't they realize that I needed their worry to assure myself that I was worth something?

▶ [Louise, in *Jacob Have I Loved*, ch 3]

(11) Punch after punch after punch. February is a mean bully. Nothing could be worse—except August.

▶ [Louise, in *Jacob Have I Loved*, ch 8]

(12) August and February are both alike in one way. They're both dream killers.

▶ [Louise, in *Jacob Have I Loved*, ch 8]

(13) I bet there's not one word in the whole blasted Bible on how to speak to cats.

▶ [Louise, in *Jacob Have I Loved*, ch 8]

▶ [Maime Trotter, in *The Great Gilly Hopkins*, "The Man Who Comes to Supper"]

(14) You ain't worthless if you can make a person laugh.

  ▶ [Jip, in *Jip: His Story*, ch 7]

(15) Now Jip was just an ignorant boy and it wasn't his business, he knew, to try to tell a writer how to write a book, but it stood to reason that if you want to catch a reader tight, the trap needs to be plain and strong with no smell of the trapper lingering on it.

  ▶ [in *Jip: His Story*, ch 11]

(16) You and me is in a pickle barrel without a fork.

  ▶ [Put Nelson, in *Jip: His Story*, ch 15]

❚ Paulsen, Gary

(1) . . . the reality of the woods. To wit: Bears and wolves did what they wanted to do, and Brian had to fit in.

  ▶ [in *Brian's Winter*, ch 2]

(2) Sometimes words lie—but the song is always true.

  ▶ [Russel's father, in *Dogsong*, ch 1]

(3) Dogs are like white people. . . . They do not know how to get a settled mind. They are always turning, looking for a better way to lie down. And if things go wrong they have anger and frustration.

  ▶ [Oogruk, in *Dogsong*, ch 2]

(4) You don't get songs, you *are* a song. When we gave up our songs . . . we gave up our insides as well.

  ▶ [Oogruk, in *Dogsong*, ch 2]

(5) Look to the center of the center of where the point [of the arrow] will go. Look *inside* the center.

  ▶ [Oogruk, in *Dogsong*, ch 3]

(6) The thing with dying was to try to not die and make death take you with surprise.

  ▶ [Russel, in *Dogsong*, ch 4]

(7) It isn't the destination that counts. It is the journey. That is what life is. A journey. Make it the right way and you will fill it correctly with days. Pay attention to the journey.

  ▶ [Oogruk, in *Dogsong*, ch 10]

(8) Come, see my dogs.
Out before me
they go,
in the long line to the sea.
Out they go.
Come, see my dogs.
They carry me
into all things, all things I will be;
all things that will come to me
will come to my dogs.
I stand on the earth and I sing.
Come, see my dogs.

  ▶ [from Russel's Dogsong, in *Dogsong*, part 3]

(9) If you keep walking back from good luck, . . . you'll come to bad luck.

  ▶ [Brian, in *Hatchet*, ch 4]

(10) Feeling sorry for yourself didn't work. It wasn't just that it was wrong to do, or that it was considered incorrect. It was more than that—it didn't work. . . . Self-pity had accomplished nothing.

▸ [Brian, in *Hatchet*, ch 8]

(11) Perhaps the greatest paradox about understanding "the woods" is that so many who enjoy it, or seem to enjoy it, spend most of their time trying to kill parts of it.

▸ [*Woodsong*, ch 1]

(12) Primarily the difference between people and animals is that people use fire. People create fire, and animals don't.

▸ [*Woodsong*, ch 4]

❧ Peck, Robert Newton

(1) A fence sets men together, not apart.

▸ [Haven Peck, in *A Day No Pigs Would Die*, ch 3]

(2) Never miss a chance . . . to keep your mouth shut.

▸ [Haven Peck, in *A Day No Pigs Would Die*, ch 10]

(3) My face was wet with the sweat of hurry. It feels worse, Papa always said, than the sweat of work.

▸ [in *A Day No Pigs Would Die*, ch 10]

(4) More than a farmer?! . . . What better can a man be? There's no higher calling than animal husbandry, and making things live and grow. We farmers are stewards. Our lot is to tend all of God's good living things, and I say there's nothing finer.

▸ [Ben Tanner, in *A Day No Pigs Would Die*, ch 13]

(5) A man's worship counts for naught, unless his dog and cat are better for it.

▸ [Shaker earthy reason, in *A Day No Pigs Would Die*, About the Author]

(6) A shut mouth can bottle up a barrel of sin.

▸ [Soup, in *Soup*, ch 4]

(7) Eddy Tacker was so mean he'd pee on a puppy.

▸ [in *Soup*, ch 9]

❧ Pene DuBois, William

(1) The wise old bear who lived at the top of the tallest Eucalyptus tree thought this behavior was TERRIBLE.

▸ [in *Bear Party*]

(2) There are two kinds of travel. The usual way is to take the fastest imaginable conveyance along the shortest road. The other way is not to care particularly where you are going or how long it will take you, or whether you will get there or not.

▸ [in *The Twenty-One Balloons*, Introduction]

(3) The best way of travel, however, if you aren't in any hurry at all, if you don't care where you are going, if you don't like to use your legs, if you want to see everything quite clearly, if you don't want to be annoyed at all by any choice of directions, is in a balloon. . . . In a balloon you can decide only when to start, and usually when to stop. The rest is left entirely to nature.

▶ [in *The Twenty-One Balloons*, Introduction]

(4) We have an unusual Constitution. It's a sort of Restaurant Government.

▶ [Mr. F., in *The Twenty-One Balloons*, ch 6]

❧ Petersham, Maud and Miska

(1) Then the surprised Mr. and Mrs. Clown saw their tent walk away.

▶ [in *The Circus Baby*]

(2) My child, you do not have to learn to eat as the circus people do because, after all, *you* are an ELEPHANT.

▶ [Mother Elephant, in *The Circus Baby*]

❧ Pilkey, Dav

(1) When cats are dreaming, they can swim with the fishes and lose their socks in the sea.

▶ [in *When Cats Dream*]

(2) When cats are dreaming, they can comb their hair with the moon.

▶ [in *When Cats Dream*]

❧ Pinkwater, Daniel Manus

(1) Melvin, Louise, Phoebe, Willie, Norman, Hortense, Bruce, Susie, Charles, Teddie, Neddie, Eddie, Freddie, and Sweetie-Pie.

▶ [sled dogs' names, in *Aunt Lulu*]

(2) My house is me and I am it. My house is where I like to be and it looks like all my dreams.

▶ [Mr. Plumbean, and later, others, in *The Big Orange Splot*]

(3) This is the life! . . . The open road, a good machine, and a whole wheat fig bar!

▶ [Uncle Borgel, in *Borgel*, ch 3]

(4) Time is like a map of New Jersey, space is like a bagel with poppy seeds, and the other is like a salad with one thing in it you like.

▶ [*Borgel*, ch 3]

(5) There is no limit to what most people don't notice.

▶ [*Borgel*, ch 26]

(6) Every boy should have a chicken.

▶ [Poppa, in *The Hoboken Chicken Emergency*, ch 1]

❚ Piper, Watty [pseud. of Mabel Caroline Bragg]

(1) I'm not very big. . . . They use me only for switching trains in the yard. I have never been over the mountain.
> ▶ [Little Blue Engine, in *The Little Engine That Could*]

(2) I think I can. I think I can. I think I can.
> ▶ [Little Blue Engine, in *The Little Engine That Could*]

❚ Polacco, Patricia

(1) Of course is true, but it may not have happened!
> ▶ [Grandmother, in *My Rotten Redheaded Older Brother*]

(2) Wishes are funny, aren't they? . . . Sometimes they come true differently than you think they will.
> ▶ [in *My Rotten Redheaded Older Brother*]

❚ Polushkin, Maria

(1) Mother, Mother, I Want Another
> ▶ [title of book]

❚ Porter, Eleanor H.

(1) the "just being glad" game
> ▶ [Pollyanna, in *Pollyanna*, throughout]

(2) Oh, of course I'd be *breathing* all the time I was doing those things, Aunt Polly, but I wouldn't be living. You breathe all the time you're asleep, but you aren't living. I mean *living*—doing the things you want to do. . . . Just breathing isn't living!
> ▶ [Pollyanna, in *Pollyanna*, ch 6]

(3) Of course things you don't know about are always nicer'n things you do, same as the pertater on 'tother side of the plate is always the biggest.
> ▶ [Jimmy Bean, in *Pollyanna*, ch 14]

(4) It takes a woman's hand and heart, or a child's presence, to make a home.
> ▶ [John Pendleton, in *Pollyanna*, ch 19]

❚ Porter, Gene Stratton. *See* Stratton-Porter, Gene

❚ Potter, Beatrix

(1) NO MORE TWIST
> ▶ [in *The Tailor of Gloucester*]

(2) . . . tippets for mice and ribbons for mobs! for mice!
> ▶ [in *The Tailor of Gloucester*]

(3) . . . an elegantly dressed gentleman reading a newspaper. He had black prick ears and sandy coloured whiskers.
> ▶ [in *The Tale of Jemima Puddle-Duck*]

(4) Jemima Puddle-Duck was a simpleton: not even the mention of sage and onions made her suspicious.

    ▶ [in *The Tale of Jemima Puddle-Duck*]

(5) Lily-white and clean, oh!
With little frills between, oh!
Smooth and hot—red rusty spot
Never more be seen, oh!

    ▶ [Mrs. Tiggy-Winkle's song, in *The Tale of Mrs. Tiggy-Winkle*]

(6) Once upon a time there were four little Rabbits, and their names were Flopsy, Mopsy, Cotton-tail, and Peter.

    ▶ [in *The Tale of Peter Rabbit*, first line]

(7) Don't go into Mr. McGregor's garden: your Father had an accident there; he was put in a pie by Mrs. McGregor.

    ▶ [mother rabbit, in *The Tale of Peter Rabbit*]

(8) I am sorry to say that Peter was not very well during the evening. His mother put him to bed, and made some camomile tea, and she gave a dose of it to Peter! "One tablespoonful to be taken at bed-time."

    ▶ [in *The Tale of Peter Rabbit*]

(9) But Flopsy, Mopsy, and Cotton-tail had bread and milk and blackberries, for supper.

    ▶ [in *The Tale of Peter Rabbit*]

(10) This is a tale about a tail—a tail that belonged to a little red squirrel, and his name was Nutkin.

    ▶ [in *The Tale of Squirrel Nutkin*, first line]

❧ Prelutsky, Jack

(1) Ride a purple pelican,
ride a silver stork,
ride them from Seattle
to the city of New York,
soar above the buildings,
bobble like a cork,
ride a purple pelican,
ride a silver stork.

    ▶ [in *Ride a Purple Pelican*]

❧ Preston, Edna Mitchell

(1) I think my breakfast is going to be YOU. [also lunch and supper]

    ▶ [cat to bluebird, in *The Sad Story of the Little Bluebird and the Hungry Cat*]

❧ Ransome, Arthur

(1) Better drowned than duffers if not duffers wont drown

    ▶ [father's telegram, in *Swallows and Amazons*, ch 1]

(2) If you want to go on liking [cooking], take my advice and make others do the washing up.

    ▶ [Mother, in *Swallows and Amazons*, ch 5]

❚ Raskin, Ellen

(1) Senseless, you say? Death is senseless yet makes way for the living. Life, too, is senseless unless you know who you are, what you want, and which way the wind blows.
  ▸ [Samuel W. Westing's will, in *The Westing Game*, ch 7]

❚ Rawlings, Marjorie Kinnan

(1) The game seemed for him [Jody] to be two different animals. On the chase, it was the quarry. He wanted only to see it fall. When it lay dead and bleeding, he was sickened and sorry. His heart ached over the mangled death. Then when it was cut into portions . . . it was only meat, like bacon, and his mouth watered at the goodness. He wondered by what alchemy it was changed, so that what sickened him one hour, maddened him with hunger, the next. It seemed as though there were either two different animals, or two different boys.
  ▸ [in *The Yearling*, ch 8]

(2) You kin tame arything, son, excusin' the human tongue.
  ▸ [Penny Baxter, in *The Yearling*, ch 9]

(3) Three things bring a man home again—his bed, his woman, and his dinner.
  ▸ [Doc Wilson, in *The Yearling*, ch 15]

(4) Words began fights and words ended them.
  ▸ [in *The Yearling*, ch 16]

(5) The devil gets blamed for a heap o' things is nothin' but human cussedness.
  ▸ [Penny Baxter, in *The Yearling*, ch 17]

(6) If I was dead, I'd set up and take notice, a day like this un.
  ▸ [Penny Baxter, in *The Yearling*, ch 30]

❚ Reid Banks, Lynne

(1) It was not that Omri didn't appreciate Patrick's birthday present to him. Far from it. He was really very grateful—sort of. It was, without a doubt, *very* kind of Patrick to give Omri anything at all, let alone a secondhand plastic Indian that he himself had finished with.
  ▸ [in *The Indian in the Cupboard*, ch 1]

(2) They're not safe with you. You *use* them. They're people. You can't use people.
  ▸ [Omri to Patrick, in *The Indian in the Cupboard*, ch 13]

❚ Rey, H. A.

(1) This is George.
  He lived in Africa. He was a good little monkey and always very curious.
  ▸ [in *Curious George*, first line]

(2) This is George. He lived with his friend, the man with the yellow hat.
> ▶ [in *Curious George Rides a Bike*, first line]

▌ Ringgold, Faith

(1) I have told him it's very easy, anyone can fly. All you need is somewhere to go that you can't get to any other way. The next thing you know, you're flying among the stars.
> ▶ [in *Tar Beach*]

▌ Robinson, Barbara

(1) The Herdmans were absolutely the worst kids in the history of the world.
> ▶ [in *The Best Christmas Pageant Ever*, ch 1, first line]

(2) Maybe they'll tell the innkeeper where to get off, and get the baby out of the barn.
> ▶ [Imogene Herdman, speaking of the Three Wise Men, in *The Best Christmas Pageant Ever*, ch 4]

(3) Hey! Unto you a child is born!
> ▶ [Gladys Herdman, as the Christmas angel, in *The Best Christmas Pageant Ever*, ch 7]

(4) But as far as I'm concerned, Mary is always going to look a lot like Imogene Herdman—sort of nervous and bewildered, but ready to clobber anyone who laid a hand on her baby.
> ▶ [in *The Best Christmas Pageant Ever*, ch 7]

▌ Rodgers, Mary

(1) When I woke up this morning, I found I'd turned into my mother.
> ▶ [in *Freaky Friday*, ch 1]

▌ Rowling, J. K.

(1) It is our choices, Harry, that show what we truly are, far more than our abilities.
> ▶ [Dumbledore, in *Harry Potter and the Chamber of Secrets*, ch 18]

▌ Ryan, Cheli Duran

(1) Hildilid was too tired from fighting the night to enjoy the day.
> ▶ [in *Hildilid's Night*]

▌ Rylant, Cynthia

(1) Henry knew it wasn't his snow glory. He knew it wasn't anybody's snow glory. Just a thing to let grow. And, if someone ate it, it was just a thing to let go.
> ▶ [in *Henry and Mudge in Puddle Trouble*]

(2) You'd have to go through at least four different hugs to get from the kitchen to the front room!
> ▶ [in *The Relatives Came*]

(3) It was different, going to sleep with all that new breathing in the house.

▸ [in *The Relatives Came*]

❨ Sachar, Louis

(1) Wayside School was accidentally built sideways. It was supposed to be only one story high, with thirty classrooms all in a row. Instead it is thirty stories high, with one classroom on each story. The builder said he was very sorry.

▸ [in *Sideways Stories from Wayside School*, Introduction]

(2) School just speeds things up. . . . Without school it might take another seventy years before you wake up and are able to count.

▸ [Mrs. Jewls, in *Sideways Stories from Wayside School*, ch 3]

(3) You need a reason to be sad. You don't need a reason to be happy.

▸ [D. J., in *Sideways Stories from Wayside School*, ch 16]

❨ Saint-Exupery, Antoine de

(1) Grown-ups never understand anything by themselves, and it is tiresome for children to be always and forever explaining things to them.

▸ [in *The Little Prince*, ch 1]

(2) It is such a secret place, the land of tears.

▸ [in *The Little Prince*, ch 7]

(3) One never ought to listen to the flowers. One should simply look at them and breathe their fragrance.

▸ [the prince, in *The Little Prince*, ch 8]

(4) One must require from each one the duty which each one can perform. . . . Accepted authority rests first of all on reason. . . . I have the right to require obedience because my orders are reasonable.

▸ [the king, in *The Little Prince*, ch 10]

(5) It is much more difficult to judge oneself than to judge others. If you succeed in judging yourself rightly, then you are indeed a man of true wisdom.

▸ [the king, in *The Little Prince*, ch 10]

(6) To me, you are still nothing more than a little boy who is just like a hundred thousand other little boys. And I have no need of you. And you, on your part, have no need of me. To you, I am nothing more than a fox like a hundred thousand other foxes. But if you tame me, then we shall need each other. To me, you will be unique in all the world. To you, I shall be unique in all the world.

▸ [the fox, in *The Little Prince*, ch 21]

(7) I do not eat bread. Wheat is of no use to me. The wheat fields have nothing to say to me. And that is sad. But you have hair that is the color of gold. Think how wonderful it will be when you have tamed me! The grain, which is also golden, will bring me back the thought of you. And I shall love to listen to the wind in the wheat.
> [the fox, in *The Little Prince*, ch 21]

(8) One only understands the things that one tames. . . . Men have no more time to understand anything. They buy things all ready made at the shops. But there is no shop anywhere where one can buy friendship, and so men have no friends any more.
> [the fox, in *The Little Prince*, ch 21]

(9) Words are the source of misunderstandings.
> [the fox, in *The Little Prince*, ch 21]

(10) It is only with the heart that one can see rightly; what is essential is invisible to the eye.
> [the fox, in *The Little Prince*, ch 21]

(11) If I had fifty-three minutes to spend as I liked, I should walk at my leisure toward a spring of fresh water.
> [the prince, in *The Little Prince*, ch 23]

◤ Sandburg, Carl

(1) Gimme the Ax lived in a house where everything is the same as it always was.
> [in *Rootabaga Stories*, part one, 1, first line]

(2) So far? So early? So soon?
> [the ticket agent, in *Rootabaga Stories*, part one, 1]

(3) If the pigs are wearing bibs then this is the Rootabaga country.
> [Gimme the Ax, in *Rootabaga Stories*, part one, 1]

◤ Schwartz, Amy

(1) Attention: All Executives
Please note that Mr. Jones will not be with us today. He is at kindergarten. Bea Jones will be taking his place.
> [in *Bea and Mr. Jones*]

(2) I love advertising! What a challenge!
> [Bea, in *Bea and Mr. Jones*]

◤ Scieszka, Jon

(1) You know, you can think of almost everything as a math problem.
> [in *Math Curse*]

(2) And everyone lived happily, though not completely honestly, ever after.
> [in "The Princess and the Bowling Ball," in *The Stinky Cheese Man and Other Fairly Stupid Tales*]

(3) Fee Fi Fum Fory.
I have made my own story.
  ▶ [the giant, in "Jack's Bean Problem," in *The Stinky Cheese Man and Other Fairly Stupid Tales*]

(4) I could probably grow hair faster than you run.
  ▶ [Rabbit, to Tortoise, in "The Tortoise and the Hair," in *The Stinky Cheese Man and Other Fairly Stupid Tales*]

(5) I mean who in his right mind would build a house of straw?
  ▶ [the wolf, in *The True Story of the 3 Little Pigs, by A. Wolf*]

❧ Seeger, Pete

(1) He had long fingernails 'cause he never cut 'em. He had slobbery teeth 'cause he didn't brush 'em, stinking feet 'cause he didn't wash 'em, matted hair 'cause he didn't comb it.
  ▶ [describing Abiyoyo, in *Abiyoyo*]

❧ Sendak, Maurice

(1) Sipping once
sipping twice
sipping chicken soup
with rice.
  ▶ [in *Chicken Soup with Rice*]

(2) fell through the dark, out of his clothes past the moon & his mama & papa sleeping tight into the light of the night kitchen
  ▶ [in *In the Night Kitchen*]

(3) I'm not the milk and the milk's not me! I'm Mickey!
  ▶ [in *In the Night Kitchen*]

(4) I'm in the milk and the milk's in me. God bless the milk and God bless me!
  ▶ [in *In the Night Kitchen*]

(5) There once was a boy named Pierre
who only would say,
"I don't care!"
  ▶ [in *Pierre*, Prologue]

(6) The moral of Pierre is: CARE!
  ▶ [in *Pierre*]

(7) Let the wild rumpus start!
  ▶ [Max, in *Where the Wild Things Are*]

(8) And Max the king of all wild things was lonely and wanted to be where someone loved him best of all.
  ▶ [in *Where the Wild Things Are*]

(9) Oh please don't go—we'll eat you up—we love you so!
  ▶ [wild things, in *Where the Wild Things Are*]

❧ Seuss, Dr. [pseud. of Theodor Seuss Geisel]

(1) But all that I've noticed,
Except my own feet,
Was a horse and a wagon
On Mulberry Street.
  ▶ [in *And to Think That I Saw It on Mulberry Street*]

(2) Shuffle, duffle, muzzle, muff.
Fista, wista, mista-cuff.
We are men of groans and
  howls,
Mystic men who eat boiled
  owls.
  ▶ [the magicians, in *Bartholomew
  and the Oobleck*]

(3) You may be a mighty king. . . .
But you're sitting in oobleck up
to your chin. And so is everyone
else in your land. And if you
won't even say you're sorry,
you're no sort of king at all!
  ▶ [Bartholomew, in *Bartholomew
  and the Ooblek*]

(4) The two biggest fools that have
  ever been seen!
And the fools that I saw were
  none other than you,
Who seem to have nothing
  else better to do
Than sit here and argue who's
  better than who!
  ▶ [the worm, in "The Big Brag,"
  in *Yertle the Turtle and Other
  Stories*]

(5) In every Zook house and in
  every Zook town
*every Zook eats his bread
with the butter side down!*
  ▶ [in *The Butter Battle Book*]

(6) Yooks are not Zooks.
Keep your butter side up!
  ▶ [sign, in *The Butter Battle Book*]

(7) The sun did not shine.
It was too wet to play.
So we sat in the house
All that cold, cold, wet day.
  ▶ [in *The Cat in the Hat*, first lines]

(8) "I know some new tricks,"
Said the Cat in the Hat.
"A lot of good tricks.
I will show them to you.
Your mother
Will not mind at all if I do."
  ▶ [in *The Cat in the Hat*]

(9) a game that I call
UP-UP-UP with a fish!
  ▶ [The Cat, in *The Cat in the Hat*]

(10) Oh, I do not like it!
Not one little bit!
  ▶ [the fish, in *The Cat in the Hat*]

(11) Thing One and Thing Two
  ▶ [in *The Cat in the Hat*]

(12) Well . . .
What would YOU do
If your mother asked YOU?
  ▶ [in *The Cat in the Hat*]

(13) Voom cleans up anything
Clean as can be!
  ▶ [in *The Cat in the Hat Comes Back*]

(14) [Mayzie] signed her name in
think-proof ink.
  ▶ [in *Daisy-Head Mayzie*]

(15) But what is money without friends?
  ▶ [in *Daisy-Head Mayzie*]

(16) trying to teach Irish ducks how
to read Jivvanese
  ▶ [in *Did I Ever Tell You How
  Lucky You Are?*]

(17) Clocks on fox tick.
Clocks on Knox tock.
Six sick bricks tick.
Six sick chicks tock.
  ▶ [in *Fox in Socks*]

(18)   a tweetle beetle
noodle poodle bottled
paddled muddled duddled
fuddled wuddled
fox in socks, sir!
▶ [in *Fox in Socks*]

(19)   I am Sam
Sam I am
▶ [signs, in *Green Eggs and Ham*]

(20)   That Sam-I-am!
That Sam-I-am!
I do not like
that Sam-I-am!
▶ [in *Green Eggs and Ham*]

(21)   I would not like them
here or there.
I would not like them
anywhere.
I do not like
green eggs and ham.
I do not like them,
Sam-I-am.
▶ [in *Green Eggs and Ham*]

(22)   You do not like them.
So you say.
Try them! Try them!
And you may.
Try them and you may, I say.
▶ [in *Green Eggs and Ham*]

(23)   I meant what I said
And I said what I meant . . .
An elephant's faithful
One hundred per cent!
▶ [Horton, in *Horton Hatches the Egg*]

(24)   And they sent him home
Happy,
One hundred per cent!
▶ [in *Horton Hatches the Egg*]

(25)   Just a very faint yelp
As if some tiny person were
calling for help.
▶ [in *Horton Hears a Who!*]

(26)   A person's a person. No matter
how small.
▶ [in *Horton Hears a Who!*]

(27)   Every *Who*
Down in *Who*-ville
Liked Christmas a lot . . .
But the Grinch,
Who lived just north of *Who*-ville,
Did *NOT!*
▶ [in *How the Grinch Stole Christmas!*]

(28)   the most likely reason of all
May have been that his heart
was two sizes too small.
▶ [in *How the Grinch Stole Christmas!*]

(29)   THE GRINCH
GOT A WONDERFUL, AWFUL
IDEA!
▶ [in *How the Grinch Stole Christmas!*]

(30)   Every *Who* down in *Who*-ville,
the tall and the small,
Was singing! Without any
presents at all!
He HADN'T stopped Christmas
from coming!
IT CAME!
Somehow or other, it came
just the same!
▶ [in *How the Grinch Stole Christmas!*]

(31)   "Maybe Christmas," he thought,
"*doesn't* come from a store.

Maybe Christmas . . . perhaps
. . . means a little bit more!"

▶ [Grinch, in *How the Grinch Stole Christmas!*]

(32) And I learned there are troubles
Of more than one kind.
Some come from ahead
And some come from behind.

▶ [in *I Had Trouble in Getting to Solla Sollew*]

(33) the City of Solla Sollew
On the banks of the beautiful
River Wah-Hoo,
Where they *never* have troubles!
At least very few.

▶ [in *I Had Trouble in Getting to Solla Sollew*]

(34) Now my troubles are going
To have trouble with *me!*

▶ [in *I Had Trouble in Getting to Solla Sollew*]

(35) I am the Lorax. I speak for the
trees.

▶ [The Lorax, in *The Lorax*]

(36) But—
Business is business! And
business must grow
regardless of crummies in
tummies, you know.

▶ [The Once-ler, in *The Lorax*]

(37) But those *trees!* Those *trees!*
Those Truffula trees!

▶ [The Once-ler, in *The Lorax*]

(38) And all that the Lorax left here
in this mess
was a small pile of rocks, with
one word . . .
"UNLESS."

▶ [in *The Lorax*]

(39) UNLESS someone like you
cares a whole awful lot,
nothing is going to get better.
It's not.

▶ [in *The Lorax*]

(40) The time has come.
The time is now.
Just go.
Go.
GO!
I don't care how.

▶ [in *Marvin K. Mooney Will You Please Go Now!*]

(41) With your head full of brains
and your shoes full of feet,
you're too smart to go down
any not-so-good street.

▶ [in *Oh, the Places You'll Go!*]

(42) I'm sorry to say so
but, sadly, it's true
that Bang-ups
and Hang-ups
can happen to you.

▶ [in *Oh, the Places You'll Go!*]

(43) Games you can't win
'cause you'll play against you.

▶ [in *Oh, the Places You'll Go!*]

(44) You can stop, if you want, with
the Z
Because most people stop
with the Z
But not me!

▶ [in *On Beyond Zebra*]

(45) Now, the Star-Belly Sneetches
Had bellies with stars.
The Plain-Belly Sneetches
Had none upon thars.

▶ [in "The Sneetches," in *The Sneetches and Other Stories*, first lines]

(46) My name is Sylvester
McMonkey McBean.
And I've heard of your troubles.
I've heard you're unhappy.
But I can fix that. I'm the
Fix-it-Up Chappie.

▶ [in "The Sneetches," in *The Sneetches and Other Stories*]

(47) On the far-away Island of
Sala-ma-Sond,
Yertle the Turtle was King of
the pond.

▶ [in "Yertle the Turtle," in *Yertle the Turtle and Other Stories*, first lines]

(48) "I'm ruler," said Yertle, "of all
that I see.
But I don't see *enough*. That's
the trouble with me."

▶ [in "Yertle the Turtle," in *Yertle the Turtle and Other Stories*]

(49) And the turtles of course . . .
all the Turtles are free
As turtles and, maybe, all
creatures should be.

▶ [in "Yertle the Turtle," in *Yertle the Turtle and Other Stories*]

(50) *Never budge!* That's my rule.
Never budge in the least!
*Not an inch to the west! Not an
inch to the east!*

▶ [in "The Zax," in *The Sneetches and Other Stories*]

❱ Sewell, Anna

(1) I never yet could make out why
men are so fond of this sport;
they often hurt themselves, often
spoil good horses, and tear up the
fields, and all for a hare or a fox
or a stag, that they could get more
easily some other way; but we
are only horses, and don't know.

▶ [Duchess, Black Beauty's mother, on hunting, in *Black Beauty,* ch 2]

(2) He used to say that a regular
course of the Birtwick horse-balls
would cure almost any vicious
horse; these balls, he said, were
made up of patience and gentle-
ness, firmness and petting, one
pound of each to be mixed up with
half a pint of common sense, and
given to the horse every day.

▶ [in *Black Beauty,* ch 8]

(3) Good Luck is rather particular
who she rides with, and mostly
prefers those who have got common sense and a good heart.

▶ [Governor Gray, in *Black Beauty,* ch 35]

❱ Sharmat, Mitchell

(1) It's all right to eat like a goat, but
you shouldn't eat like a pig.

▶ [Mother Goat, in *Gregory the Terrible Eater*]

❱ Sharp, Margery

(1) It was a full meeting of the Prisoner's Aid Society. Everyone
knows that mice are the prisoner's
friends—sharing his dry bread
crumbs even when they are not
hungry, allowing themselves to
be taught all manner of foolish
tricks, such as no self-respecting

mouse would otherwise contemplate, in order to cheer his lonely hours; what is less well known is how splendidly they are organized. Not a prison in any land but has its own national branch of a wonderful, worldwide system. It is on record that long, long ago a Norman mouse took ship all the way to Turkey, to join a French sailor-boy locked up in Constantinople! The Jean Fromage Medal was Struck in his honor.

▶ [in *The Rescuers*, ch 1]

(2) What happened subsequently will be forever famous in naval annals. With a hundred miles to go, and navigating solely by Miss Bianca's sketch of a garden-party hat, Nils actually succeeded in reaching the Capital.

▶ [in *The Rescuers*, ch 4]

❧ Shaw, Charles

(1) Sometimes it looked like Spilt Milk. But it wasn't Spilt Milk.

▶ [in *It Looked Like Spilt Milk*]

❧ Sidney, Margaret [pseud. of Harriet Mulford Lothrop]

(1) Is she a Pepper? . . . and are you a Pepper?

▶ [Jasper, in *Five Little Peppers*, ch 11]

❧ Silverstein, Shel

(1) Once there was a tree . . . and she loved a little boy.

▶ [in *The Giving Tree*, first line]

(2) Here comes summer,
Here comes summer—
Whoosh—shiver—there it goes.

▶ [in "Here Comes," in *A Light in the Attic*]

(3) What do I do?
What do I do?
This library book is 42
Years overdue.

▶ [in "Overdues," in *A Light in the Attic*]

(4) I tried on the summer sun,
Felt good. . . .
Finally, finally felt well dressed,
Nature's clothes just fit me best.

▶ [in "Tryin' on Clothes," in *A Light in the Attic*]

(5) But this bridge will only take you halfway there—
The last few steps you'll have to take alone.

▶ [in "This Bridge," in *A Light in the Attic*]

(6) I am not your missing piece. I am nobody's piece. I am my own piece. And even if I was somebody's missing piece I don't think I'd be yours!

▶ [in *The Missing Piece*]

(7) Now that it was complete it could not sing at all.

▶ [in *The Missing Piece*]

(8) Corners wear off and shapes change.

 ▶ [The Big O, in *The Missing Piece Meets the Big O*]

(9) I will not play at tug o' war.
I'd rather play at hug o' war . . .
And everyone cuddles,
And everyone wins.

 ▶ [in "Hug o' War," in *Where the Sidewalk Ends*]

(10) If you're a bird, be an early
early bird—
But if you're a worm, sleep late.

 ▶ [in "Early Bird," in *Where the Sidewalk Ends*]

(11) Oh, I'm being eaten
By a boa constrictor, . . .
Oh, heck,
It's up to my neck.
Oh, dread,
It's upmmmmmmmmmmm-
ffffffffff . . .

 ▶ [in "Boa Constrictor," in *Where the Sidewalk Ends*]

(12) We all look the same
When we turn off the light.
So maybe the way
To make everything right
Is for God to just reach out
And turn off the light!

 ▶ [in "No Difference," in *Where the Sidewalk Ends*]

(13) A hippo sandwich is easy to
make. . . .
And now comes the problem . . .
Biting into it!

 ▶ [in "Recipe for a Hippopotamus Sandwich," in *Where the Sidewalk Ends*]

(14) So only the biggest fish get fat.
Do you know any folks like that?

 ▶ [in "Fish?" in *Where the Sidewalk Ends*]

(15) If the track is tough and the hill
is rough,
THINKING you can just ain't
enough!

 ▶ [in "The Little Blue Engine," in *Where the Sidewalk Ends*]

◤ Slepian, Jan

(1) Death was in the air, stilling talk, finding inside every onlooker the place it owns.

 ▶ [in *Back to Before*, ch 2]

◤ Slobodkina, Esphyr

(1) Once there was a peddler who sold caps. But he was not like an ordinary peddler carrying his wares on his back. He carried them on top of his head.

 First he had on his own checked cap, than a bunch of gray caps, then a bunch of brown caps, then a bunch of blue caps, and on the very top a bunch of red caps.

 ▶ [in *Caps for Sale*]

(2) Caps! Caps for sale! Fifty cents a cap!

 ▶ [in *Caps for Sale*]

(3) On every branch sat a monkey. On every monkey was a gray, or a brown, or a blue, or a red cap!

 ▶ [in *Caps for Sale*]

(4)   But the monkeys only shook their fingers back at him and said, "Tsz, tsz, tsz."
▶ [in *Caps for Sale*]

❧ Smith, Dodie [Smith, Dorothy Gladys]

(1)   Pain hurts more when one is angry.
▶ [Pongo, in *The Hundred and One Dalmatians*, ch 9]

(2)   the Hundred and Oneth Dalmatian
▶ [chapter title, in *The Hundred and One Dalmatians*, ch 18]

❧ Smith, Doris Buchanan

(1)   It was hard to think about God when something as small as a bee could kill your best friend.
▶ [in *A Taste of Blackberries*, ch 7]

❧ Snyder, Zilpha Keatley

(1)   Only evil comes from great changes made too swiftly.
▶ [Hiro D'anhk, in *Below the Root*, ch 19]

(2)   Dad says being a baby offended Marshall's dignity.
▶ [Melanie, in *The Egypt Game*, "Eyelashes and Ceremony"]

(3)   It seemed that sixth grade boys just normally kept a lot of things around that were perfect for the altar of an evil god.
▶ [in *The Egypt Game*, "Hiero-gylphics"]

(4)   Wasn't that like a boy. They got things into a mess, and then expected a girl to get them out of it.
▶ [in *The Egypt Game*, "Confession and Confusion"]

(5)   Imagination is a great thing in long dull hours, but it's a real curse in a dark alley.
▶ [in *The Egypt Game*, "Fear Strikes"]

(6)   It's just awful when you go back to something that was so great the way you remembered it and it's not good anymore. It even ruins remembering.
▶ [April, in *The Egypt Game*, "Christmas Keys"]

❧ Spinelli, Jerry

(1)   That kind of thinking [that math is men's stuff] . . . will make *you* [daughter Abby] a second-class citizen.
▶ [Jess Coogan, in *Crash*, ch 13]

(2)   Football isn't for fruitcakes. Football doesn't take any crap from the weather.
▶ [in *Crash*, ch 25]

(3)   It's not the sneakers that count, it's the feet.
▶ [Scooter, in *Crash*, ch 34]

(4)   You don't feel so safe being captain.
▶ [Crash Coogan, in *Crash*, ch 44]

(5) Ma-niac, Ma-niac
He's so *cool*
Ma-niac, Ma-niac
Don't go to *school*
Runs all *night*
Runs all *right*
Ma-niac, Ma-niac
Kissed a *bull!*
> [jump-rope rhyme in *Maniac Magee*, "Before the Story"]

(6) The history of a kid is one part fact, two parts legends, and three parts snowball.
> [in *Maniac Magee*, "Before the Story"]

(7) Inside his house, a kid gets one name, but on the other side of the door, it's whatever the rest of the world wants to call him.
> [in *Maniac Magee*, ch 14]

(8) The saddest shower of all is the one you take the night before school starts in September. It's like you're not just washing the day's dirt away, you're washing the whole summer down the drain—all the fun, all the long, free days.
> [in *Who Put That Hair in My Toothbrush?* first line]

❧ Spyri, Johanna

(1) Zeal in learning never does any harm.
> [Frau Sesemann, in *Heidi*, part 1, ch 10]

(2) In anger we are all foolish.
> [Frau Sesemann, in *Heidi*, part 2, ch 9]

(3) Whoever does a wicked thing and thinks no one knows about it is mistaken.
> [Frau Sesemann, in *Heidi*, part 2, ch 9]

❧ Steele, Mary Q. *See* Gage, Wilson

❧ Steig, William

(1) Only when taking it easy . . . could one do one's wondering.
> [in *Abels' Island*, ch 10]

(2) It's me all right. . . . It's more me than what I see in the mirror. It's what I see when I imagine how I look. It's a work of art, that's what it is!
> [Gower the frog, when looking at his statue, in *Abels' Island*, ch 15]

(3) Amos, a little speck of a living thing in the vast living universe, felt thoroughly akin to it all.
> [in *Amos & Boris*]

(4) You have to be *out* of the sea really to know how good it is to be *in* it. . . . That is, if you're a whale.
> [Boris, in *Amos & Boris*]

(5) Caleb the carpenter and Kate the weaver loved each other, but not every single minute.
> [in *Caleb and Kate*]

(6)   How I love them raw . . . with just a pinch of salt, and a . . . dry . . . white wine.
▸ [Fox, dreaming about mice, in *Doctor De Soto*]

(7)   On his way home, he [the fox] wondered if it would be shabby of him to eat the De Sotos when the job was done.
▸ [in *Doctor De Soto*]

(8)   Once I start a job . . . I finish it. My father was the same way.
▸ [Dr. De Soto, in *Doctor De Soto*]

❚ Stevenson, James

(1)   Deep in our earth so wondrous . . .
With dirt above us and under us.
▸ [worm national anthem, in *National Worm Day*, ch 1]

❚ Stevenson, Robert Louis

(1)   In winter I get up at night
And dress by yellow candle-light.
In summer, quite the other way,
I have to go to bed by day.
▸ [in "Bed in Summer," in *A Child's Garden of Verses*]

(2)   When I was down beside the sea
A wooden spade they gave to me
To dig the sandy shore.
▸ [in "At the Seaside," in *A Child's Garden of Verses*]

(3)   A child should always say what's true,
And speak when he is spoken to,
And behave mannerly at table:
At least as far as he is able.
▸ ["Whole Duty of Children," in *A Child's Garden of Verses*]

(4)   Whenever the moon and stars are set,
Whenever the wind is high,
All night long in the dark and wet,
A man goes riding by. . . .
By at the gallop he goes, and then
By he comes back at the gallop again.
▸ [in "Windy Nights," in *A Child's Garden of Verses*]

(5)   Dark brown is the river,
Golden is the sand.
It flows along forever,
With trees on either hand. . . .
Boats of mine a-boating—
Where will all come home? . . .
Other little children
Shall bring my boats ashore.
▸ [in "Where Go the Boats?" in *A Child's Garden of Verses*]

(6)   When I was sick and lay a-bed,
I had two pillows at my head. . . .
I was the giant great and still
That sits upon the pillow-hill,
And sees before him, dale and plain,
The pleasant land of counterpane.
▸ [in "The Land of Counterpane," in *A Child's Garden of Verses*]

(7) I have a little shadow that goes
    in and out with me. . . .
    The funniest thing about him is
    the way he likes to grow—
    Not at all like proper children,
    which is always very slow.

    ▶ [in "My Shadow," in *A Child's Garden of Verses*]

(8) The friendly cow, all red and
    white,
    I love with all my heart.

    ▶ [in "The Cow," in *A Child's Garden of Verses*]

(9) The world is so full
    of a number of things,
    I'm sure we should all
    be as happy as kings.

    ▶ ["Happy Thought," in *A Child's Garden of Verses*]

(10) How do you like to go up in a
     swing,
     Up in the air so blue? . . .
     Up in the air I go flying again,
     Up in the air and down!

     ▶ [in "The Swing," in *A Child's Garden of Verses*]

(11) Faster than fairies, faster than
     witches,
     Bridges and houses, hedges
     and ditches.

     ▶ [in "From a Railway Carriage," in *A Child's Garden of Verses*]

(12) Sing a song of seasons!
     Something bright in all!
     Flowers in the summer,
     Fires in the fall!

     ▶ [in "Autumn Fires," in *A Child's Garden of Verses*]

❧ Stolz, Mary

(1) No place is big enough if you
    can't get out of it.

    ▶ [Martin, in *The Bully of Barkham Street*, ch 2]

(2) Remember it's one of the surest
    signs of maturity, the day you
    find yourself accepting people
    for what they are, with their good
    points and their bad.

    ▶ [Martin's mother, in *The Bully of Barkham Street*, ch 6]

(3) Some of us [slaves], defeated in
    spirit and body, knocked at
    Death's door, and were kindly
    taken in.

    ▶ [in *Cezanne Pinto*, ch 1]

(4) The human species, in its many
    hues, with its many gods and
    countless ways of thinking and
    behaving, is braided together in
    one long, thick strand, and . . . if
    we don't come to understand—
    to concede—this large and simple
    truth, our world will ravel past
    repair.

    ▶ [in *Cezanne Pinto*, ch 1]

(5) Kings and tyrants, emperors and
    dictators, have always known
    that to keep a people in harness,
    you put blinders on them, seal-
    ing away the light of learning.

    ▶ [in *Cezanne Pinto*, ch 1]

(6) Never . . . use a simple word if
    you have at hand a fancy one.

    ▶ [Tamar, in *Cezanne Pinto*, ch 2]

(7)   Let no one persuade you that there are two sides to every question. There is only one side to *any* question.

▶ [Tamar, in *Cezanne Pinto*, ch 2]

\ Stratton-Porter, Gene

(1)   I believe the best way to get an answer to prayer is to work for it.

▶ [Elnora, in *A Girl of the Limberlost*, ch 3]

(2)   What you are lies with you. If you are lazy, and accept your lot, you may live in it. If you are willing to work, you can write your name anywhere you choose, among the only ones who live beyond the grave in this world.

▶ [The Bird Woman, in *A Girl of the Limberlost*, ch 3]

(3)   The wages of sin are the hardest debts on earth to pay, and they are always collected at inconvenient times and unexpected places.

▶ [in *A Girl of the Limberlost*, ch 12]

(4)   It wouldn't be a gentlemanly thing to do, and first of all, the Almighty is bound to be a gentleman.

▶ [Mrs. Comstock, in *A Girl of the Limberlost*, ch 12]

\ Swift, Hildegarde, and Lynd Ward

(1)   "I call to the airplanes," cried the bridge. "I flash to the ships of the air. But you are still master of the river. Quick, let your light shine again. Each to his own place, little brother!"

▶ [in *The Little Red Lighthouse and the Great Gray Bridge*]

\ Taylor, Jane

(1)   Twinkle, twinkle, little star,
How I wonder what you are!
Up above the world so high,
Like a diamond in the sky.

▶ [in Baring-Gould, *The Annotated Mother Goose*]

\ Taylor, Mildred

(1)   White people may demand our respect, but what we give them is not respect but fear. What we give to our own people is far more important because it's given freely.

▶ [Mama, in *Roll of Thunder, Hear My Cry*, ch 6]

(2)   A black man's always gotta be ready to die. And it don't make me any difference if I die today or tomorrow. Just as long as I die right.

▶ [David Logan (Papa), in *Song of the Trees*]

❚ Thayer, Jane [pseud. of Catherine Woolley]

(1) I'd like a boy for Christmas.
  ▶ [Petey, the puppy, in *The Puppy Who Wanted a Boy*]

❚ Thomas, Patricia

(1) Oh, *please,*
   Don't sneeze!
  ▶ [various animals, in *"Stand Back," Said the Elephant, "I'm Going to Sneeze!"*]

(2) And all of the hair
   Fell off of the bear.
  ▶ [in *"Stand Back," Said the Elephant, "I'm Going to Sneeze!"*]

❚ Thompson, Kay

(1) I am Eloise
   I am six
   I am a city child
   I live at The Plaza
  ▶ [in *Eloise*, first lines]

❚ Thurber, James

(1) Now has warmth and urgency, and Then is dead and buried.
  ▶ [in *The Thirteen Clocks*, ch 1]

(2) Time is for dragonflies and angels. The former live too little and the latter live too long.
  ▶ [Golux, in *The Thirteen Clocks*, ch 3]

(3) We all have flaws . . . and mine is being wicked.
  ▶ [The duke, in *The Thirteen Clocks*, ch 8]

❚ Titus, Eve

(1) In all France there was no happier, more contented mouse than Anatole.
  ▶ [in *Anatole*]

(2) A friend is never insulted—a friend has faith.
  ▶ [Gaston, in *Anatole*]

❚ Tolkien, J. R. R.

(1) In a hole in the ground there lived a hobbit. Not a nasty, dirty, wet hole, filled with the ends of worms and an oozy smell, nor yet a dry, bare, sandy hole with nothing in it to sit down on or to eat: it was a hobbit-hole, and that means comfort.
  ▶ [in *The Hobbit*, ch 1, first line]

(2) We are plain quiet folk and have no use for adventures. Nasty disturbing uncomfortable things! Make you late for dinner!
  ▶ [Bilbo Baggins, in *The Hobbit*, ch 1]

(3) I wish I was at home in my nice hole by the fire, with the kettle just beginning to sing!
  ▶ [Bilbo Baggins, in *The Hobbit*, ch 2, also later]

(4) There is nothing like looking, if you want to find something. . . . You certainly usually find something, if you look, but it is not always quite the something you were after.
  ▶ [in *The Hobbit*, ch 4]

(5) Escaping goblins to be caught by wolves!
  ▶ [Bilbo Baggins, in *The Hobbit*, ch 6]

(6) Farewell! . . . wherever you fare, till your eyries receive you at the journey's end! . . . May the wind under your wings bear you where the sun sails and the moon walks.
  ▶ [eagles' saying, in *The Hobbit*, ch 7]

(7) It does not do to leave a live dragon out of your calculations, if you live near him.
  ▶ [in *The Hobbit*, ch 12]

(8) Never laugh at live dragons!
  ▶ [Bilbo Baggins, in *The Hobbit*, ch 12]

(9) If more of us valued food and cheer and song above hoarded gold, it would be a merrier world.
  ▶ [Thorin Oakenshield, in *The Hobbit*, ch 18]

❧ Travers, P. L.

(1) I'll stay till the wind changes.
  ▶ [Mary Poppins, in *Mary Poppins*, ch 1]

(2) It may be that to eat and be eaten are the same thing in the end. . . . We are all made of the same stuff . . . we are all one, all moving to the same end.
  ▶ [the Hamadryad, in *Mary Poppins*, ch 10]

❧ Treviño, Elizabeth Bolton de

(1) The eye is complicated. It mixes the colors for you. . . . The painter must unmix them.
  ▶ [Velazquez, in *I, Juan de Pareja*, ch 4]

(2) Art must be true. . . . It is the one thing in life that must rest on solid truth. Otherwise, it is useless.
  ▶ [Velazquez, in *I, Juan de Pareja*, ch 4]

(3) Space is medicine for eyes that have always to look at things too closely.
  ▶ [Velazquez, in *I, Juan de Pareja*, ch 5]

(4) Say to yourselves, "I would rather paint exactly what I see, even if it is ugly, perfectly, than indifferently paint something superficially lovely." Say to yourselves, "Art is Truth, and to serve Art, I will never deceive."
  ▶ [Velazquez, in *I, Juan de Pareja*, ch 5]

❧ Udry, Janice May

(1) Trees are very nice. They fill up the sky.
  ▶ [in *A Tree Is Nice*, first line]

❧ Ungerer, Tomi

(1) On clear, starry nights the Moon Man can be seen curled up in his shimmering seat in space.
  ▶ [in *Moon Man*, first line]

(2) Once upon a time there were three fierce robbers. They went about hidden under large black capes and tall black hats. The first had a blunderbuss. The second had a pepper-blower. And the third had a huge red axe.
  ▶ [in *The Three Robbers*, first lines]

❧ Van Allsburg, Chris

(1) Jumanji. A jungle game. . . . Free game, fun for some but not for all. P.S. Read instructions carefully.
  ▶ [in *Jumanji*]

(2) Once a game of Jumanji is started it will not be over until one player reaches the golden city.
  ▶ [in *Jumanji*]

(3) He threw with all his might, but the third stone came skipping back.
  ▶ [in *The Mysteries of Harris Burdick*]

(4) What I wanted more than anything was one silver bell from Santa's sleigh.
  ▶ [in *The Polar Express*]

(5) At one time most of my friends could hear the bell, but as years passed, it fell silent for all of them. . . . Though I've grown old, the bell still rings for me as it does for all who truly believe.
  ▶ [in *The Polar Express*]

❧ Viorst, Judith

(1) I could tell it was going to be a terrible, horrible, no good, very bad day.
  ▶ [in *Alexander and the Terrible, Horrible, No Good, Very Bad Day*]

(2) I think I'll move to Australia.
  ▶ [in *Alexander and the Terrible, Horrible, No Good, Very Bad Day*]

(3) They made me buy plain old white ones [sneakers], but they can't make me wear them.
  ▶ [in *Alexander and the Terrible, Horrible, No Good, Very Bad Day*]

(4) I was careful as could be except for my elbow.
  ▶ [in *Alexander and the Terrible, Horrible, No Good, Very Bad Day*]

(5) My mom says some days are like that. Even in Australia.
  ▶ [in *Alexander and the Terrible, Horrible, No Good, Very Bad Day*]

(6) Mother says deep down in his heart Anthony loves me. Anthony says deep down in his heart he thinks I stink.

▶ [in *I'll Fix Anthony*]

(7) But if it [heaven] is there . . . it's bound to have room for Barney and tuna and cream.

▶ [Annie, in *The Tenth Good Thing About Barney*]

(8) Barney is in the ground and he's helping grow flowers. You know, I said, that's a pretty nice job for a cat.

▶ [in *The Tenth Good Thing About Barney*]

❚ Voigt, Cynthia

(1) One advantage of having a strict teacher, who you suspect might be a witch, is that you can feel safe with her.

▶ [in *Bad Girls*, ch 2]

(2) You have to reach out to people. To your family too. You can't just let them sit there, you should put your hand out. If they slap it back, well you reach out again if you care enough.

▶ [Gram, in *Dicey's Song*, ch 7]

(3) It's still true.

▶ [that their mother is gone; what James says every morning as he wakes up; in *Homecoming*, throughout part one]

(4) Maybe life was like a sea, and all the people were like boats. . . . Everybody who was born was cast into the sea. Winds would blow them in all directions. Tides would rise and turn, in their own rhythm. And the boats—they just went along as best they could, trying to find a harbor.

▶ [in *Homecoming*, part two, ch 3]

(5) Rebellion is necessary for the development of character.

▶ [Jerry, in *Homecoming*, part two, ch 3]

(6) You could say all of life is a series of last chances.

▶ [Will, in *Homecoming*, part two, ch 7]

(7) You had to understand that some of his wrong thinking was right for a smart kid in fifth grade and trust him to grow out of it at the proper time.

▶ [in *A Solitary Blue*, ch 10]

(8) It's so easy to fall in love—the way you fall into the water when the weather is hot—but living in love is different.

▶ [The Professor, in *A Solitary Blue*, ch 11]

(9) Love is just the beginning. . . . I think we can't help loving, but what matters is what we do about it. What we do with love. Do for it. What love does with us.

▶ [The Professor, in *A Solitary Blue*, ch 11]

(10) The things that grow upward like the sunlight. The things that grow downward like the rain.

▶ [Jeb Twohey, in *Tree by Leaf*, ch 7]

(11) The worst things weren't outside of you.

▶ [in *Tree by Leaf*, ch 15]

❚ Waber, Bernard

(1) There's a crocodile in the bathtub.

▶ [Mrs. Primm, in *The House on East 88th Street*]

(2) So now if you should happen to be walking past the house on East 88th Street and if you should happen to hear sounds that go: SWISH, SWASH, SPLASH, SWOOSH! Don't be surprised. It's only Lyle. Lyle the crocodile.

▶ [in *The House on East 88th Street*]

❚ Waddell, Martin

(1) How goes the work? Quack!

▶ [in *Farmer Duck*]

❚ Ward, Lynd. *See* Swift, Hildegarde

❚ Weller, Frances Ward

(1) It was pretty scary to think he [Jonno] might just get his life under control sometime, only to change in a couple of seasons into an almost different person.

▶ [in *Boat Song*, ch 5]

(2) There's a woman . . . who's in danger of wearing out the English language single-handed.

▶ [Rob Loud, in *Boat Song*, ch 10]

(3) The rotten thing [about being eleven] . . . is that you're expected to think like a grown-up while still being treated like a little kid.

▶ [Jonno, in *Boat Song*, ch 13]

(4) Ye must give him more to listen to [if you want your father to listen to you].

▶ [Rob Loud, in *Boat Song*, ch 15]

(5) A friend can tell you things you don't want to tell yourself.

▶ [Rob Loud, in *Boat Song*, ch 18]

❚ White, E. B.

(1) No, I only distribute pigs to early risers. . . . Fern was up at daylight, trying to rid the world of injustice. As a result, she now has a pig. A small one, to be sure, but nevertheless, a pig. It just shows what can happen if a person gets out of bed promptly.

▶ [Mr. Arable, in *Charlotte's Web*, ch 1]

(2) What do you mean, *less* than nothing? . . . I don't think there is any such thing as *less* than nothing. Nothing is absolutely the limit of nothingness. It's the lowest you can go. It's the end of the line. How can something be less than nothing? If there were something that was less

than nothing, then nothing would not be nothing, it would be something—even though it's just a very little bit of something. But if nothing is *nothing*, then nothing has nothing that is less than *it* is.

▶ [Wilbur, in *Charlotte's Web*, ch 4]

(3) **SOME PIG**
TERRIFIC
RADIANT
HUMBLE

▶ [words about Wilbur in Charlotte's web, in *Charlotte's Web*, ch 11, 13, 15, 19]

(4) After all, what's a life, anyway? We're born, we live a little while, we die. . . . By helping you, perhaps I was trying to lift up my life a trifle. Heaven knows anyone's life can stand a little of that.

▶ [Charlotte, in *Charlotte's Web*, ch 21]

(5) It is not often that someone comes along who is a true friend and a good writer. Charlotte was both.

▶ [in *Charlotte's Web*, ch 22]

◣ White, T. H.

(1) Education is experience, and the essence of experience is self-reliance.

▶ [the tench, in *The Sword in the Stone*, ch 5]

(2) The best thing for disturbances of the spirit . . . is to learn. That is the only thing that never fails.

▶ [Merlyn, in *The Sword in the Stone*, ch 21]

(3) As for you, Man, you will be a naked tool all your life, though a user of tools. . . . You will always remain *potential* in Our image.

▶ [God, in a story told by the badger, in *The Sword in the Stone*, ch 21]

(4) Whoso Pulleth Out This Sword of this Stone and Anvil, is Rightwise King Born of All England.

▶ [words on the sword in the stone, in *The Sword in the Stone*, ch 22]

◣ Wiggin, Kate Douglas

(1) It *is* a journey when you carry a nightgown!

▶ [Rebecca, in *Rebecca of Sunnybrook Farm*, ch 1]

(2) I only wish I'd known how to take a little of my foolishness along with me, as some folks do, to brighten my declining years.

▶ [Aunt Jane, when told she was a fool as a child, in *Rebecca of Sunnybrook Farm*, ch 6]

(3) The soul grows into lovely habits as easily as into ugly ones, and the moment a life begins to blossom into beautiful words and deeds, that moment a new standard of conduct is established, and your eager neighbors look to you for a continuous manifestation of the good cheer, the sympathy, the ready wit, the comradeship, or the inspiration,

you once showed yourself capable of. Bear figs for a season or two, and the world outside the orchard is very unwilling you should bear thistles.

▶ [in *Rebecca of Sunnybrook Farm*, ch 20]

◣ Wilder, Laura Ingalls

(1) [Laura] was glad that the cozy house, and Pa and Ma and the firelight and the music, were now. They could not be forgotten, she thought, because now is now. It can never be a long time ago.

▶ [in *Little House in the Big Woods*, ch 13]

◣ Wildsmith, Brian

(1) Every night I see something which you have never seen, nor ever will—the dark.

▶ [moon to sun, in *What the Moon Saw*]

◣ Williams, Jay

(1) We know what a dragon looks like. He looks like a small, fat, bald old man.

▶ [in *Everyone Knows What a Dragon Looks Like*]

◣ Williams, Linda

(1) Two shoes go CLOMP, CLOMP,
One pair of pants go WIGGLE, WIGGLE,
One shirt go SHAKE, SHAKE,
Two gloves go CLAP, CLAP,
One hat go NOD, NOD,
And one scary pumpkin head go BOO, BOO!

▶ [in *The Little Old Lady Who Was Not Afraid of Anything*]

◣ Williams, Margery

(1) Real isn't how you are made. . . . It's a thing that happens to you. When a child loves you for a long, long time, not just to play with, but REALLY loves you, then you become Real.

▶ [The Skin Horse, in *The Velveteen Rabbit*]

(2) When you are Real you don't mind being hurt.

▶ [The Skin Horse, in *The Velveteen Rabbit*]

(3) It [becoming Real] doesn't happen all at once. . . . You become. It takes a long time. . . . Generally, by the time you are Real, most of your hair has been loved off, and your eyes drop out and you get loose in the joints and very shabby. But these things don't matter at all, because once you are Real you can't be ugly, except to people who don't understand.

▶ [The Skin Horse, in *The Velveteen Rabbit*]

▌ Wojciechowska, Maia

(1) In Spain, however, people have found a way of cheating death. They summon it to appear in the afternoon in the bull ring, and they make it face a man. Death—a fighting bull with horns as weapons—is killed by a bullfighter. And the people are there watching death being cheated of its right.
▸ [in *Shadow of a Bull*, ch 1]

(2) Christopher Columbus had a son, but no one expected him to discover another New World!
▸ [Manolo, in *Shadow of a Bull*, ch 12]

(3) A man is not like a fighting bull. A man's life should not be all fighting, but also giving, loving.
▸ [Alfonso Castillo, in *Shadow of a Bull*, ch 15]

(4) You cannot confuse bravery or courage with lack of fear. Real courage, true bravery is doing things in spite of fear, knowing fear.
▸ [Alfonso Castillo, in *Shadow of a Bull*, ch 15]

▌ Wood, Audrey

(1) "Help! Help!" cried the Page when the sun came up. "King Bidgood's in the bathtub and he won't get out! Oh, who knows what to do?"
▸ [in *King Bidgood's in the Bathtub*]

(2) "Come in!" cried the King, with a jig, jig, jig. "Tonight we dance in the tub!"
▸ [in *King Bidgood's in the Bathtub*]

(3) a cozy bed in a napping house, where everyone is sleeping
▸ [in *The Napping House*]

(4) Silly Sally went to town, walking backwards, upside down.
▸ [in *Silly Sally*]

▌ Woolley, Catherine. *See* Thayer, Jane

▌ Wortis, Avi. *See* Avi

▌ Wrede, Patricia C.

(1) Who ever heard of a polite cat?
▸ [Archaniz, in *Calling on Dragons*, ch 1]

(2) You shouldn't give advice you don't follow.
▸ [Queen Cimorene, in *Calling on Dragons*, ch 6]

(3) Winged horses eat pretty much the same thing as regular horses, plus a little birdseed.
▸ [Farmer MacDonald, in *Calling on Dragons*, ch 11]

(4) Nine times out of ten, talking is a way of avoiding doing things.
▸ [frog, in *Dealing with Dragons*, ch 1]

(5) NONE OF THIS NONSENSE, PLEASE

▶ [sign over Morwen's door, in *Dealing with Dragons*, ch 8]

(6) What difference does that make to a cat? [that Kazul is a dragon]

▶ [Kazul, in *Dealing with Dragons*, ch 8]

❚ Yates, Elizabeth

(1) There's a fire that burns fast the more fuel goes on it and that's shiftlessness.

▶ [Violet, in *Amos Fortune Free Man*, "Amos on the Mountain"]

❚ Yee, Wong Herbert

(1) I'm a BIG BLACK BEAR, and I do as I please.

▶ [in *Big Black Bear*]

(2) He [Fireman Small] pulls back into station number nine, Walks upstairs one step at a time. Closes the curtains, gets in bed And pulls the covers over his head.

▶ [repeated with slight variations, in *Fireman Small*]

❚ Yep, Laurence

(1) It's hard to order someone to believe.

▶ [Moon Shadow, in *Dragonwings*, ch 3]

❚ Yolen, Jane

(1) In that hole, dark was light, day was night, and summer and winter seemed the same.

▶ [in *Eeny, Meeny, Miney Mole*]

(2) She [Eeny] thought all these new and complicated thoughts for hour after hour.

▶ [in *Eeny, Meeny, Miney Mole*]

(3) We watched silently with heat in our mouths, the heat of all the words we had not spoken.

▶ [in *Owl Moon*]

(4) When you go owling you don't need words or warm or anything but hope. The kind of hope that flies on silent wings under a shining Owl Moon.

▶ [in *Owl Moon*]

❚ Yorinks, Arthur

(1) But ripe fruit soon spoils.

▶ [in *Hey, Al*]

(2) Paradise lost is sometimes Heaven found.

▶ [in *Hey, Al*]

(3) One day last spring, Louis, a butcher, turned into a fish.

▶ [in *Louis the Fish*]

❚ Zemach, Harve

(1) A horrible thing is coming this way, Creeping closer day by day.

▶ [in *The Judge*]

\ Zion, Gene

(1) Harry was a white dog with black spots who liked everything, except . . . getting a bath.

▶ [in *Harry the Dirty Dog*]

\ Zolotow, Charlotte

(1) He needs it [a doll] to hug and to cradle and to take to the park so that when he's a father like you, he'll know how to take care of his baby and feed him and love him and bring him the things he wants, like a doll, so that he can practice being a father.

▶ [grandmother, in *William's Doll*]

QUOTATIONS FROM TRADITIONAL SOURCES

❧ Arabian Nights

(1) Who will change old lamps for new?
  ▶ [African magician, in "The Story of Aladdin; or, the Wonderful Magic Lamp"]

(2) Open, Sesame!
  ▶ [robbers' magic words to open hidden door, in "The Story of Ali Baba and the Forty Thieves"]

❧ Fairy Tales

(1) Up stick and bang him.
  ▶ [in "The Ass, the Table, and the Stick," in Jacobs, *English Fairy Tales*]

(2) Seven at one blow.
  ▶ [tailor's belt, in "The Brave Little Tailor," in Grimm, *Grimms' Fairy Tales*]

(3) I love you as fresh meat loves salt.
  ▶ [Third daughter, to father, in "Cap o' Rushes," in Jacobs, *English Fairy Tales*]

(4) Top-off. Half-gone. All-gone.
  ▶ [names the cat gives to the imaginary kittens he claims to be attending the christening of, when he is really eating the stored jar of fat, in "The Cat Who Married a Mouse," in Grimm, *Complete Brothers Grimm Fairy Tales*]

(5) The fair Burd Ellen . . . must have been carried off by the fairies, because she went round the church "widershins"—the opposite way to the sun.
  ▶ [Warlock Merlin, in "Childe Rowland," in Jacobs, *English Fairy Tales*]

(6) Turn again, Whittington,
Thrice Lord Mayor of London.

▶ [bells of Bow Church, in "Dick Whittington and His Cat," in Jacobs, *English Fairy Tales*]

(7) Flounder, flounder in the sea,
Come, I pray, and talk to me.

▶ [fisherman, in "The Fisherman and His Wife," in Grimm, *Complete Brothers Grimm Fairy Tales*]

(8) She was not satisfied even now, and at last she told her husband that she wished to be the Pope.

▶ [in "The Fisherman and His Wife," in Grimm, *Complete Brothers Grimm Fairy Tales*]

(9) How surprised she was to see the frog change into a handsome young prince.

▶ [in "The Frog Prince," in Grimm, *Complete Brothers Grimm Fairy Tales*]

(10) The house was made of gingerbread.

▶ [in "Hansel and Gretel," in Grimm, *Favorite Fairy Tales told in Germany*]

(11) Nibble, nibble, little mouse,
Who is gnawing at my house?

▶ [witch, in "Hansel and Gretel," in Grimm, *The Juniper Tree*]

(12) The sky is falling! The sky is falling. I must go and tell the King.

▶ [Henny Penny, in Zimmerman, *Henny Penny*]

(13) Fee-fi-fo-fum,
I smell the blood of an Englishman,

Be he alive, or be he dead
I'll grind his bones to make me bread!

▶ [ogre, in "Jack and the Beanstalk," in Steel, *English Fairy Tales*. Also in "Jack the Giant-Killer" and other English tales containing giants]

(14) Oh, Grandmamma, Grandmamma, what big ears you've got!
All the better to hear with, my dear.
But Grandmamma, Grandmamma, what big eyes you've got!
All the better to see you with, my dear.
Oh, Grandmamma, Grandmamma, what big teeth you've got!
All the better to eat you with, my dear.

▶ [Red Riding Hood and the Wolf, in "Little Red Riding Hood," Steel, *English Fairy Tales*]

(15) Be bold, be bold, but not too bold,
Lest that your heart's blood should run cold.

▶ [writing over the door, in "Mr. Fox," in Jacobs, *English Fairy Tales*]

(16) It is not so, nor it was not so.
And God forbid that it should be so.
But it is so, and it was so.
Here's hand and ring I have to show.

▶ [Mr. Fox and Lady Mary, in "Mr. Fox," in Jacobs, *English Fairy Tales*]

(17) Piggy won't go over the stile; and I shan't get home tonight.

▸ [old woman, in "The Old Woman and Her Pig," in Jacobs, *English Fairy Tales*]

(18) Help! Help! The Marquis of Carabas is drowning!

▸ [Puss, in "Puss in Boots," in Perrault, *The Sleeping Beauty and Other . . .*]

(19) Rapunzel, Rapunzel, let down your hair.

▸ [witch and, later, the prince, in "Rapunzel," in Grimm, *Complete Brothers Grimm Fairy Tales*]

(20) My wicked mother slew me,
My dear father ate me,
My little brother whom I love
Sits below, and I sing above
Stick, stock, stone dead.

▸ [in "The Rose-Tree," in Jacobs, *English Fairy Tales*]

(21) My daughter can spin straw into gold.

▸ [bragging miller, in "Rumpelstilt-skin," in Grimm, *Fairy Tales of Brothers Grimm*]

(22) He [Rumpelstiltskin] was so angry that he stamped his right foot so deep into the ground that his whole leg went in. Then in his rage he pulled his left foot so hard that he tore himself in two.

▸ [in "Rumpelstiltskin," in Grimm, *Fairy Tales of Brothers Grimm*]

(23) In the fifteenth year of her age the princess shall prick herself with a spindle, and shall fall down dead.

▸ [uninvited wise woman (in some versions, a fairy), in "Sleeping Beauty," in Grimm, *Household Stories*]

(24) The princess shall not die, but fall into a deep sleep for a hundred years.

▸ [wise woman (in some versions, a fairy), in "Sleeping Beauty," in Grimm, *Household Stories*]

(25) Mirror, mirror on the wall,
Who is the fairest of them all?

▸ [queen, in "Snow-White and the Seven Dwarfs," in Grimm, *Fairy Tales of Brothers Grimm*]

(26) You are fairest in this hall,
Snow-White is the fairest of them all.

▸ [mirror, in "Snow-White and the Seven Dwarfs," in Grimm, *Fairy Tales of Brothers Grimm*]

(27) Once upon a time there were three Bears. . . . One of them was a Little Wee Bear, and one was a Middle-sized Bear, and the other was a Great Big Bear.

▸ [in "The Story of the Three Bears," in Steel, *English Fairy Tales*] (Modern versions usually substitute Mother Bear, Father Bear, and Baby Bear.)

(28) First she [Goldilocks] tasted the porridge of the Great Big Bear, and that was too hot for her. Next she tasted the porridge of the Middle-sized Bear, but that was too cold for her. And then she went to the porridge of the Little Wee Bear, and . . . that was neither too hot

nor too cold, but just right, and she . . . ate it all up!

> ▶ [in "The Story of the Three Bears," in Steel, *English Fairy Tales*]

(29) Somebody has been sitting in my chair!

> ▶ [Bears, in "The Story of the Three Bears," in Steel, *English Fairy Tales*]

(30) Somebody has been lying in my bed,—and here she is still!

> ▶ [Wee Little Bear (Baby Bear), in "The Story of the Three Bears," in Steel, *English Fairy Tales*]

(31) Give me my bone!

> ▶ [in "Teeny-Tiny," in Jacobs, *English Fairy Tales*]

(32) Trip, trap, trip, trap, trip, trap, went the bridge.

> ▶ [in "Three Billy Goats Gruff," in Asbjørnsen, *East of the Sun . . .*]

(33) Who's that tripping over my bridge?

> ▶ [troll, in "Three Billy Goats Gruff," in Asbjørnsen, *East of the Sun . . .*]

(34) Wait a bit till the second billy goat Gruff comes. He's much bigger.

> ▶ [little billy goat, in "Three Billy Goats Gruff," in Asbjørnsen, *East of the Sun . . .*]

(35) So snip, snap, snout
This tale's told out.

> ▶ [in "Three Billy Goats Gruff," in Asbjørnsen, *East of the Sun . . .*]

(36) "Little pig, little pig, let me come in."
"No, no, by the hair of my chiny chin chin."
"Then I'll huff, and I'll puff, and I'll blow your house in."

> ▶ [wolf and pigs, in "The Story of the Three Little Pigs," in Jacobs, *English Fairy Tales*]

(37) Here lies Tom Thumb, King Arthur's Knight,
Who died by a spider's cruel bite. . . .
And on a mouse a-hunting went. . . .
Wipe, wipe your eyes and shake your head,
And cry, "Alas! Tom Thumb is dead!"

> ▶ [Epitaph, in "The History of Sir Thomas Thumb," in Jacobs, *English Fairy Tales*]

(38) Nimmy nimmy not
My name's Tom Tit Tot.

> ▶ [in "Tom Tit Tot," in Jacobs, *English Fairy Tales*]

◣ Nursery Rhymes

(1) Algy met a bear,
A bear met Algy,
The bear was bulgy,
The bulge was Algy.

> ▶ [in Prelutsky, *Poems of A. Nonny Mouse*]

(2) All around the cobbler's bench
The monkey chased the weasel;
That's the way the money goes,
Pop goes the weasel!

> ▶ [in Lobel, *The Random House Book of Mother Goose*]

(3) All work and no play makes
     Jack a dull boy;
     All play and no work makes
     Jack a mere toy.
     ▸ [in Baring-Gould, *The Annotated
       Mother Goose*]

(4) As I was going to St. Ives,
     I met a man with seven wives.
     Each wife had seven sacks,
     Each sack had seven cats,
     Each cat had seven kits;
     Kits, cats, sacks, and wives,
     How many were going to St.
     Ives?
     ▸ [in Baring-Gould, *The Annotated
       Mother Goose*]

(5) Baa, baa, black sheep,
     Have you any wool?
     Yes, sir, yes, sir,
     Three bags full,
     One for the master,
     One for the dame,
     One for the little boy
     Who lives in the lane.
     ▸ [in Foreman, *Michael Foreman's
       Mother Goose*]

(6) Bobby Shafto's gone to sea,
     Silver buckles on his knee;
     He'll come back and marry me!
     Bonny Bobby Shafto!
     ▸ [in Baring-Gould, *The Annotated
       Mother Goose*]

(7) Boys and girls come out to play;
     The moon doth shine as bright
     as day.
     ▸ [in Foreman, *Michael Foreman's
       Mother Goose*]

(8) Bye baby bunting,
     Daddy's gone a-hunting
     Gone to get a rabbit skin
     To wrap a baby bunting in.

     ▸ [in Foreman, *Michael Foreman's
       Mother Goose*]

(9) A centipede was happy quite,
     Until a frog in fun
     said, "Pray, which leg comes
     after which?"
     This raised her mind to such a
     pitch,
     She lay distracted in the ditch,
     Considering how to run.
     ▸ [in Prelutsky, *Poems of A. Nonny
       Mouse*]

     ▸ [sometimes attributed to Mrs.
       Edmund Caster]

(10) Curly locks, Curly locks,
     Wilt thou be mine?
     Thou shalt not wash dishes
     Nor yet feed the swine,
     But sit on a cushion
     And sew a fine seam,
     And feed upon strawberries,
     Sugar, and cream.
     ▸ [in Foreman, *Michael Foreman's
       Mother Goose*]

(11) Diddle, diddle, dumpling, my
     son John,
     Went to bed with his trousers
     on;
     One shoe off, and one shoe on,
     Diddle, diddle, dumpling, my
     son John.
     ▸ [in Baring-Gould, *The Annotated
       Mother Goose*]

(12) Ding, dong, bell.
     Pussy's in the well.
     Who put her in?
     Little Johnny Green.
     Who pulled her out?
     Little Tommy Stout.
     ▸ [in Foreman, *Michael Foreman's
       Mother Goose*]

(13) A diller, a dollar,
A ten o'clock scholar,
What makes you come so soon?
You used to come at ten o'clock,
And now you come at noon.

> ▶ [in Baring-Gould, *The Annotated Mother Goose*]

(14) Don't worry if your job is small
And your rewards are few,
Remember that the mighty oak
Was once a nut like you.

> ▶ [in Prelutsky, *Poems of A. Nonny Mouse*]

(15) One fell off and bumped his head.

> ▶ [in Christelow, *Five Little Monkeys Jumping on the Bed*]

(16) No more monkeys jumping on the bed.

> ▶ [in Christelow, *Five Little Monkeys Jumping on the Bed*]

(17) A frog he would a-wooing go,
Heigho, says Rowley!
Whether his Mother would let
him or no.
*With a rowley-powley, gammon
and spinach,*
Heigho, says Anthony Rowley!

> ▶ [in Caldecott, *R. Caldecott's Second Collection . . .*]

(18) Fuzzy Wuzzy was a bear,
Fuzzy Wuzzy had no hair,
Fuzzy Wuzzy wasn't fuzzy,
Was he?

> ▶ [in Prelutsky, *Poems of A. Nonny Mouse*]

(19) Georgie Porgie, pudding and pie,
Kissed the girls and made
them cry;
When the boys came out to play,
Georgie Porgie ran away.

> ▶ [in Baring-Gould, *The Annotated Mother Goose*]

(20) Goosey, goosey, gander,
Whither shall I wander?
Upstairs and downstairs
and in my lady's chamber.

> ▶ [in Baring-Gould, *The Annotated Mother Goose*]

(21) Hark, hark,
The dogs do bark,
The beggars are coming to town;
Some in rags,
And some in jags,
And one in a velvet gown.

> ▶ [in Foreman, *Michael Foreman's Mother Goose*]

(22) Hey diddle, diddle,
The cat and the fiddle,
The cow jumped over the moon;
The little dog laughed
To see such sport,
And the dish ran away with the
spoon.

> ▶ [in Foreman, *Michael Foreman's Mother Goose*]

(23) Hickety, pickety, my black hen,
[variant: Higgledy, piggledy]
She lays eggs for gentlemen;
Sometimes nine and
sometimes ten,
Hickety, pickety, my black hen.

> ▶ [in Baring-Gould, *The Annotated Mother Goose*]

(24) Hickory, dickory, dock,
The mouse ran up the clock.
The clock struck one,
Down the mouse did run.
[Variant: The mouse ran down.]
Hickory, dickory, dock.

> ▶ [in Foreman, *Michael Foreman's Mother Goose*]

(25) Hot cross buns!
Hot cross buns!
One a penny, two a penny,
Hot cross buns!

   ▶ [in Baring-Gould, *The Annotated Mother Goose*]

(26) How many miles to Babylon?
Threescore miles and ten.

   ▶ [in Foreman, *Michael Foreman's Mother Goose*]

(27) How much wood would a
    woodchuck chuck
If a woodchuck could chuck
    wood?

   ▶ [in Prelutsky, *Poems of A. Nonny Mouse*]

(28) Humpty dumpty sat on a wall,
Humpty dumpty had a great
    fall;
All the king's horses and all
    the king's men
Couldn't put Humpty together
    again.

   ▶ [in Baring-Gould, *The Annotated Mother Goose*]

(29) Hush, little baby, don't say a
    word,
Papa's going to buy you a
    mockingbird.

   ▶ [in Baring-Gould, *The Annotated Mother Goose*]

(30) I had a little nut tree,
Nothing would it bear
But a silver nutmeg
And a golden pear.

   ▶ [in Baring-Gould, *The Annotated Mother Goose*]

(31) I love little pussy,
Her coat is so warm,
And if I don't hurt her,
She'll do me no harm.

   ▶ [in Baring-Gould, *The Annotated Mother Goose*]

(32) If all the seas were one sea,
What a great sea that would be!

   ▶ [in Baring-Gould, *The Annotated Mother Goose*]

(33) Jack and Jill went up the hill
To fetch a pail of water;
Jack fell down and broke his
    crown,
And Jill came tumbling after.

   ▶ [in Foreman, *Michael Foreman's Mother Goose*]

(34) Jack be nimble,
Jack be quick,
Jack jump over
The candlestick.

   ▶ [in Foreman, *Michael Foreman's Mother Goose*]

(35) Jack Sprat could eat no fat,
His wife could eat no lean,
And so between them both,
    you see,
They licked the platter clean.

   ▶ [in Lobel, *The Random House Book of Mother Goose*]

(36) Ladybird, ladybird,
[Variant: Ladybug, ladybug]
Fly away home,
Your house is on fire
Your children will burn.
[Variant: And your children all
    gone.]

   ▶ [in Baring-Gould, *The Annotated Mother Goose*]

(37) Little Boy Blue,
Come blow your horn,
The sheep's in the meadow,
The cow's in the corn;
But where is the boy
Who looks after the sheep?
He's under the haystack,
Fast asleep.
  ▶ [in Foreman, *Michael Foreman's Mother Goose*]

(38) Little Bo-Peep has lost her
    sheep
And doesn't know where to
    find them;
Leave them alone, and they'll
    come home,
Bringing their tails behind them.
[Variant: Dragging their tails
    behind them]
  ▶ [in Foreman, *Michael Foreman's Mother Goose*]

(39) Little Jack Horner
Sat in a corner,
Eating a Christmas pie;
He put in his thumb
And pulled out a plum
And said, "What a good boy
    am I."
  ▶ [in Foreman, *Michael Foreman's Mother Goose*]

(40) Little Miss Muffet
Sat on a tuffet
Eating her curds and whey;
There came a big spider,
[Variant: Along came a spider]
Who sat down beside her
And frightened Miss Muffet
    away.
  ▶ [in Baring-Gould, *The Annotated Mother Goose*]

(41) Little Tommy Tucker
Sings for his supper.

  ▶ [in Foreman, *Michael Foreman's Mother Goose*]

(42) London Bridge is falling down,
Falling down, falling down,
London Bridge is falling down,
My fair lady.
  ▶ [in Foreman, *Michael Foreman's Mother Goose*]

(43) Mary, Mary, quite contrary,
How does your garden grow?
With silver bells and cockleshells,
And pretty maids all in a row.
  ▶ [in Foreman, *Michael Foreman's Mother Goose*]

(44) Methuselah ate what he found
    on his plate,
And never, as people do now,
Did he note the amount of the
    calorie count:
He ate it because it was chow.
  ▶ [in Prelutsky, *A. Nonny Mouse Writes Again!*]

(45) "Where are you going, my
    Pretty Maid?"
"I'm going a-milking, Sir," she
    said.
  ▶ [in "The Milkmaid," in Caldecott, *R. Caldecott's Second Collection . . .*]

(46) "But what is your fortune, my
    pretty Maid?"
"My face is my fortune, Sir,"
    she said.
"Then I can't marry you, my
    Pretty Maid!"
"Nobody asked you, Sir," she
    said.
  ▶ [in "The Milkmaid," in Caldecott, *R. Caldecott's Second Collection . . .*]

(47) Monday's child is fair of face,
Tuesday's child is full of grace,
Wednesday's child is full of woe,
Thursday's child has far to go,
Friday's child is loving and giving,
Saturday's child works hard for
his living,
And the child that is born on
the Sabbath day
Is bonny and blithe, and good
and gay.
▶ [in Baring-Gould, *The Annotated
Mother Goose*]

(48) The north wind doth blow,
And we shall have snow,
And what will poor robin do then?
Poor thing!
He'll sit in a barn
And keep himself warm
And hide his head under his
wing.
Poor thing!
▶ [in Baring-Gould, *The Annotated
Mother Goose*]

(49) Now I lay me down to rest,
I pray I pass tomorrow's test,
If I should die before I wake,
That's one less test I'll have to
take.
▶ [in Prelutsky, *Poems of A. Nonny
Mouse*]

(50) Now I lay me down to sleep,
I pray the Lord my soul to keep;
And if I die before I wake,
I pray the Lord my soul to take.
▶ [in Baring-Gould, *The Annotated
Mother Goose*]

(51) Oh, the grand old Duke of York
He had ten thousand men;
He marched them up to the
top of the hill,

And he marched them down
again.
▶ [in Foreman, *Michael Foreman's
Mother Goose*]

(52) Old King Cole
Was a merry old soul,
And a merry old soul was he;
He called for his pipe,
And he called for his bowl,
And he called for his fiddlers
three.
▶ [in Baring-Gould, *The Annotated
Mother Goose*]

(53) One, two, buckle my shoe;
Three, four, open the door;
[Variants: shut the door, knock
at the door]
Five, six, pick up sticks.
▶ [in Baring-Gould, *The Annotated
Mother Goose*]

(54) Pat a cake, pat a cake, baker's
man,
Bake me a cake as fast as you
can.
▶ [in Foreman, *Michael Foreman's
Mother Goose*]

(55) A peanut sat on a railroad track
His heart was all aflutter.
The five fifteen came rushing
by—
[Variant: Around the bend
came number ten]
Toot! Toot! Peanut butter!
▶ [in Prelutsky, *Poems of A. Nonny
Mouse*]

(56) Pease porridge hot,
Pease porridge cold,
Pease porridge in the pot
Nine days old.
Some like it hot,

Some like it cold,
Some like it in the pot
Nine days old.

▸ [in Baring-Gould, *The Annotated Mother Goose*]

(57) Peter, Peter, pumpkin eater,
Had a wife and couldn't keep her;
He put her in a pumpkin shell
And there he kept her very well.

▸ [in Baring-Gould, *The Annotated Mother Goose*]

(58) Peter Piper picked a peck of pickled peppers.

▸ [in Baring-Gould, *The Annotated Mother Goose*]

(59) Polly, put the kettle on,
We'll all have tea.

▸ [in Baring-Gould, *The Annotated Mother Goose*]

(60) Pussycat, pussycat, where have you been?
I've been to London to look at the queen.
Pussycat, pussycat, what did you there?
I frightened a little mouse under her chair.

▸ [in Baring-Gould, *The Annotated Mother Goose*]

(61) The Queen of Hearts,
She made some tarts,
All on a summer's day;
The Knave of Hearts,
He stole the tarts
And took them clean away.

▸ [in Baring-Gould, *The Annotated Mother Goose*]

(62) Rich man, poor man,
beggarman, thief,

Doctor, lawyer, merchant, chief,
Tinker, tailor, soldier, sailor.

▸ [in Lobel, *The Random House Book of Mother Goose*]

(63) Ride a cock-horse to Banbury Cross
To see a fine lady upon a white horse;
Rings on her fingers and bells on her toes,
And she shall have music wherever she goes.

▸ [in Baring-Gould, *The Annotated Mother Goose*]

(64) Rub-a-dub-dub,
Three men in a tub,
And who do you think they be?
The butcher, the baker, the candlestick maker,
Turn 'em out, knaves all three!

▸ [in Emerson, *The Nursery Treasury*]

(65) See-saw, Margery Daw,
Jacky shall have a new master;
Jacky shall have but a penny a day
Because he can't work any faster.

▸ [in Lobel, *The Random House Book of Mother Goose*]

(66) She sells sea shells on the seashore.

▸ [Variant: by the sea shore]

▸ [in Lobel, *The Random House Book of Mother Goose*]

(67) Simple Simon met a pieman
Going to the fair;
Says Simple Simon to the pieman,
Let me taste your ware.

▸ [in Baring-Gould, *The Annotated Mother Goose*]

(68) Sing a song of sixpence,
A pocket full of rye;
Four and twenty blackbirds
Baked in a pie.

▶ [in Foreman, *Michael Foreman's Mother Goose*]

(69) Star light, star bright,
First star I see tonight,
I wish I may, I wish I might,
Have the wish I wish tonight.

▶ [in Baring-Gould, *The Annotated Mother Goose*]

(70) This is the farmer sowing his corn,
That kept the cock that crowed in the morn,
That waked the priest all shaven and shorn,
That married the man all tattered and torn,
That kissed the maiden all forlorn,
That milked the cow with the crumpled horn,
That tossed the dog
That worried the cat
That killed the rat
That ate the malt
That lay in the house that Jack built.

▶ [in Baring-Gould, *The Annotated Mother Goose*]

(71) There was a crooked man,
And he walked a crooked mile.
He found a crooked sixpence
Against a crooked stile.
[Variant: upon a crooked stile]

▶ [in Baring-Gould, *The Annotated Mother Goose*]

(72) There was a little girl, and she had a little curl,
Right in the middle of her forehead;

When she was good she was very, very good,
But when she was bad she was horrid.

▶ [in Baring-Gould, *The Annotated Mother Goose*]

(73) There was a young lady of Niger
Who smiled as she rode on a tiger.
They returned from the ride
With the lady inside—
And the smile on the face of the tiger.

▶ [in Prelutsky, *Poems of A. Nonny Mouse*]

(74) There was a young woman named Bright,
Whose speed was much faster than light.
She set out one day
In a relative way
And returned on the previous night.

▶ [in Prelutsky, *A. Nonny Mouse Writes Again!*]

(75) There was an old woman who lived in a shoe,
She had so many children,
She didn't know what to do,
She gave them some broth without any bread;
She whipped them all soundly and put them to bed.

▶ [in Baring-Gould, *The Annotated Mother Goose*]

(76) This little pig went to market,
[Variant: this little piggy]
This little pig stayed home,
This little pig had roast beef,
This little pig had none,
And this little pig cried Wee-wee-wee
All the way home.

▶ [in Baring-Gould, *The Annotated Mother Goose*]

(77) Three blind mice, see how
        they run!
      They all ran after the farmer's
        wife,
      Who cut off their tails with a
        carving knife;
      Did you ever see such a sight
        in your life
      As three blind mice?

      ▶ [in Baring-Gould, *The Annotated
        Mother Goose*]

(78) Three little kittens, they lost
        their mittens,
      And they began to cry,
      Oh, Mother dear, we sadly fear
      That we have lost our mittens.
      [Variant: Our mittens we have
        lost]
      What! lost your mittens, you
        naughty kittens!
      Then you shall have no pie.
      Mee-ow, mee-ow, mee-ow.
      No, you shall have no pie.

      ▶ [in Baring-Gould, *The Annotated
        Mother Goose*]

(79) Three wise men of Gotham,
      They went to sea in a bowl.
      And if the bowl had been
        stronger,
      My song would be longer.

      ▶ [in Prelutsky, *A. Nonny Mouse
        Writes Again!*]

(80) To market, to market, to buy a
        fat pig
      Home again, home again,
        jiggety-jig.

      ▶ [in Baring-Gould, *The Annotated
        Mother Goose*]

(81) Tom, Tom, the piper's son,
      Stole a pig and away did run;

The pig was eat, and Tom was
  beat,
Till he run crying down the street.
[Variant: Then Tom went crying
  down the street]

▶ [in Baring-Gould, *The Annotated
  Mother Goose*]

(82) What are little boys made of?
      What are little boys made of?
      Frogs and snails
      [Variant: Snips and snails]
      And puppy dogs' tails,
      That's what little boys are
        made of.

      What are little girls made of?
      What are little girls made of?
      Sugar and spice
      And all things nice,
      [Variant: And everything nice]
      That's what little girls are
        made of.

      ▶ [in Baring-Gould, *The Annotated
        Mother Goose*]

(83) Wee Willie Winkie runs
        through the town,
      Upstairs and downstairs in his
        nightgown,
      Rapping at the window, crying
        through the lock,
      Are the children all in bed, for
        now it's eight o'clock?

      ▶ [in Baring-Gould, *The Annotated
        Mother Goose*]

(84) Who killed Cock Robin?
      "I," said the sparrow,
      "With my little bow and arrow,
      I killed Cock Robin."

      ▶ [in Lobel, *The Random House
        Book of Mother Goose*]

KEYWORD INDEX

The boldface single letters in the keyword phrases represent the keyword, e.g., **a** for accepting, **a** for accident, etc.

◣ A

adults
    expect to be perfect because they're **a**   Greene, C. (1)

adventure
    a is something unexpected   Gates (2)
    longing for **a** result of reading   McKinley (1)
    to die will be awfully big **a**   Barrie (17)

adventures
    best and raciest **a**   Grahame (13)
    no use for **a**   Tolkien (2)

adversity
    brought up as though living in **a**   Hale, L. (4)

advertising
    I love **a**   Schwartz (2)

advice
    a from friends like the weather   Lobel (6)
    learned how to take **a**   Craik (2)
    lords of creation don't take **a**   Alcott (7)
    shouldn't give **a** you don't follow   Wrede (2)

advisers
    when women are **a**   Alcott (7)

afraid
    courage is facing danger when **a**   Baum (11)
    enemies who have learned to be **a**   Merrill (5)
    I'm **a** it won't come up   Krauss (1)
    I'm never **a** with you   Milne (16)
    poor seeds are **a** to grow   Lobel (15)
    to be **a** and to be brave   Dalgliesh (2)

airplanes
    I call to the **a**   Swift (1)

ale
    cakes and **a** in fear   Aesop (7)

Algy
    A met a bear   Nursery rhymes (1)

alike
    still change color but always be **a**   Lionni (1)

alive
    being **a** is magic   Burnett (13)

all
    a you get by giving stuff up   Brooks (3)
    top-off, half-gone, **a**-gone   Fairy tales (4)

Allah
    ninety-nine names for **A**   Oppenheim (1)
    when **A** created the horse   Henry (1)

Almighty
    A is bound to be a gentleman   Stratton-Porter (4)

alone
    a no one wins freedom   Le Guin (2)
    last few steps have to take **a**   Silverstein (5)
    left him stranded there **a**   Paterson (2)
    memory is happiness of being **a**   Lowry (3)
    moving makes you feel all **a**   Park (1)
    when he comes to bat he stands **a**   Lord, B. (1)
    why only feel [God] when I'm **a**   Blume (3)

alphabet (subj.)
    you can stop if you want with Z   Seuss (44)

altar
    perfect for the **a** of an evil god   Snyder (3)

Amaroq
    A wolf my friend   George (2)

America
    to bring to the wild **A**   Edmonds (1)

American
    as **A** as pizza pie   Konigsburg (27)

amir
    your **A** whom you do not obey   Kipling (9)

Amy
    A's nose still afflicted her   Alcott (5)

Andrew
    A Marcus wanted freckles   Blume (4)

angel
    a dance no faster than music   Hite (2)

angels
    time is for dragonflies and **a**   Thurber (2)

anger
    in **a** we are all foolish   Spyri (2)
    no sight so ugly as face in **a**   Fitzhugh (9)

angry
    a every day of my life   Alcott (3)
    is everyone still **a** at me   Aardema (1)
    pain hurts more when one is **a** Smith, Dodie (1)
    so **a** that he stamped his foot   Fairy tales (22)

Angus
    each day as **A** grew older   Flack (1)

animal
    a fed comes back   Napoli (4)
    don't know what kind of **a** I am Jackson, K. & B.(1)

authority
accepted **a** rests on reason — Saint-Exupery (4)
words author and **a** — Byars (2)

authorship (subj.)
allow me to introduce myself — Howe (1)
wasn't his business to tell a writer — Paterson (15)
when I type a title page — Byars (1)

automobiles (subj.)
most motorcars are conglomerations — Fleming (1)

avoiding
talking is a way of **a** — Wrede (4)

◣ B

baa
b b black sheep — Nursery rhymes (5)

Babar
B then buys himself — Brunhoff (2)

babies (subj.)
this is Sophie — MacLachlan (1)
will live to regret that bump — Henkes (4)
Zeek Silver Moon was born — Ehrlich (1)

baby
as long as I'm living my **b** you'll be — Munsch (1)
b is a very heavy thing — Lyon (2)
b was a changeling — McGraw (1)
being a **b** offended dignity — Snyder (2)
clobber anyone who laid hand on **b** — Robinson (4)
first **b** laughed — Barrie (11)
get the **b** out of the barn — Robinson (2)
he'll know how to take care of his **b** — Zolotow (1)
hush little **b** don't say a word — Nursery rhymes (29)
Mama loved her **b** Ben — Lindgren, B. (1)

Babylon
how many miles to **B** — Nursery rhymes (26)

back
just can't **b** down — Butterworth (1)

backson
gon out **b** bisy **b** — Milne (9)
spotted or herbaceous **b** — Milne (10)

backwards
memory that only works **b** — Carroll (30)
walking **b** upside down — Wood (4)

backwater
all along the **b**   Grahame (7)

bacon
better beans and **b** in peace   Aesop (7)

bad
beautiful things grow **b** by doing **b**   MacDonald, G. (1)
nothing all **b** either   Gray, E. (1)
one **b** turn deserves   Aesop (12)

baddest
b dude on the block   Myers (1)

bagel
space is like a **b** with poppy seeds   Pinkwater (4)

bags
yes sir yes sir three **b** full   Nursery rhymes (5)

Bagthorpian
greatest and best **B** Party   Cresswell (5)

bait
everyone else with same **b**   Aldrich (2)

balance
world is in **b**   Le Guin (5)

balloon
best way of travel is in a **b**   Pene DuBois (3)

ballpoint
b pen factor in decline   Konigsburg (25)

banana
best friend not a **b**   Gackenbach (3)

bananas
we **b** should have warned you   Kimmel (3)

Banbury
there's **B** cakes and lollipops   de la Mare (6)

bang
b-ups and hang-ups can happen   Seuss (42)
up stick and **b** him   Fairy tales (1)

bank
as hard to find as **b** presidents   Konigsberg (11)

banks
b of great gray-green greasy Limpopo   Kipling (25)

banquet
b comes when something's over   Grahame (3)

barks
each dog **b** in his own yard   Kipling (3)

baseball
> father do with son but talk **b**   Feiffer (2)
> isn't a game, it's real, it's **b**   Levy (2)

baseball (subj.)
> in our national pastime   Lord, B. (1)

bat
> twinkle twinkle little **b**   Carroll (12)
> when he comes to **b** he stands alone   Lord, B. (1)

bath
> liked everything except getting a **b**   Zion (1)

bathrobes
> always wear **b** when our dinosaurs   Butterworth (2)

bathtub
> King Bidgood's in the **b**   Wood (1)
> my **b** is in the living room   Lobel (19)
> there's a crocodile in the **b**   Waber (1)
> won't sail in a **b**   Crampton (1)

battle
> soldiers don't really like going into **b**   Burnett (6)

battles
> **b** are ugly when women fight   Lewis (4)

bean
> Boggis and Bunce and **B**   Dahl (16)
> human **b** has two legs   Dahl (3)
> liked to practice with a string **b**   Hoban (9)

beans
> better **b** and bacon in peace   Aesop (7)
> tickled the ground and it laughed **b**   Cushman (2)

bear
> Algy met a **b**   Nursery rhymes (1)
> all of the hair fell off of the **b**   Thomas (2)
> **B** of Very Little Brain   Milne (35)
> **b** went walking   Kuskin (3)
> big birthday **b** hug   Flack (5)
> boy and his **b** will always be playing   Milne (13)
> for you are my little **b**   Minarik (1)
> Fuzzy Wuzzy was a **b**   Nursery rhymes (18)
> I'm a big black **b** and I do   Yee (1)
> inside the **b** you would be you   Joosse (1)
> isn't it funny how a **b** likes honey   Milne (31)
> Little **B** and Little Sal's mother   McCloskey (1)
> please look after this **b**   Bond (2)
> silly old **B**   Milne (32)
> that **b** did greet and eat   Kuskin (3)
> wise old **b** who lived at the top   Pene DuBois (1)

beard
 I pity him who has a **b**   Field, E. (12)
 there was an old man with a **b**   Lear (2)

bears
 b always land on their feet   Bond (5)
 b is sixpence extra   Bond (3)
 b steal ice cream   Duvoisin (4)
 home for retired **b** in Lima   Bond (4)
 there were three **b**   Fairy tales (27)

beast
 man who mistreats poor dumb **b**   DeFelice (1)
 war is **b** with long claws   Hunt (2)

Beatrice
 B Quimby's biggest problem   Cleary (1)

beaus
 ever so many **b** on the string   Montgomery (7)

beautiful
 b things grow bad by doing bad   MacDonald, G. (1)
 something to make the world more **b**   Cooney (4)

beauty
 b lives in heart of its holder   Hite (1)
 black is **b**   O'Neill (2)
 pay back to world in **b** and caring   Paterson (5)

become
 can **b** anything you want to be   Kerr (3)

bed
 cozy **b** in a napping house   Wood (3)
 God knows what was in that **b**   Andersen (6)
 my **b**'s not big enough for three   Mayer (2)
 no more monkeys jumping on the **b**   Nursery rhymes (16)
 somebody has been lying in my **b**   Fairy tales (30)
 up the tree in the window back in **b**   Berenstain (1)
 winter may be beautiful but **b** is better   Lobel (8)

bedroom
 remembered where **b** window was   Johnson (2)

bedstead
 on bare **b** put a pea   Andersen (5)

bed-time
 to be taken at **b**   Potter (8)

bee
 only reason for being a **b**   Milne (30)
 something as small as a **b** could kill   Smith, Doris (1)
 you were a bumble **b** and a bull sat   Leaf (3)

beg
    didn't **b** borrow or steal   Alcott (4)

beggars
    the **b** are coming to town   Nursery rhymes (21)

begin
    b at the beginning   Carroll (21)

beginning
    hold that **b** in his being   Le Guin (8)

behave
    must be the way people **b**   Fatio (1)

behavior
    thought this **b** was terrible   Pene DuBois (1)

behavior (subj.)
    jest 'fore Christmas I'm as good   Field, E. (11)
    Mama loved her baby Ben   Lindgren, B. (1)
    never do anything by halves   Dahl (21)
    when I'm very good my dear   de la Mare (6)

believe
    bell still rings for all who truly **b**   Van Allsburg (5)
    can't **b** that said Alice   Carroll (31)
    do you **b** in fairies   Barrie (18)
    hard to order someone to **b**   Yep (1)
    if you **b** clap you hands   Barrie (20)
    one can't **b** impossible things   Carroll (31)

bell
    b still rings for me   Van Allsburg (5)
    ding dong **b**, pussy's in the well   Nursery rhymes (12)
    one silver **b** from Santa's sleigh   Van Allsburg (4)

belling
    b the cat   Aesop (17)

bells
    rings on her fingers and **b** on her toes   Nursery rhymes (63)

belly
    full **b** contented heart   Cushman (12)

beloved
    O my Best **B**   Kipling (18)

bench
    all around the cobbler's **b**   Nursery rhymes (2)

bend
    better to **b** than break   Aesop (22)

Bergen
    bought it in **B** op Zoom   Edmonds (1)

while you waited in darkness	Frasier (1)
Zeek Silver Moon was born	Ehrlich (1)

birthday

Alice does not have a **b**	Hoban (4)
appreciate Patrick's **b** present	Reid Banks (1)
big **b** bear hug	Flack (5)
b party had been the greatest	Cresswell (5)
happy **b** Little Gorilla	Bornstein (2)
spoiled two **b** cakes	Cleary (2)
your **b** is always the one not now	Hoban (5)

bison (subj.)

for centuries he ran	Ciardi (7)

bisy

gon out backson **b** backson	Milne (9)

bit

b by fleas and plagued by family	Cushman (6)
I do not like it not one little **b**	Seuss (10)

bite

don't get a **b** until you start to take	Butterworth (3)

black

b is beauty	O'Neill (2)
b man gotta be ready to die	Taylor, M. (2)
can't be Peter Pan, he isn't **b**	Hoffman (1)
one of them **b** as a mussel shell	Lionni (8)

blackberries

bread and milk and **b**	Potter (9)

blackbirds

four and twenty **b** baked in a pie	Nursery rhymes (68)

blade

wants that **b** of grass	Hedderwick (1)

blamed

devil gets **b**	Rawlings (5)

blanket

heard of the **b** fairy	Henkes (6)
summer comes like hairy **b**	Napoli (1)

blaze

b kin destroy him that makes it	Hunt (1)

bless

b the world feels like tip-tapping	Gray, L. (3)

blessing

greet the sun with some kind of **b**	Baylor (1)

blind

three **b** mice	Nursery rhymes (77)

blood
    I smell the **b** of an Englishman   Fairy tales (13)
    price paid in **b** is heavy reckoning   Alexander (9)
    your heart's **b** should run cold   Fairy tales (15)

bloodier
    hockey's a lot **b** than football   Blume (7)

bloomed
    one day in his own good time Leo **b**   Kraus (2)

bloomer
    watched **b** doesn't bloom   Kraus (1)

blow
    come **b** your horn   Nursery rhymes (37)
    seven at one **b**   Fairy tales (2)

blue
    heads are green, hands are **b**   Lear (11)
    Little Boy **B** come blow your horn   Nursery rhymes (37)
    what kind of berries make pancakes **b**   Devlin (1)

blueberries
    among the **b** on Blueberry Hill   McCloskey (1)

bluebird
    in like a crow out like a **b**   Bailey (4)

boa
    I'm being eaten by a **b**   Silverstein (11)

board
    loose **b** on stairs a little creak   Bright (1)

boat
    beautiful pea-green **b**   Lear (8)
    home was a **b** with two wise eyes   Flack (6)
    sometimes a **b**, sometimes an accident   Milne (47)

boats
    life like a sea, people like **b**   Voigt (4)
    shall bring my **b** ashore   Stevenson, R. (5)
    simply messing about in **b**   Grahame (6)

Bobby
    B Shafto's gone to sea   Nursery rhymes (6)

bodyguard
    Denmark must be **b** for Jews   Lowry (4)

Boggis
    B and Bunce and Bean   Dahl (16)

boil
    b a cauldron make a brew   Devlin (1)

bold
    be **b** but not too **b**   Fairy tales (15)

bondage
    don't thank people who set you in **b**   Cleaver (2)

bone
    give me my **b**   Fairy tales (31)
    to fetch her poor dog a **b**   Martin, S. (1)

bones
    I'll grind his **b** to make me bread   Fairy tales (13)

bong
    land where the **b**-tree grows   Lear (9)

book
    ain't the **b** what's sacred   Fitzhugh (11)
    b-learning often came in useful   Grahame (1)
    disturbed while absorbed in **b**   Burnett (8)
    library **b** is 42 years overdue   Silverstein (3)
    nothing to say in the **b** he tried to write   Hale, L. (2)
    sentences to go I'll have a **b**   Byars (1)
    what is the use of a **b**   Carroll (2)

books
    b that cannot be read   Lobel (22)

boots
    gunpowder ran out at heels of **b**   Caldecott (1)

Bo-Peep
    little **B** has lost her sheep   Nursery rhymes (38)

boredom
    every job some built-in **b**   Konigsburg (18)

born
    b at sea in teeth of gale   Brown (8)
    b in henyard   Andersen (12)
    if you were **b** to walk ground   Belloc (7)
    we're **b**, we live a little while, we die   White, E. (4)
    Zeek Silver Moon was **b**   Ehrlich (1)

borogoves
    all mimsy were the **b**   Carroll (23)

borrowed
    they're every one **b**   Lyon (5)

bother
    long words **b** me   Milne (35)

bottle
    drink much from **b** marked poison   Carroll (3)

bottom
    honey right down to the **b** of the jar   Milne (36)

bubble
    b b pasta pot   dePaola (5)

bucket
    Charlie **B** the hero   Dahl (9)

Buckingham
    changing the guard at **B** Palace   Milne (21)

buckles
    silver **b** on his knee   Nursery rhymes (6)

Buddha
    great **B** whom he had painted   Coatsworth (1)

budge
    never **b** in the least   Seuss (50)

buffalo (subj.)
    for centuries he ran   Ciardi (7)

bulge
    the **b** was Algy   Nursery rhymes (1)

bull
    man is not like a fighting **b**   Wojciechowska (3)
    Maniac Maniac kissed a **b**   Spinelli (5)
    were a bumble bee and a **b** sat   Leaf (3)

bullets
    b made of platinum   Belloc (3)

bullfighting (subj.)
    a way of cheating death   Wojciechowska (1)

bullies (subj.)
    any excuse will serve tyrant   Aesop (2)

bulls (subj.)
    they called him Ferdinand   Leaf (4)

bully
    February is a mean **b**   Paterson (11)

bum
    look like real prince but you are a **b**   Munsch (2)

bumble
    were a **b** bee and a bull sat   Leaf (3)

bumblebees
    wasps and **b** have a party   Hoban (3)

bump
    b b b on the back of his head   Milne (27)
    live to regret that **b**   Henkes (4)

bumped
    one fell off and **b** his head   Nursery rhymes (15)

Bunce
Boggis and **B** and Bean — Dahl (16)

bunny
b who wanted to run away — Brown (7)
one day **b** said going to be Indian — Bornstein (1)

buns
hot cross **b** — Nursery rhymes (25)

bunting
bye baby **b** — Nursery rhymes (8)

Burd
fair **B** Ellen — Fairy tales (5)

burden
any great gift is a **b** — Cooper (2)

buried
civilized men **b** their dead — DeFelice (2)

bush
four times as big as the **b** — Lear (1)

business
being king is a **b** — Konigsburg (19)
b is **b**, and **b** must grow — Seuss (36)

bust
we must increase our **b** — Blume (2)

butcher
the **b**, the baker, the candlestick maker — Nursery rhymes (64)
Louis a **b** turned into a fish — Yorinks (3)

butter
do like a little bit of **b** to my bread — Milne (25)
keep your **b** side up — Seuss (6)
nothing left but pool of melted **b** — Bannerman (3)
Zook eats bread with the **b** side down — Seuss (5)

button
that is not my **b** — Lobel (12)

buttons
whole world is covered with **b** — Lobel (13)

buy
had to **b** man to get [dog] — Knight (3)

buzz
nobody comes that can't **b** — Hoban (3)

bye
b baby bunting — Nursery rhymes (8)

◣ C

hurrah for that chocolate **c**   Field, E. (2)
I am the **c** who walks by himself   Kipling (30)
men will always throw things at a **c**   Kipling (31)
once our only now no longer lonely **c**   DeRegniers (7)
one reason I got a **c**   Neville (1)
pretty nice job for a **c**   Viorst (8)
pussy **c** does not tell a lion   Konigsburg (20)
the truth about the **c** and pup   Field, E. (9)
under holy hand knelt **c**   Coatsworth (1)
up in that tree sits chocolate **c**   Field, E. (1)
watched a **c** try to decide where to sit   Howe (2)
what difference does that make to a **c**   Wrede (6)
who ever heard of a polite **c**   Wrede (1)
wildest of all wild animals was the **c**   Kipling (28)

catch-as-catch-can
fell to playing the game of **c**   Caldecott (1)

caterpillar
tiny and very hungry **c**   Carle (2)

cathedral
than in destroying **c**   Greene, B. (2)

cats
c here **c** there **c** and kittens everywhere   Gag (1)
how to speak to **c**   Paterson (13)
millions and billions and trillions of **c**   Gag (1)
when **c** are dreaming   Pilkey (1, 2)

cats (subj.)
dog growls when it's angry   Carroll (7)
I love little pussy, her coat is so warm   Nursery rhymes (31)
soft paws sharp claws   DeRegniers (1)
waving wild tail, walking by wild lone   Kipling (32)

cellar
something terrible down in the **c**   Gackenbach (1)

center
look to the **c** of the **c**   Paulsen (5)

centers
different people have different **c**   Lyon (3)

centipede
c was happy quite   Nursery rhymes (9)

centuries
for **c** he ran and ran   Ciardi (7)

cereal
know what breakfast **c** made of   Dahl (11)

chair
more time in the uncooperative **c**   Henkes (3)
somebody has been sitting in my **c**   Fairy tales (29)

challenge (subj.)
I thought they were sort of fun   Fisher (4)

challenges
obstacles are **c** for winners   Kerr (2)

chameleons (subj.)
we will still change color   Lionni (1)

chances
do best he can and take his **c**   Gates (3)
life is series of last **c**   Voigt (6)

Chang
C which meant little or nothing   Mosel (1)

change
c into an almost different person   Weller (1)
c people's habits make all trouble   Fitzhugh (7)
c your ways when fear seizes   George (1)
must not **c** one thing   Le Guin (5)
still **c** color but always be alike   Lionni (1)
to stay young is also not to **c**   Blos (1)

changed
they **c** my gun, everything's **c**, I'm **c**   Irving (5)
think themselves **c** when only mood **c**   MacDonald, G. (7)

changeling
baby was a **c**   McGraw (1)

changes
great **c** made too swiftly   Snyder (1)
I'll stay till the wind **c**   Travers (1)
life's all about **c**   Blos (1)

changing
minds like diapers need **c**   Cushman (5)
they're **c** the guard at Buckingham   Milne (21)

character
rebellion necessary for **c**   Voigt (5)

charity
c seldom of real service   Cleaver (1)
like **c**, stealing begins at home   Blos (2)

Charlie
C Bucket the hero   Dahl (9)

cheat
creatures had begun to **c**   Harris (5)
when stakes are high, I never **c**   Konigsburg (6)

cheating
found a way of **c** death   Wojciechowska (1)

cheer
if more of us valued food and **c** — Tolkien (9)

cheers
3 **c** for Pooh — Milne (48)

cherries
made believe **c** were eyes — Henkes (7)

Cheshire Cat (subj.)
cat without a grin — Carroll (9)
dog growls when it's angry — Carroll (7)
vanished quite slowly — Carroll (8)

Chewandswallow
different about **C** was its weather — Barrett (1)

chewing
repulsive bum **c c** gum — Dahl (10)

chicken
every boy should have a **c** — Pinkwater (6)
more nobility in building **c** coop — Greene, B. (2)
sipping **c** soup with rice — Sendak (1)

chickens
do not count your **c** — Aesop (28)

child
c should always say what's true — Stevenson, R. (3)
c's presence to make a home — Porter (4)
hey unto you a **c** — Robinson (3)
Monday's **c** is fair of face — Nursery rhymes (47)
no **c** likes to be ordered to be nice — Cleary (8)
one **c** a week is fifty-two a year — Dahl (22)
own **c** is disgusting little blister — Dahl (20)

children
all **c** except one grow up — Barrie (1)
as friend to **c**, yak — Belloc (1)
best thing about havin' fourteen **c** — Henry (2)
c could say anything — Norton (4)
other little **c** shall bring my boats — Stevenson, R. (5)
so many **c** she didn't know what to do — Nursery rhymes (75)
when **c** died he went part way — Barrie (4)

children (subj.)
they're every one borrowed — Lyon (5)

chin
by the hair of my chiny **c c** — Fairy tales (36)

chocolate
cash reward or **c** eclairs — Marshall (2)
hurrah for that **c** cat — Field, E. (2)
up in that tree sits **c** cat — Field, E. (1)

choice
    freedom, not gift but **c**   Le Guin (3)

choices
    our **c** show what we truly are   Rowling (1)

chomps
    C Bars are nice to get   Hoban (6)

choose
    very wise to let children **c**   Nesbit (1)

chops
    c is to magic what scales   Konigsburg (28)

chose
    until he **c** they were all his   O'Hara (3)

Christmas
    always winter and never **C**   Lewis (1)
    C won't be **C** without presents   Alcott (1)
    down in Who-ville liked **C** a lot   Seuss (27)
    he hadn't stopped **C** from coming   Seuss (30)
    I'd like a boy for **C**   Thayer (1)
    jest 'fore **C** I'm as good as I kin be   Field, E. (11)
    maybe **C** doesn't come from a store   Seuss (31)
    'twas the night before **C**   Moore (1)

Christmas (subj.)
    villagers all this frosty tide   Grahame (11)

chuck
    how much wood would a woodchuck **c**   Nursery rhymes (27)

church
    went round the **c** widershins   Fairy tales (5)

cigars
    c should be like onions   McKinley (3)

circles
    life is made up of **c**   MacLachlan (8)

city
    one player reaches the golden **c**   Van Allsburg (2)
    road to the **C** of Emeralds   Baum (3)

civilized
    c men buried their dead   DeFelice (2)

clap
    if you believe in fairies **c** your hands Barrie (20)

class
    how was your **c** trip to the farm   Noble (1)
    our **c** really has bad luck   Cole, J. (1)

clown
surprised Mr. and Mrs. C saw their tent ..... Petersham (1)

coal
Brownie who lived in a c cellar ..... Craik (1)

coat
beautiful little red c ..... Bannerman (1)

cobbler
all around the c's bench ..... Nursery rhymes (2)

cock
who killed c robin ..... Nursery rhymes (84)

coconut
I'll meet you at the top of the c tree ..... Martin, B. (1)

coffee
gave it points over c ..... McKinley (4)

cold
how c my toes tiddely pom ..... Milne (1)
just about to come down with terrible c ..... Fitzhugh (8)

color
still change c but always be alike ..... Lionni (1)

colors
eye mixes c for you ..... Treviño (1)
I gather c for winter is gray ..... Lionni (4)

Columbus
C had a son but no one expected ..... Wojciechowska (2)

comb
c their hair with the moon ..... Pilkey (2)

come
I'm afraid it won't c up ..... Krauss (1)

command
learned to obey before he could c ..... Craik (2)

common
own predicament c fate of millions ..... Kindl (1)

common sense
caught a handful of c ..... Harris (4)
prefers those who have c ..... Sewell (3)

complaining
doing what is expected without c ..... Cleary (15)

complete
now it was c it could not sing ..... Silverstein (7)

complexions
not able to keep our c ..... Field, R. (3)

complications
Jamie liked perspiration and **c**   Konigsburg (2)

compliment
sometimes it is a **c** to be admired   Morris (4)

confidence
a man's **c**, that's his capacity   Kerr (3)

confusing
everything more **c** on empty stomach   Alexander (5)

conscience
mosquito has a guilty **c**   Aardema (1)

Constitution
unusual **C,** a restaurant government   Pene DuBois (4)

contempt
familiarity breeds **c**   Aesop (18)

contrary
Mary Mary quite **c**   Nursery rhymes (43)

control
can't **c** your sadness   Park (3)
people who try to **c** people   Fitzhugh (7)

conversations
use of a book without pictures or **c**   Carroll (2)

convictions
your father had strong **c**   Conly (2)

cookie
if you give a mouse a **c**   Numeroff (1)

cookies
all the sandwich **c** sweet   Hoban (15)
no one makes **c** like Grandma   Hutchins (1)

cooking (subj.)
it you want to go on liking it   Ransome (2)

coquette
undisputed sway over heart of **c**   Irving (2)

corn
c be high as heaven   Hamilton (7)
getting in **c** prose of farm child's life   Blos (6)

corner
found the **c** that spring was around   Lobel (9)
leave your **c** for a while   Hill (1)

corners
c wear off and shapes change   Silverstein (8)

cost
    he **c** me much   Konigsburg (21)

could
    I **c** do that but I wouldn't   Cole, B. (3)

count
    do not **c** your chickens   Aesop (28)

counterpane
    pleasant land of **c**   Stevenson, R. (6)

courage
    cannot confuse **c** with lack of fear   Wojciechowska (4)
    followed them that takes **c**   Conly (2)
    great **c** to appear with empty truth   Demi (1)
    have **c** to look upon evil   Alexander (3)
    keep up your **c** Sarah Noble   Dalgliesh (1)
    takes more **c** to be a passenger   Konigsburg (29)
    to be afraid best kind of **c**   Dalgliesh (2)
    true **c** is facing danger   Baum (11)
    your **c** lights the way   Martin, B. (3)

courage (subj.)
    if people expect you to be brave   Creech (6)
    it is hard to be brave   Milne (41)

Coven Tree
    here in **C** we're no strangers to magic   Brittain (1)

cow
    c jumped over the moon   Nursery rhymes (22)
    c who wants to be different   Duvoisin (2)
    friendly **c** all red and white   Stevenson, R. (8)
    milked the **c** with the crumpled horn   Nursery rhymes (70)
    understanding mother even though **c**   Leaf (2)
    until the **c** started crying   Noble (1)

cowardly
    C Lion   Baum (15)
    realio trulio **c** dragon   Nash (1)

crane
    old story about the **c**   Coerr (1)

cranes
    folds one thousand paper **c**   Coerr (1)

cream
    even a very special cat likes **c**   Jeter (1)

create
    all hate what we **c**   Cole, B. (1)

creature
    not a **c** was stirring   Moore (1)

credentials
ask for **c** before they give food — Greene, B. (3)

credit
if succeeds give weaker vessel half **c** — Alcott (7)

creeping
c closer day by day — Zemach (1)

cried
c till you have no more tears — Lewis (6)
when his parrot died he **c** and **c** — Fox, M. (1)

crimson
purple shoes with **c** soles — Bannerman (1)

crocodile
c would have had me — Barrie (14)
got a new [nose] from the **c** — Kipling (25)
it's only Lyle, Lyle the **c** — Waber (2)
terrible tick-tock of the **c** — Barrie (21)
there's a **c** in the bathtub — Waber (1)

crocus
for **C** it's his teeth — Duvoisin (1)

crooked
there was a **c** man — Nursery rhymes (71)

croquet
c balls were live hedgehogs — Carroll (15)

cross
add to their suffering by being **c** — MacDonald, G. (4)

crosses
anyone **c** this line I shoot — Gardiner (2)

crossing
think only of **c** to the end — McCully (2)

crow
in like a **c** out like a bluebird — Bailey (4)
Johnny **C** would dig and sow — Brooke (1)

crowns
numbskulls put **c** on heads — Alexander (16)

cruelty (subj.)
I tend to believe in demons — Fox, P. (4)

crumbs
a lap is so you don't get **c** — Krauss (4)

cry
all pirates **c** and so do I — Fox, M. (1)

◣ D

tonight we **d** in the tub	Wood (2)
when didst thou see elephants **d**	Kipling (6)
will you join the **d**	Carroll (18)

danced
d by the light of the moon	Lear (10)

dancing
tap **d** on God's piano	Park (6)

danger
not as much **d** about uncommon things	Hale, L. (5)
true courage is facing **d**	Baum (11)

Danny
D gave his mother a bear hug	Flack (5)

dare
fortune often smiles on those who **d**	Gerrard (1)

dark
all I know is the **d**	Le Guin (1)
d mountains are always around us	Martin, B. (2)
fell through the **d** out of his clothes	Sendak (2)
for the **D** the **D** is rising	Cooper (3)
in that hole, **d** was light	Yolen (1)
it was a **d** and stormy night	L'Engle (1)
long **d** thought of something to eat	Ciardi (1)
once on **d** winter's day	Burnett (4)
when the **D** comes rising	Cooper (4)
you have never seen, the **d**	Wildsmith (1)

darkest
I was brought up in **D** Peru	Bond (4)

darkness
d has way of falling down on you	Hamilton (2)
while you waited in **d**	Frasier (1)
you have raced **d** and won	Martin, B. (3)

dasher
Now **D** now Dancer	Moore (3)

daughter
my **d** can spin straw into gold	Fairy tales (21)

daughters (subj.)
mothers have need of sharp eyes	Alcott (8)

dawn
sun begins its life at **d**	Baylor (2)

dawn (subj.)
way to start a day	Baylor (1)

day
d deserves good loud trumpet	Lobel (25)
if I was dead I'd set up, a **d** like this	Rawlings (6)

new sun every **d** — Baylor (2)
terrible horrible no good very bad **d** — Viorst (1)
today was a difficult **d** — Henkes (5)
too tired from fighting night to enjoy **d** — Ryan (1)
way to start a **d** is this — Baylor (1)

days

some **d** are like that — Viorst (5)

dead

civilized men buried their **d** — DeFelice (2)
fairy somewhere falls down **d** — Barrie (12)
if I was **d** I'd set up — Rawlings (6)
in war the **d** pay debts for the living — Collier (7)
think you feel when you **d** — Brooks (1)
use of principles if you have to be **d** — Collier (4)
wouldn't be any **d** people — Myers (2)

death

border between life and **d** — Orr (1)
d is senseless yet makes way — Raskin (1)
D itself start working backwards — Lewis (7)
d was in the air — Slepian (1)
don't need anybody's **d** — Collier (5)
found a way of cheating **d** — Wojciechowska (1)
make **d** take you by surprise — Paulsen (6)
Nag come up and dance with **d** — Kipling (4)
only ending in this world is **d** — Paterson (9)
silence deep as **d** — Dahl (14)
some of us knocked at **D**'s door — Stolz (3)
watching **d** being cheated of its right — Wojciechowska (1)
young men never think about **d** — O'Dell (2)

death (subj.)

as Beth had hoped — Alcott (6)
Barney is in the ground — Viorst (8)
black man gotta be ready to die — Taylor, M. (2)
eaten up by rhinoceros — Dahl (17)
hard to think about God — Smith, Doris (1)
he cost me much — Konigsburg (21)
he's never going to be lost — Park (7)
I go to enjoy the freedom — Collier (6)
if crying was going to bring anybody — Myers (2)
soul should be stolen — Fox, P. (7)
Teunis riding in with half a dozen — Edmonds (2)
think you feel when you dead — Brooks (1)
when his parrot died he cried — Fox, M. (1)
when somebody goes away — Fitzhugh (6)

debts

in war dead pay **d** for the living — Collier (7)
wages of sin hardest **d** — Stratton-Porter (3)

died
 d because she never knew   Belloc (12)
 when children **d** he went part way   Barrie (4)
 when his parrot **d** he cried   Fox, M. (1)

dies
 look to **D** and run   Hamilton (3)
 when somebody **d** want to tell   Fitzhugh (6)

difference
 d between savages and civilized   DeFelice (2)
 he by himself can make a **d**   Lord, B. (1)
 what **d** does that make to a cat   Wrede (6)

different
 cow who wants to be **d**   Duvoisin (2)
 d people have **d** centers   Lyon (3)

dig
 could **d** as much in a day as a hundred   Burton (4)
 I have to **d** a hole just for myself   Hurd (1)

dignity
 being a baby offended **d**   Snyder (2)

diller
 a **d**, a dollar, a ten o'clock scholar   Nursery rhymes (13)

ding
 d dong bell, pussy's in the well   Nursery rhymes (12)

dinosaurs
 wear our bathrobes when our **d** hatch   Butterworth (2)

direction
 general **d** was up   Holman (3)

direction (subj.)
 would you tell me please   Carroll (6)

dirt
 with **d** above us and under us   Stevenson, J. (1)

disappointment (subj.)
 worst part of growing up   Montgomery (8)

discover
 d another New World   Wojciechowska (2)

disease
 d like Selfishness or Answerbackism   MacDonald, B. (1)

dish
 and the **d** ran away with the spoon   Nursery rhymes (22)

dishonesty
 d goes very far to make man no value   MacDonald, G. (3)

dolls
    d can do things   Burnett (7)

dolls (subj.)
    he needs it to hug   Zolotow (1)

donkeys
    transformed into so many little **d**   Collodi (9)

door
    at my wee small **d**   de la Mare (2)
    follow wall there will be **d**   De Angeli (1)
    parlor **d** a little squeak   Bright (1)

doorbell
    said Ma as the **d** rang   Hutchins (1)

door-mat
    ever heard of **d** telling one anything   Grahame (8)

doors
    all **d** hard to unlock until find key   O'Brien (1)

Dorothy
    D lived in midst of Kansas prairies   Baum (1)
    I am **D** the small and meek   Baum (9)
    my name is **D**   Baum (4)

double
    d-headed three-clawed whatzit   Gackenbach (2)

doubt
    if it is a good morning, which I **d**   Milne (38)
    never **d** what nobody is sure   Belloc (14)

down
    d Spook Hill through the woods   Berenstain (1)
    d the rabbit hole   Carroll (1)

downstairs
    only way of coming **d**   Milne (27)

dragon
    does not do to leave a live **d** out   Tolkien (7)
    realio trulio cowardly **d**   Nash (1)
    we know what a **d** looks like   Williams, J. (1)

dragonflies
    time is for **d** and angels   Thurber (2)

dragons
    never laugh at live **d**   Tolkien (8)

draught
    d out of Rip Van Winkle's flagon   Irving (6)

dream
    August and February both **d** killers   Paterson (12)

only a sort of thing in his **d**   Carroll (28)
people who think lies likely to **d** lies   MacDonald, G. (6)

dreaming
when cats are **d**   Pilkey (1, 2)

dreams
my house looks like all my **d**   Pinkwater (2)

dresses
a hundred **d** all lined up   Estes (1)

drink
delicious is **d** of cool water   Babbitt (8)
d much from bottle marked poison   Carroll (3)
rather die than **d** bitter medicine   Collodi (4)
to **d** life from only the good   Konigsburg (24)

drowned
better **d** than duffers   Ransome (1)

drowning
Marquis of Carabas is **d**   Fairy tales (18)
reason for swimming to escape **d**   Cresswell (3)

drummer
D Hoff fired it off   Emberley (1)

duck
I wish that I had **d** feet   Le Sieg (1)
last **d** always got a spank   Flack (7)

duckling
failure is the ugly **d**   Feiffer (4)
ugly **d**   Andersen (11)

ducklings (subj.)
Jack, Kack, Lack, Mack   McCloskey (3)

ducks
d are a-dabbling up tails all   Grahame (7)
Irish **d** how to read Jivvanese   Seuss (16)
two white **d** marching   Flack (3)

duffers
better drowned than **d**   Ransome (1)

dug
we've **d** so fast   Burton (5)

duke
grand old **D** of York   Nursery rhymes (51)

dumpster
life is like a **d**   Naylor (1)

dusk (subj.)
darkness has a way of falling   Hamilton (2)

dust
> little toy dog is covered with **d**   Field, E. (5)

duty
> require from each one the **d**   Saint-Exupery (4)
> to be conceited of doing one's **d**   MacDonald, G. (9)

dying
> can't have living without **d**   Babbitt (11)
> they can stop **d**   Collier (5)
> thing with **d** was to try to not die   Paulsen (6)

◣ E

eagles (subj.)
> farewell wherever you fare   Tolkien (6)

earl
> I should rather not be an **e**   Burnett (1)

earlier
> not to get up any **e** than necessary   Hale, L. (3)

early
> be an **e e** bird   Silverstein (10)
> so far, so **e**, so soon   Sandburg (2)
> wake up so dreadfully **e**   Lewis (8)

ears
> what big **e** you've got   Fairy tales (14)

earth
> deep in our **e** so wondrous   Stevenson, J. (1)

easily
> only thing can do **e** is be wrong   Juster (7)

east
> go outside and face the **e**   Baylor (1)

easy
> do only the **e** and useless jobs   Juster (8)
> only when taking it **e**   Steig (1)

eat
> all right to **e** like a goat   Sharmat (1)
> all the better to **e** you with   Fairy tales (14)
> **e** as the circus people do   Petersham (2)
> Jack Sprat could **e** no fat   Nursery rhymes (35)
> long dark thought of something to **e**   Ciardi (1)
> people only **e** stupid animals   King-Smith (1)
> shabby of him to **e** the De Sotos   Steig (7)
> that bear did greet and **e**   Kuskin (3)
> to **e** and be eaten are same thing   Travers (2)
> we'll **e** you up we love you so   Sendak (9)

England
    rightwise king born of all **E**   White, T. (4)

English
    E is a strong language   Konigsburg (23)
    wearing out **E** language   Weller (2)

enjoy
    can nearly always **e** things   Montgomery (3)

enough
    I don't see **e**   Seuss (48)
    there is **e** for all   Lawson (1)

epitaphs (subj.)
    here lies Tom Thumb   Fairy tales (37)
    she lived among us   Blos (5)

equal
    like and **e** two different things   L'Engle (5)

equilibrium
    world is in balance, in **e**   Le Guin (5)

escaping
    e goblins to be caught by wolves   Tolkien (5)

essential
    what is **e** is invisible   Saint-Exupery (10)

eucalyptus
    top of the tallest **e** tree   Pene DuBois (1)

even
    sandwich, pickle, egg come out **e**   Hoban (10)

everyone
    e and everything was stopped   Burton (1)

everywhere
    if you're **e** how can you be lost   Park (7)

evil
    have courage to look upon **e**   Alexander (3)
    only **e** comes from great changes   Snyder (1)
    perfect for the altar of an **e** god   Snyder (3)
    problem of God allowing **e**   Cushman (8)

examinations (subj.)
    I thought they were sort of fun   Fisher (4)

excellence
    can you know **e** if never seen it   Konigsburg (30)

excellent
    doesn't get any better than **e**   MacLachlan (3)

excited
    don't get **e** about a thing until   Butterworth (3)

exciting
    really **e** things scare us   Dahl (13)

excuse
    any **e** will serve tyrant   Aesop (2)

expect
    for those who don't **e** miracles   Alexander (15)

expectations
    e is place must always go before   Juster (1)
    some people never go beyond **e**   Juster (1)

expected
    doing what is **e** of me   Cleary (15)

expecting
    e other people to tune into our agenda   Creech (7)

experience
    education is **e**   White, T. (1)

ewe
    I may be **e** I may be ram   King-Smith (3)

extinction (subj.)
    for centuries he ran and ran   Ciardi (7)

eye
    e mixes colors for you   Treviño (1)
    I'll be the **e**   Lionni (11)

eyes
    boat with two wise **e**   Flack (6)
    e a mother leaves behind   Barrie (5)
    made believe cherries were **e**   Henkes (7)
    space is medicine for **e**   Treviño (3)
    Wynken and Blynken are two little **e**   Field, E. (4)

eyries
    till your **e** receive you   Tolkien (6)

◣ F

face
    my **f** is my fortune   Nursery rhymes (46)
    no sight so ugly as **f** in anger   Fitzhugh (9)
    what wisdom does for an old **f**   Hunt (4)

faces
    very unlovely old **f**   Hunt (5)

fact
    one part **f**, two parts legends   Spinelli (6)

fear (subj.)
    dark mountains are always around us   Martin, B. (2)
    most frightened seeds in world   Lobel (16)
    poor seeds are afraid to grow   Lobel (15)
    they called him Ferdinand   Leaf (4)

fears
    lay aside our little **f**   Kipling (11)

feathers
    not only fine **f**   Aesop (14)

February
    August and **F** both dream killers   Paterson (12)
    F is a mean bully   Paterson (11)

fed
    animal **f** comes back   Napoli (4)

fee
    f fi fo fum   Fairy tales (13)
    f fi fum fory   Scieszka (3)

feed
    when you **f** a fish never **f** him a lot   Palmer (1)

feet
    bears always land on their **f**   Bond (5)
    f are never happy again on the ground   McCully (1)
    I wish that I had duck **f**   LeSieg (1)
    not the sneakers, it's the **f**   Spinelli (3)
    shoes full of **f**   Seuss (41)

felt
    don't seem to have **f** at all how   Milne (34)

fence
    f sets men together   Peck (1)

Ferdinand
    They called him **F** the Fierce   Leaf (4)

Ferris wheel
    August hangs like highest seat of **F**   Babbitt (9)

fetched
    Rabbit always went and **f** them   Milne (11)

fiddle
    hey diddle diddle the cat and the **f**   Nursery rhymes (22)

fiddlers
    he called for his **f** three   Nursery rhymes (52)

fierce
    they called him Ferdinand the **F**   Leaf (4)

fig
    whole wheat **f** bar   Pinkwater (3)

flying
if this is **f**   Milne (43)

flying (subj.)
just think lovely thoughts   Barrie (8)

foam
f rubber son with no emotions   Park (2)

foes
see how he treats his defeated **f**   Morris (1)

fog
ground-hugging California tule **f**   Fleischman, S. (1)
yellow **f** hung so thick and heavy   Burnett (4)

food
ask for credentials before they give **f**   Greene, B. (3)
if more of us valued **f**   Tolkien (9)

food (subj.)
everything everyone ate came from sky   Barrett (1)
made believe cherries were eyes   Henkes (7)
Methuselah ate what he found   Nursery rhymes (44)
sandwich, pickle, egg come out even   Hoban (10)
whatever Miss T. eats   de la Mare (4)
when you wake up in the morning   Milne (50)

fool
even a prince may be a **f**   Paterson (1)
f would not know what to do with heart   Baum (7)

foolish
better to be **f** enjoying yourself   Babbitt (2)
in anger we are all **f**   Spyri (2)

foolishly
so sure you will never love **f**   Morris (3)

foolishness
take a little of my **f** along   Wiggin (2)

foolishness (subj.)
nobody can make a monkey   Forbes, E. (1)

fools
two biggest **f** ever been seen   Seuss (4)

foot
one-**f**-up and one-**f**-down   Flack (3)
stamped his right **f** so deep   Fairy tales (22)

football
f isn't for fruitcakes   Spinelli (2)
hockey's a lot bloodier than **f**   Blume (7)

forest
enchanted place on the top of the **f**   Milne (13)

friendship (subj.)
I do not eat bread — Saint-Exupery (7)
no child likes to be ordered — Cleary (8)
to me you are still nothing more — Saint-Exupery (6)

frighten
how to **f** Miss Clavell — Bemelmans (3)

frightened
most **f** seeds in whole world — Lobel (16)

Frizzle
Ms. **F** the strangest teacher — Cole, J. (1)
with teacher like Ms. **F** — Cole, J. (2)

frog
an egg a **f** could get attached to — Joyce (1)
f change into a handsome prince — Fairy tales (9)
f he would a-wooing go — Nursery rhymes (17)
kind and tender to the **F** — Belloc (4)
lonely people say who keep **f** — Belloc (5)

frogs
f and snails and puppy dogs' tails — Nursery rhymes (82)
f are **f** and fish is fish — Lionni (2)
sit there like big damp **f** — Fox, P. (6)

frogs (subj.)
I'm De Fawg Pin — Napoli (3)

fromage
Jean **F** medal — Sharp (1)

front
sort of Tigger who was always in **f** — Milne (8)

frosty
villagers all this **f** tide — Grahame (11)

fruit
ripe **f** soon spoils — Yorinks (1)

fuel
fire that burns fast the more **f** — Yates (1)

full
world is so **f** of a number of things — Stevenson, R. (9)

fungus
forty-two pounds of edible **f** — McCloskey (2)

funny
f thing about mothers and fathers — Dahl (20)

fur
little **f** family warm as toast — Brown (4)
sleep sleep my little **f** child — Brown (5)

Geoppolis
    city of **G** covered with snow   Burton (1)

George
    this is **G**, he lived in Africa   Rey (1)

Georgie
    G Porgie pudding and pie   Nursery rhymes (19)

get
    not to **g** up any earlier than necessary   Hale, L. (3)
    only **g** what you give   Krumgold (2)

ghosts (subj.)
    every night at the same time   Bright (1)

giant
    I is the Big Friendly **G**   Dahl (4)
    just because I is a **g**   Dahl (2)
    only nice and jumbly **g**   Dahl (4)

gift
    any great **g** is a burden   Cooper (2)
    thought she was a **g** from God   Blos (5)

giggle
    no reason on earth why they should **g**   Fisher (5)

gimble
    did gyre and **g** in the wabe   Carroll (23)

gimme
    G the Ax lived in a house   Sandburg (1)

gingerbread
    g dog prowls below   Field, E. (1)
    house was made of **g**   Fairy tales (10)

gingham
    g dog and the calico cat   Field, E. (8)

girl
    expected a **g** to get them out   Snyder (4)
    g had won Grand National   Bagnold (3)
    no little **g** to pull it   Field, E. (12)
    only **g** with large, black moustache   Hurwitz (1)
    same **g** and yet not the same   Brink (1)
    thirteen-year-old **g** accused of murder Avi (2)

girls
    g discovered that boys awful in sixth Cleary (5)
    need sharp eyes when have **g**   Alcott (8)
    twelve little **g** in two straight lines Bemelmans (1)
    what are little **g** made of   Nursery rhymes (82)

give
    men **g** up many things   Alexander (14)

only get what you **g**   Krumgold (2)
we **g** all we have   Forbes, E. (3)

giving
all you get by **g** stuff up   Brooks (3)

glad
g that I am not a Goop   Burgess (2)
g when you're **g**   DeRegniers (2)
just being **g** game   Porter (1)

glide
makes men **g** from one state of mind   Fox, P. (2)

gloop
Augustus **G** a greedy boy   Dahl (9)

glory
man's life weighs more than **g**   Alexander (9)

glove
g is a house for a hand   Hoberman (1)

gnawing
who is **g** at my house   Fairy tales (11)

goat
all right to eat like a **g**   Sharmat (1)
billy **g** Gruff   Fairy tales (34)

goblins
escaping **g** to be caught by wolves   Tolkien (5)

god
easier than praying directly to **G**   Creech (5)
hard to think about **G**   Smith, Doris (1)
looking for you **G**   Blume (3)
people made up **G**   Fitzhugh (14)
perfect for the altar of an evil **g**   Snyder (3)
rather lonely to be a **g**   Field, R. (2)
thought she was a gift from **G**   Blos (5)

God (subj.)
Almighty is bound to be a gentleman   Stratton-Porter (4)

gods
g help them that help   Aesop (30)

gold
couldn't be sold for **g** or silver   Burton (2)
my daughter can spin straw into **g**   Fairy tales (21)
that **g** you claimed is lying   Cushman (1)
valued food and cheer above **g**   Tolkien (9)

golden
until one player reaches the **g** city   Van Allsburg (2)

grandma
  no one makes cookies like **G**   Hutchins (1)
  Strega Nona which meant **G** Witch   dePaola (3)

grandmother
  don't hate **g**, hate it that she's old   Lowry (2)

grapes
  sour **g**   Aesop (20)

grass
  wants that blade of **g**   Hedderwick (1)

grassy
  g g garter snake   Gray, L. (4)

gratitude
  no **g** from wicked   Aesop (13)

gray
  great **g**-green greasy Limpopo   Kipling (25)

great
  g things wound up with things little   Montgomery (6)
  I am Oz the **g** and terrible   Baum (9)
  in the **g** green room   Brown (1)

Grecian
  nose never would grow **G**   Alcott (5)

green
  G Noah Demon Tree   Boston (1)
  heads are **g**, hands are blue   Lear (11)
  I do not like **g** eggs and ham   Seuss (21)
  in the great **g** room   Brown (1)
  suit of a becoming shade of **g**   Brunhoff (2)
  where the world is **g** and blue   Duvoisin (4)

green thumb (subj.)
  tickled the ground and it laughed   Cushman (2)

grew
  Angus **g** older he grew longer   Flack (1)

grin
  cat without a **g**   Carroll (9)
  vanished ending with the **g**   Carroll (8)

Grinch
  G got a wonderful awful idea   Seuss (29)

gringy
  going to have its **g** moments   Naylor (5)

ground
  if you were born to walk the **g**   Belloc (7)
  in a hole in the **g** there lived a hobbit   Tolkien (1)
  in the **g** helping grow flowers   Viorst (8)
  tickled the **g** and it laughed   Cushman (2)

grow

    all children except one **g** up   Barrie (1)

    just a thing to let **g**   Rylant (1)

    one side make you **g** taller   Carroll (5)

    poor seeds are afraid to **g**   Lobel (15)

    real reason I had wanted to **g** up   Byars (4)

    things that **g** upward like sunlight   Voigt (10)

    when I **g** up I will go to faraway   Cooney (3)

    you'd never **g** up   Babbitt (10)

growing

    keep **g** from one person into another   Brink (1)

    keep it from **g** anymore, that's sin   Krumgold (1)

    now seeds, start **g**   Lobel (14)

    worst part of **g** up   Montgomery (8)

growing up (subj.)

    doing what is expected   Cleary (15)

    Little Gorilla was big   Bornstein (2)

    real reason I had wanted to grow up   Byars (4)

    what a lot has happened   Brink (1)

growls

    dog **g** when it's angry   Carroll (7)

grown-up

    expected to think like a **g**   Weller (3)

grown-ups

    g always talking   Andersen (2)

    g appear as giants   Dahl (7)

    g never understand anything   Saint-Exupery (1)

    g often forget no child likes   Cleary (8)

guard

    changing the **g** at Buckingham Palace   Milne (21)

guest

    g lists a way of choosing sides   Konigsburg (26)

guilty conscience

    mosquito has a **g**   Aardema (1)

gun

    Edward sitting up with the **g**   Edmonds (2)

gunpowder

    till the **g** ran out of the heels   Caldecott (1)

guns (subj.)

    he bought it in Bergen op Zoom   Edmonds (1)

gutter

    beloved has lain in **g**   Andersen (10)

gyre

    did **g** and gimble in the wabe   Carroll (23)

\ H

habits
 soul grows in to lovely **h**   Wiggin (3)

hair
 all of the **h** fell off of the bear   Thomas (2)
 by the **h** of my chiny chin chin   Fairy tales (36)
 Fuzzy Wuzzy had no **h**   Nursery rhymes (18)
 grow **h** faster than you run   Scieszka (4)
 h the color of a carrot was braided   Lindgren, A. (1)
 most of your **h** has been loved off   Williams, M. (3)
 Rapunzel let down your **h**   Fairy tales (19)
 took off her long stringy red **h**   Balian (2)

hair (subj.)
 only sold what was my own   Alcott (4)

half
 top-off, **h**-gone, all-gone   Fairy tales (4)

halves
 never do anything by **h**   Dahl (21)

ham
 I do not like green eggs and **h**   Seuss (21)

hammock
 someone to sew **h**   Avi (4)

hand
 h in **h** on the edge of the sand   Lear (10)
 here's **h** and ring I have to show   Fairy tales (16)
 woman's **h** and heart   Porter (4)

hands
 heads are green, **h** are blue   Lear (11)

happened
 true but it may not have **h**   Polacco (1)
 what might have **h** had I only thought   Grahame (13)

happier
 pobbles are **h** without their toes   Lear (6)

happily
 h though not completely honestly   Scieszka (2)

happiness
 can't pursue **h**   Fox, P. (8)
 h is best thing in world   Baum (8)
 memory is **h** of being alone   Lowry (3)

happy
 brains do not make one **h**   Baum (8)
 don't need reason to be **h**   Sachar (3)

I am singing **H** Thursday to her   Hoban (4)
sent him home **h** one hundred   Seuss (24)
should all be as **h** as kings   Stevenson, R. (9)
stuff about **h** endings is lies   Paterson (9)

hard
    h times aren't only about money   Hesse (2)

hark
    h h the dogs do bark   Nursery rhymes (21)

hat
    farmer had a **h**, an old brown **h**   Nodset (1)
    man with the yellow **h**   Rey (2)

hatched
    count chickens before **h**   Aesop (28)

hate
    all **h** what we create   Cole, B. (1)
    maybe all the kids would **h** me   Blume (6)

hated
    h math with every bone   Fitzhugh (5)

hating
    spent so much time **h** it   Fitzhugh (5)

hats
    not here eating **h**   Krasilovsky (1)

haul
    can **h** as big a load as his father   Gramatky (2)

head
    and Nod is a little **h**   Field, E. (4)
    carried [caps] on top of his **h**   Slobodkina (1)
    h full of brains   Seuss (41)
    hide his **h** under his wing   Nursery rhymes (48)
    off with her **h**   Carroll (14)
    one fell off and bumped his **h**   Nursery rhymes (15)
    put your **h** inside wolf's mouth   Aesop (6)
    when do they make a **h** of lettuce   Hamilton (6)
    with his **h** up in the air   Burnett (15)

headache
    could cure a **h** with oil   dePaola (4)

headless
    h heedless happy Miss Hickory   Bailey (5)
    h horseman of Sleepy Hollow   Irving (1)

headmasters
    h and policemen biggest giants   Dahl (7)

heads
    h are green, hands are blue   Lear (11)

if your **h** were stuffed with straw	Baum (6)
off with their **h**	Carroll (14)

hear

all the better to **h** with	Fairy tales (14)
could Muffin **h** that	Brown (6)
to **h** one must be silent	Le Guin (4)

heart

beauty lives in **h** of its holder	Hite (1)
deep down in his **h** Anthony loves me	Viorst (6)
fool would not know what to do with **h**	Baum (7)
h was two sizes too small	Seuss (28)
I shall take the **h**	Baum (8)
only with **h** one can see rightly	Saint-Exupery (10)
prefers common sense and good **h**	Sewell (3)
undisputed sway over **h** of coquette	Irving (2)
wrong to want a **h**	Baum (12)
you now can see with your **h**	Martin, B. (3)

hearts

he who wins a thousand common **h**	Irving (2)

heat

h of all the words we had not spoken	Yolen (3)

heaven

corn be high as **h**	Hamilton (7)
how supremely **h** playing piano	Hesse (1)
in **h** lawyers are as hard to find	Konigsburg (11)
isn't **h** this is Cleveland	Allard (2)
paradise lost sometimes **h** found	Yorinks (2)

heaven (subj.)

room for Barney and tuna and cream	Viorst (7)

heavy

baby is a very **h** thing	Lyon (2)

hedgehogs

croquet balls were live **h**	Carroll (15)

heel

walk on your **h** and favor your toe	Paterson (8)

heels

gunpowder ran out at **h** of boots	Caldecott (1)
knock the **h** together	Baum (13)

heffalump

help help a **H** a horrible **H**	Milne (37)

heigho

h says Rowley	Nursery rhymes (17)

Helen

H was too fast for him	Graham (1)

hell
man in gov't bound for **H**   Konigsburg (12)

hello
good-bye is always **h** to something else   Lyon (6)

help
gods **h** them that **h** themselves   Aesop (30)
h h a horrible Heffalump   Milne (37)
h h cried the Page   Wood (1)
if you don't **h** the other animals   Lofting (2)
some tiny person were calling for **h**   Seuss (25)

hen
hickety pickety my black **h**   Nursery rhymes (23)

Hendrika
H, I thought you were home   Krasilovsky (1)

herbaceous
spotted or **h** backson   Milne (10)

Herdmans
H were worst kids in history   Robinson (1)

here
why into **h** often equals there   Hoban (24)

hero
decisive action denotes **h**   Belloc (6)

heroes
h let your voices ring   Kellogg (3)

hey
h unto you a child   Robinson (3)

hickety
h pickety my black hen   Nursery rhymes (23)

hickory
headless heedless happy Miss **H**   Bailey (5)
h dickory dock   Nursery rhymes (24)
Miss **H** had difficulty turning   Bailey (1)
Miss **H** real person   Bailey (2)

hide
royalty isn't allowed to **h**   McKinley (7)

higgledy
h piggledy my black hen   Nursery rhymes (23)

high
h and mighty have longest distance   Lobel (5)

high school
two kinds of people go to **h**   Cleary (14)

homework
 h sits on top of Sunday   Hoban (20)

honest
 clings to being **h** harder than ever   Knight (2)

honestly
 happily though not completely **h**   Scieszka (2)

honesty
 h, there's no two ways about it   Knight (2)

honey
 h right down to the bottom   Milne (36)
 isn't it funny how a bear likes **h**   Milne (31)
 only reason for making **h**   Milne (30)

honor
 h our friends too   Fitzhugh (10)

hope
 don't expect miracles but **h**   Alexander (15)
 hard times about losing spirit and **h**   Hesse (2)
 h is forward-looking part of memory   Jones (2)
 h that flies on silent wings   Yolen (4)

horn
 come blow your **h**   Nursery rhymes (37)

horrible
 don't let New Jersey be too **h**   Blume (1)
 a **h** Heffalump   Milne (37)
 h thing is coming this way   Zemach (1)

horse
 cure almost any vicious **h**   Sewell (2)
 got **h** for a shilling   Bagnold (5)
 h and a wagon on Mulberry Street   Seuss (1)
 wind condensed itself and result was **h**   Henry (1)

horse-balls
 regular course of Birtwick **h**   Sewell (2)

horseman
 headless **h** of Sleepy Hollow   Irving (1)

horses
 all the king's **h** and all the king's men   Nursery rhymes (28)
 often spoil good **h**   Sewell (1)
 winged **h** eat pretty much the same   Wrede (3)

horses (subj.)
 simply born to get to know one person   Bagnold (2)

hot
 h cross buns   Nursery rhymes (25)
 some like it **h**   Nursery rhymes (56)

hour
good to take an **h** or two off · · · · · · · · Hoff (1)

house
blow your **h** in · · · · · · · · · · · · · · Fairy tales (36)
box is a **h** for a teabag · · · · · · · · · · Hoberman (2)
cozy bed in a napping **h** · · · · · · · · · Wood (3)
glove is a **h** for a hand · · · · · · · · · Hoberman (1)
h is a **h** for me · · · · · · · · · · · · Hoberman (1)
the **h** that Jack built · · · · · · · · · · Nursery rhymes (70)
h was made of gingerbread · · · · · · · · Fairy tales (10)
I will be my own **h** · · · · · · · · · · · · Kindl (2)
in old **h** in Paris · · · · · · · · · · · · Bemelmans (1)
little **h** looks just like the little **h** · · · · Burton (3)
my **h** is me and I am it · · · · · · · · · · Pinkwater (2)
played **h** and Wendell made rules · · · · · Henkes (8)
who in right mind build **h** of straw · · · · Scieszka (5)
who is gnawing at my **h** · · · · · · · · · Fairy tales (11)

houses
women are **h** for our children · · · · · · · Kindl (2)

houses (subj.)
couldn't be sold for gold or silver · · · · · · Burton (2)

how
not very **h** · · · · · · · · · · · · · · · · Milne (34)

howling
if we listened to the **h** of every jackal · · · · Kipling (13)

Hubbard
old mother **H** · · · · · · · · · · · · · · Martin, S. (1)

Hudson
Hendrick **H**, crew at game of ninepins · · · · Irving (6)

huff
I'll **h** and I'll puff · · · · · · · · · · · · Fairy tales (36)

huffle
h of a snail in danger · · · · · · · · · · Milne (22)

hug
big birthday bear **h** · · · · · · · · · · · · Flack (5)
I'd rather play at **h** o' war · · · · · · · · Silverstein (9)

hugs
go through four different **h** · · · · · · · · Rylant (2)

human
h bean has two legs · · · · · · · · · · · Dahl (3)
h beans are for borrowers · · · · · · · · Norton (5)
h species braided together · · · · · · · · Stolz (4)
h voice, no sound like this · · · · · · · · O'Dell (1)
put you into **h** shape · · · · · · · · · · · Alexander (7)

❚ I

◣J

� K

key

all doors hard to unlock until find **k**   O'Brien (1)

with a teenytiny **k**   de la Mare (5)

kid

still being treated like little **k**   Weller (3)

kids

Herdmans were worst **k** in history   Robinson (1)

kill

something as small as a bee could **k**   Smith, Doris (1)

killed

who **k** Cock Robin   Nursery rhymes (84)

kind

be **k** and tender to frog   Belloc (4)

kindness

k must be highest virtue   Blos (3)

king

all the **k**'s horses   Nursery rhymes (28)

being **k** is a business   Konigsburg (19)

cried the **k** with a jig jig jig   Wood (2)

didn't want to be **k** if people threw   Levine (1)

k and queen invited me   DeRegniers (3)

K Bidgood's in the bathtub   Wood (1)

k is not a free man   Konigsburg (19)

K John was not a good man   Milne (14)

like being born a **k**   Burnett (3)

no sort of **k** at all   Seuss (3)

old **K** Cole was a merry old soul   Nursery rhymes (52)

rightwise **k** born of all England   White, T. (4)

want to know a **k**, see how he treats   Morris (1)

Yertle the Turtle was **k** of the pond   Seuss (47)

kings

here we can all feel like **k**   Kellogg (2)

kiss

dogs are to **k** people   Krauss (3)

perhaps that was **k** from Nana   dePaola (1)

sweet mocking mouth had one **k**   Barrie (2)

kissed

k the girls and made them cry   Nursery rhymes (19)

since he **k** them and put them there   Field, E. (6)

kitchen

into the light of the night **k**   Sendak (2)

kits

k, cats, sacks, and wives   Nursery rhymes (4)

◣ L

L Bo-Peep has lost her sheep   Nursery rhymes (38)
L Boy Blue come blow your horn   Nursery rhymes (37)
l by l does trick   Aesop (26)
l friends may prove great   Aesop (10)
L Jack Horner sat in a corner   Nursery rhymes (39)
L Miss Muffet sat on a tuffet   Nursery rhymes (40)
l pig let me come in   Fairy tales (36)
L Tommy Tucker sings for his supper   Nursery rhymes (41)
when I was l didn't know   Curtis (2)

live
former l too little and latter l too long   Thurber (2)
to l on alone for ever and ever   Norton (3)
we're born, we l a little while, we die   White, E. (4)
would all l in beautiful places   Baum (6)

lives
comparing our l to a sonnet   L'Engle (6)

living
as long as I'm l my baby you'll be   Munsch (1)
can't have l without dying   Babbitt (11)
in war dead pay debts for the l   Collier (7)
just breathing isn't l   Porter (2)
l in love is different   Voigt (8)

load
haul as big a l as his father   Gramatky (2)

lobster
'tis the voice of the l   Carroll (20)

locks
curly l curly l   Nursery rhymes (10)

locomotives
baby l go there to learn   Crampton (2)

logic
as it isn't it ain't that's l   Carroll (26)
l has little to do with government   McKinley (6)

lollipops
there's a jar of l   de la Mare (5)
there's Banbury cakes and l   de la Mare (6)

London
I've been to L to look at the queen   Nursery rhymes (60)
L Bridge is falling down   Nursery rhymes (42)
thrice Lord Mayor of L   Fairy tales (6)

loneliness
sense of l was overwhelming   Dahl (14)

lone
walking by his wild l   Kipling (32)

▌M

mackerel
everyone with same bait catching **m**   Aldrich (2)

mad
therefore I'm **m**   Carroll (7)

Madeline
M just said pooh pooh   Bemelmans (2)
smallest one was **M**   Bemelmans (1)

Magi (subj.)
maybe they'll tell the innkeeper   Robinson (2)

magic
chops is to **m** what scales   Konigsburg (28)
here in Coven Tree no strangers to **m**   Brittain (1)
I put the **m** finger on them all   Dahl (18)
m can begin to change things   Lisle (1)
m can't work miracles   Alexander (19)
m is in everything   Burnett (11)
sun is shining that is **m**   Burnett (13)
warts have a kind of **m**   Lowry (1)

magnificent
if man paid homage to someone **m**   Konigsburg (16)

maid
where are you going my pretty **m**   Nursery rhymes (45)

maids
pretty **m** all in a row   Nursery rhymes (43)

make-believe
m was so real to him   Barrie (15)

mallets
m live flamingoes   Carroll (15)

malt
that ate the **m** that lay in the house   Nursery rhymes (70)

mama
M loved her baby Ben   Lindgren, B. (1)

man
boy in time of peace, **m** in time of war   Forbes, E. (4)
had to buy the **m** to get [dog]   Knight (3)
m-eaters become mangy   Kipling (2)
m is not like a fighting bull   Wojciechowska (3)
m will be naked tool   White, T. (3)
m with the yellow hat   Rey (2)
no one catch me and make me a **m**   Barrie (23)
only that a **m** can stand up   Forbes, E. (3)
other **m** has always got to pay   Belloc (8)

real person better than being real **m**   Myers (3)
really a very good **m**   Baum (10)

manger
dog in **m**   Aesop (19)

mangy
man-eaters become **m**   Kipling (2)

maniac
M M he's so cool   Spinelli (5)

mannerly
behave **m** at table   Stevenson, R. (3)

manners
between his table **m** and guitar   Hoban (14)
good **m** very important   Fitzhugh (2)
had no **m** then and has no **m** now   Kipling (22)

manners (subj.)
The Goops they lick their fingers   Burgess (2)

maples
m are such sociable trees   Montgomery (5)

March
M in like crow   Bailey (4)

marched
he **m** them up to the top of the hill   Nursery rhymes (51)

Margery
see-saw **M** Daw   Nursery rhymes (65)

market
to **m** to **m** to buy a fat pig   Nursery rhymes (80)

marquis
the **M** of Carabas is drowning   Fairy tales (18)

marriage
m spinning bearing children   Cushman (9)

marry
he'll come back and **m** me   Nursery rhymes (6)

Mary
M had a little lamb   Hale, S. (1)
M is always going to look like   Robinson (4)
M M quite contrary   Nursery rhymes (43)
steam shovel her name was **M** Anne   Burton (4)
when **M** found this garden   Burnett (12)

master
any boy in Yorkshire **M** Colin   Burnett (15)
one **m** on this ship   Avi (5)
which is to be **m**   Carroll (34)

medicine
rather die then drink bitter **m** — Collodi (4)
space is **m** for eyes — Treviño (3)

meet
I'll **m** you at the top of the coconut tree — Martin, B. (1)

melons
I'm not the one who talks to **m** — Kimmel (2)
talking **m** are nothing but trouble — Kimmel (3)

melted
nothing left but pool of **m** butter — Bannerman (3)
[tigers] all just **m** away — Bannerman (3)

Melvin
M, Louise, Phoebe, Willie — Pinkwater (1)

memories (subj.)
on a journey without a suitcase — Christiansen (1)

memory
hope is forward-looking part of **m** — Jones (2)
m is happiness of being alone — Lowry (3)
m that only works backwards — Carroll (30)
poet has spiritual **m** — Andersen (3)

men
m give up many things — Alexander (14)
tell you about **m**: wolves gentler — Alexander (4)

men (subj.)
when women are advisers — Alcott (7)

messing
simply **m** about in boats — Grahame (6)

Methuselah
M ate what he found on his plate — Nursery rhymes (44)

mice
friends forever skog and **m** — Kellogg (3)
m are the prisoner's friends — Sharp (1)
three blind **m** — Nursery rhymes (77)
tippets for **m** and ribbons for mobs — Potter (2)

Mickey
milk's not me, I'm **M** — Sendak (3)

Mike
M Mulligan had a steam shovel — Burton (4)

miles
how many **m** to Babylon — Nursery rhymes (26)

military
logic has nothing to do with **m** — McKinley (6)

milk
he's going to ask for a glass of **m**   Numeroff (1)
I'm in the **m** and the **m**'s in me   Sendak (4)
I'm not the **m** and the **m**'s not me   Sendak (3)
sometimes it looked like spilt **m**   Shaw (1)

milking
I'm going a **m** sir   Nursery rhymes (45)

mimsy
all **m** were the borogoves   Carroll (23)

Minchin
Miss **M** Select Seminary   Burnett (5)

mind
don't **m** because no one knows   Myers (4)
how to get a settled **m**   Paulsen (3)
rather have just one in right **m**   Montgomery (7)
to let a sad thought get into your **m**   Burnett (14)
who did not **m** not being like   Duvoisin (3)

minds
m like diapers need changing   Cushman (5)

minstrel
road home to a **m**   Gray, E. (2)

minutes
if I had fifty-three **m**   Saint-Exupery (11)

miracles
for those who don't expect **m**   Alexander (15)
magic can't work **m**   Alexander (19)

mirror
m m on the wall   Fairy tales (25)

miss
always things to **m**   MacLachlan (10)
M Minchin Select Seminary   Burnett (5)
whatever **M** T. eats   de la Mare (4)

missed
I guess I would have **m** her   Hoban (17)

missing
I am not your **m** piece   Silverstein (6)

missus
m on a farm or ranch   O'Hara (1)

mistake
I create illusions, I don't **m** them   Alexander (22)

mistakes
jails are for the really big **m**   Park (4)
never feel badly about making **m**   Juster (9)

mistreats
man who **m** poor dumb beast

DeFelice (1)

misunderstandings
words are source of **m**

Saint-Exupery (9)

mittens
they lost their **m**

Nursery rhymes (78)

mixed
all **m** up with each other

McCloskey (1)

moan
mournful **m** and silken tone

Moss (1)

mobs
ribbons for **m**

Potter (2)

mockingbird
papa's going to buy you a **m**

Nursery rhymes (29)

modern art (subj.)
I could do that but I wouldn't

Cole, B. (3)

mome
m raths outgrabe

Carroll (23)

Monday
homework has the smell of **M**
M's child is fair of face

Hoban (20)
Nursery rhymes (47)

money
don't have to spend **m** on sadness
may be wonder in **m**
what is **m** without friends

Greene, B. (4)
Bagnold (4)
Seuss (15)

mongoose
motto of all **m** family

Kipling (5)

monkey
good little **m** and always curious
the **m** chased the weasel
nobody can make a **m** out of anyone
on every branch sat a **m**

Rey (1)
Nursery rhymes (2)
Forbes, E. (1)
Slobodkina (3)

monkeys
he chased **m** on Monday
no more **m** jumping on the bed

Jackson, K. (1)
Nursery rhymes (16)

monsters
m and people made a deal
m only shook their fingers back

Crowe (1)
Slobodkina (4)

mood
only their **m** that is changed

MacDonald, G. (7)

moon
comb their hair with the **m**

Pilkey (2)

you are a bird and you are my **m**   Eastman (3)
your **m** will not mind at all   Seuss (8)

mothers
funny thing about **m** and fathers   Dahl (20)
m have need of sharp eyes   Alcott (8)
world be without nagging **m**   Cleary (13)

motor car
m went poop-poop-poop   Grahame (12)

motorcars
most **m** are conglomerations   Fleming (1)

motorcycle
as fast as the **m** would go   Cleary (7)

motto
m of mongoose family   Kipling (5)
that is the **m** of all witches   Dahl (22)

mound
time runs different in the **M**   McGraw (2)

mountain
I am on my **m** in a tree home   George (3)
I have never been over the **m**   Piper (1)

mountains
dark **m** are always around us   Martin, B. (2)

mournful
m moan and silken tone   Moss (1)

mouse
has anybody seen my **m**   Milne (24)
if you give a **m** a cookie   Numeroff (1)
m a day keeps vet away   King-Smith (5)
the **m** ran up the clock   Nursery rhymes (24)
m soup must be mixed with stories   Lobel (21)
nibble nibble little **m**   Fairy tales (11)
no happier more contented **m**   Titus (1)
not a creature was stirring, not even **m**   Moore (1)
on a **m** a-hunting went   Fairy tales (37)
only string and not **m**   Babbitt (3)

moustache
only girl in class with large, black **m**   Hurwitz (1)

mouth
never miss chance to keep **m** shut   Peck (2)
opens his huge **m** ever so wide   Hadithi (1)
put your head inside a wolf's **m**   Aesop (6)
shut **m** can bottle up barrel   Peck (6)
sweet mocking **m** had one kiss   Barrie (2)

mouths
    animals don't always speak with **m**   Lofting (1)

move
    I think I'll **m** to Australia   Viorst (2)
    m slowly think fast   Hamilton (1)

moved
    just **m** in down the street   Kellogg (1)

moves
    and so one **m** about   Hoban (24)

moving
    m makes you feel all alone   Park (1)

much
    m outcry little outcome   Aesop (4)

mud
    face full of swamp **m**   Creech (4)
    more children tumble into **m** puddles   Hale, L. (5)
    sinks down in good soft **m**   Lobel (24)

Muffet
    little Miss **M** sat on a tuffet   Nursery rhymes (40)

muffin
    could **M** hear that   Brown (6)

Mulligan
    Mike **M** had a steam shovel   Burton (4)

Munchkins
    M   Baum (16)

murder
    thirteen-year-old girl accused of **m**   Avi (2)

mush
    smucky **m** smacky **m**   Knutson (1)

mushroom
    what happens to **m** when it rains   Ginsburg (1)

music
    angel dance no faster than **m** plays   Hite (2)
    orange is **m** of the tango   O'Neill (3)

mussel
    black as a **m** shell   Lionni (8)

must
    does only and wholly what he **m** do   Le Guin (7)
    we **m** increase our bust   Blume (2)

mystic
    m men who eat boiled owls   Seuss (2)

◣ N

nag
N come up and dance with death — Kipling (4)

nagging
world be without **n** mothers — Cleary (13)

naked
man will be **n** tool — White, T. (3)

nakedness (subj.)
doesn't have anything on — Andersen (1)
I tried on the summer sun — Silverstein (4)

name
camel knows the hundredth **n** — Oppenheim (1)
did not think **n** absolutely perfect — Henkes (1)
inside his house a kid gets one **n** — Spinelli (7)
my **n**'s Tom Tit Tot — Fairy tales (38)
n over the door in gold letters — Milne (29)
signed her **n** in think-proof ink — Seuss (14)
under the **n** of Sanders — Milne (29)
useful to the people that **n** them — Carroll (25)

names
little short **n** instead of great long **n** — Mosel (2)
use of their having **n** — Carroll (25)

names (subj.)
her second son she called Chang — Mosel (1)
I hope that he does not kill another — O'Dell (5)
whenever new scholar came to school — Aldrich (1)

Nana
now you are both **N** Upstairs — dePaola (2)
perhaps that was kiss from **N** Upstairs — dePaola (1)

napping
cozy bed in a **n** house — Wood (3)

narrower
the way he can follow grows **n** — Le Guin (7)

natural
large as life and twice as **n** — Carroll (35)

nature
n's clothes just fit me best — Silverstein (4)

navigating
n solely by Miss Bianca's sketch — Sharp (2)

necessity
spring is a wondrous **n** — Cleaver (4)

never going to stand by and say **n** — Estes (2)
n on other side of **n** but us — Hoban (25)
soon have **n** to yield — Aesop (24)
very easy to take more than **n** — Carroll (13)
what do you mean, less than **n** — White, E. (2)

notice
no limit to what most people don't **n** — Pinkwater (5)

noticed
all that I've **n** except my own feet — Seuss (1)

now
n has warmth and urgency — Thurber (1)
n I lay me down to rest — Nursery rhymes (49)
n I lay me down to sleep — Nursery rhymes (50)
n is **n**, can never be long ago — Wilder (1)

nut
I had a little **n** tree — Nursery rhymes (30)
mighty oak was once a **n** like you — Nursery rhymes (14)

nutmeg
but a silver **n** and a golden pear — Nursery rhymes (30)

nutting
n's the poetry — Blos (6)

◣ O

oak
mighty **o** was once a nut like you — Nursery rhymes (14)

oath
ancient **o** of the Krakow Trumpeter — Kelly (1)

obedience
right to require **o** because orders — Saint-Exupery (4)

obey
learned to **o** before he could command — Craik (2)
your Amir whom you do not **o** — Kipling (9)

object
Large **O** Theory of History — Merrill (3)

obstacles
o are challenges for winners — Kerr (2)

occupation
my full-time **o** is dog — Howe (1)

occupations (subj.)
no matter what you decide to be — Naylor (5)

ocean (subj.)
  break now waves and split your ribs .... Fleischman, P. (1)
  sea can swallow ships .... Babbitt (1)

off
  o with her head .... Carroll (14)

old
  goodness knows how o .... Milne (45)
  hate it that [grandmother's] so o .... Lowry (2)
  might have wished never to grow o .... Blos (1)
  o King Cole was a merry old soul .... Nursery rhymes (52)
  o lamps for new .... Arabian nights (1)
  when I grow o I will live beside sea .... Cooney (3)

one
  o two buckle my shoe .... Nursery rhymes (53)
  rule of O times O .... Ciardi (2)
  when I was o I had just begun .... Milne (19)

oneth
  hundred and o Dalmatian .... Smith, Dodie (1)

onions
  cigars should be like o .... McKinley (3)
  people are like o .... Cushman (11)

oobleck
  you're sitting in o up to your chin .... Seuss (3)

open
  o sesame .... Arabian nights (2)

opinion
  own o of yourself that matters .... Cresswell (4)

orange
  o is music of the tango .... O'Neill (3)

orchestra
  members of the Philharmonic O .... Kuskin (1)

order
  hard to o someone to believe .... Yep (1)
  such a thing as too much o .... Lobel (4)

orders
  your Amir must take o from our Viceroy .... Kipling (9)

ought
  I know what I o to be .... Konigsburg (10)

ounce
  such a thing as an o .... Fisher (2)

outcome
  much outcry little o .... Aesop (4)

outcry
    much **o** little outcome   Aesop (4)

outside
    everything that matters is **o** time   Cooper (5)
    worst things weren't **o** of you   Voigt (11)

over
    First do it **o**   Ciardi (3)

overdue
    library book is 42 years **o**   Silverstein (3)

overworked
    o sounded important   Feiffer (1)

owl
    o and pussy-cat went to sea   Lear (8)
    when hoot **o** screeching westward flies   Hamilton (3)

owling
    when you go **o**   Yolen (4)

owls
    mystic men who eat boiled **o**   Seuss (2)
    where the **o** sing   Duvoisin (4)

oyster
    played part of **o**   Gray, E. (3)

Oz
    I am **O** great and terrible   Baum (9)
    great **O** to send me back to Kansas   Baum (4)

◣ P

pain
    p hurts more when one is angry   Smith, Dodie (1)
    real **p** is a black vortex   Orr (1)

paint
    would rather **p** exactly   Treviño (4)

painter
    p must unmix [colors]   Treviño (1)

pajamas
    father never goes out in **p**   Joyce (3)

pale
    turn not **p** beloved snail   Carroll (19)

pancakes
    what kind of berries make **p** blue   Devlin (1)

papa
    as if **p** was pickle bottle   Alcott (2)
    p's going to buy you a mockingbird   Nursery rhymes (29)
    tell your **p** where the yak   Belloc (2)

paradise
    p lost is sometimes heaven found   Yorinks (2)

parent
    stodgy **p** is no fun at all   Dahl (15)

parents
    p were right, not children   Norton (4)

parents (subj.)
    funny thing about mothers and fathers   Dahl (20)
    irregular seconds folks   Greene, B. (5)
    James's mother and father went to   Dahl (17)

Paris
    in old house in **P**   Bemelmans (1)

parrot
    when his **p** died he cried and cried   Fox, M. (1)

part
    think they take another's **p**   MacDonald, G. (8)

party
    greatest and best Bagthorpian **P**   Cresswell (5)
    wasps and bumblebees have a **p**   Hoban (3)

passenger
    takes more courage to be a **p**   Konigsburg (29)

pasta
    bubble bubble **p** pot   dePaola (5)
    you wanted **p** from magic **p** pot   dePaola (6)

pat
    p a cake **p** a cake baker's man   Nursery rhymes (54)

patience
    biding one's time different from **p**   Konigsburg (9)

paws
    soft **p** sharp claws   DeRegniers (1)

pay
    other man has always got to **p**   Belloc (8)
    p back to world in beauty and caring   Paterson (5)

pea
    on bare bedstead put a **p**   Andersen (5)

peace
    better beans and bacon in **p**   Aesop (7)
    boy in time of **p** man in time of war   Forbes, E. (4)
    cannot have **p** until understand wars   Merrill (1)

peacefully
    live together **p** here   Grifalconi (1)

peach
    each **p** pear plum   Ahlberg (1)

peaches
    big ripe **p** and threw them   Gage (1)

peanut
    p sat on a railroad track   Nursery rhymes (55)
    toot toot **p** butter   Nursery rhymes (55)

pear
    but a silver nutmeg and a golden **p**   Nursery rhymes (30)
    each peach **p** plum   Ahlberg (1)

pease
    p porridge hot **p** porridge cold   Nursery rhymes (56)

peddler
    once was a **p** who sold caps   Slobodkina (1)

pee
    so mean he'd **p** on a puppy   Peck (7)

pelican
    ride a purple **p**   Prelutsky (1)

pen
    ballpoint **p** factor in decline   Konigsburg (25)

pencils
    this writing business, **p** and what-not   Milne (49)

penny
    Jacky shall have but a **p** a day   Nursery rhymes (65)
    rich people have **p** wishes   Konigsburg (3)

people
    difference between **p** and animals   Paulsen (12)
    monsters and **p** made a deal   Crowe (1)
    must be the way **p** behave   Fatio (1)
    p come stay for awhile   Grahame (10)
    you can't use **p**   Reid Banks (2)

pepper
    is she a **P**   Sidney (1)

peppers
    picked a peck of pickled **p**   Nursery rhymes (58)

perfect
    expect people to be **p** because adults   Greene, C. (1)
    his truck's got to be **p**   Naylor (4)

person
    every **p** has kind of animal   Brooks (2)

keep growing from one **p** into another ... Brink (1)
p's a **p** no matter how small ... Seuss (26)
real **p** better than being real man ... Myers (3)

perspective (subj.)
in the course of a lifetime ... Creech (8)

perspiration
Jamie liked **p** and complications ... Konigsburg (2)

Peru
brought up in Darkest **P** ... Bond (4)

pet
rather be your **p** than your breakfast ... King-Smith (4)

Peter
can't be **P**, that's boy's name ... Hoffman (1)
P P pumpkin eater ... Nursery rhymes (57)
P Piper picked a peck ... Nursery rhymes (58)

Peter Pan
can't be **P P**, he isn't black ... Hoffman (1)

Peter Pan (subj.)
make-believe was so real to him ... Barrie (15)
odd stories about him ... Barrie (4)

Peterkin
sad blow to the **P** family ... Hale, L. (2)

pets
I could have as many **p** ... Byars (4)

pets (subj.)
every boy should have a chicken ... Pinkwater (6)

Philadelphia
the lady from **P** ... Hale, L. (1)

piano
how supremely heaven playing **p** ... Hesse (1)
tap dancing on God's **p** ... Park (6)

picked
p a peck of pickled peppers ... Nursery rhymes (58)

pickle
as if papa was **p** bottle ... Alcott (2)
in a **p** barrel without a fork ... Paterson (16)

pictures
use of a book without **p** ... Carroll (2)

pie
four and twenty blackbirds baked in a **p** ... Nursery rhymes (68)
he was put in a **p** by Mrs. MacGregor ... Potter (7)

poison
    drink much from bottle marked **p**   Carroll (3)

poke
    P once our only cat   DeRegniers (7)

poky
    where in the world is **p** little puppy   Lowrey (1)

polar bear
    what if I turned into a **p**   Joosse (1)

pole
    North **P** discovered by Pooh   Milne (44)

policemen
    headmasters and **p** biggest giants   Dahl (7)

polite
    who ever heard of a **p** cat   Wrede (1)

Polly
    P put the kettle on   Nursery rhymes (59)

pond
    Yertle the Turtle was king of the **p**   Seuss (47)

pooh
    Madeline just said **p p**   Bemelmans (2)
    wherever I am there's always **P**   Milne (15)

poop
    motor car went **p p p**   Grahame (12)

pop
    p goes the weasel   Nursery rhymes (2)
    p out of the egg came   Carle (2)

pope
    she wished to be the **p**   Fairy tales (8)

porpoise
    there's a **p** close behind us   Carroll (17)

porridge
    tasted the **p** of the great big bear   Fairy tales (28)

possible
    so many things are **p**   Juster (10)

potential
    p in our image   White, T. (3)

potions
    made special **p** for girls who wanted   dePaola (4)

poverty
    p will not make a man worthless   MacDonald, G. (3)

power
    any great gift or **p** is a burden   Cooper (2)
    loves the feel of **p**   Cleary (4)
    men give up **p** never   Alexander (14)

practice
    liked to **p** with a string bean   Hoban (9)

practice (subj.)
    writing is like anything   Byars (3)

pram
    one morning in her **p**   de la Mare (1)

prayed
    I **p** to trees   Creech (5)

prayer
    best way to get an answer to **p**   Stratton-Porter (1)

prayers
    Christopher Robin is saying his **p**   Milne (26)
    saying one's **p** isn't same as praying   Montgomery (4)

praying
    saying one's prayers isn't same as **p**   Montgomery (4)

precious
    p things for those that prize   Aesop (9)

preparing
    so little time **p** the one that must follow   McKinley (5)

present
    p of a friend, it was Tacy   Lovelace (1)

presents
    singing without any **p**   Seuss (30)
    won't be Christmas without **p**   Alcott (1)

pretty
    p maids all in a row   Nursery rhymes (43)

previous
    and returned on the **p** night   Nursery rhymes (74)

price
    p paid in blood is heavy reckoning   Alexander (9)

prick
    princess shall **p** herself   Fairy tales (23)

pride
    eat two fine slices of your **p**   Collodi (6)

prince
    even a **p** may be a fool   Paterson (1)
    frog change into a handsome **p**   Fairy tales (9)
    look like real **p** but you are a bum   Munsch (2)

❧ Q

quietly
    sit just **q** and smell the flowers   Leaf (1)

◣ R

rabbit
    down the **r** hole   Carroll (1)
    R never let things come to him   Milne (11)

rabbits
    four little **r** and their names were   Potter (6)
    r don't like rabbit stew   Kuskin (2)

race
    slow and steady wins the **r**   Aesop (33)

race relations (subj.)
    white people may demand our respect   Taylor, M. (1)

raced
    you have **r** darkness and won   Martin, B. (3)

radiant
    some pig, terrific, **r**, humble   White, E. (3)

radish
    the **r** cure   MacDonald, B. (2)

railroad
    peanut sat on a **r** track   Nursery rhymes (55)

rails
    staying on the **r** no matter what   Crampton (3)

rain
    never had he seen so much **r**   Milne (45)

rains
    what happens to mushroom when it **r**   Ginsburg (1)

ram
    I may be ewe, I may be **r**   King-Smith (3)

ran
    he **r** so fast that he began   Ciardi (7)

Rapunzel
    R let down your hair   Fairy tales (19)

raspberries
    never eat **r** like these again   Hunt (3)

raspberry
    r strawberry gooseberry I'm very   Hoban (8)

raven
    why is a **r** like a writing desk   Carroll (10)

right

as long as answer is **r**   Juster (6)
don't be **r** till it's time to be   Ciardi (4)
learn more being wrong for **r** reasons   Juster (9)
man has a **r** to be judged   Eckert (1)
parents were **r**, not children   Norton (4)
people have **r** to be losers   Avi (1)
quite often I is left instead of **r**   Dahl (5)
second to the **r** and straight on   Barrie (9)
wrong will be **r** when Aslan comes   Lewis (2)

rights

judgments as to **r** and wrongs   Avi (3)
no one's private **r** ought to get invaded   Krumgold (4)

ring

with a **r** at the end of his nose   Lear (9)

rings

r on her fingers and bells on her toes   Nursery rhymes (63)

Rio

roll down to **R**   Kipling (27)

ripe

r fruit soon spoils   Yorinks (1)

risers

only distribute pigs to early **r**   White, E. (1)

river

beautiful **R** Wah-Hoo   Seuss (33)
great gray-green greasy Limpopo **R**   Kipling (25)
r sleek sinuous full-bodied animal   Grahame (5)
to a **r** most things are same   Ciardi (6)
you are still master of the **r**   Swift (1)

road

one **r** talk never finds   MacDonald, G. (10)
r paved with yellow brick   Baum (3)
r's a kind of holy thing   Gray, E. (2)

roads

all **r** are hard   Hoban (21)

robbed

pobble was **r** of his twice five toes   Lear (5)

robbers

three fierce **r**   Ungerer (2)

robin

what will poor **r** do then   Nursery rhymes (48)
who killed cock **r**   Nursery rhymes (84)

rock

isn't this a strange moss-covered **r**   Kimmel (1)

rock-a-by
    R Lady from Hushaby street   Field, E. (7)

roll
    r down to Rio   Kipling (27)

room
    in the great green **r**   Brown (1)
    r for Barney and tuna and cream   Viorst (7)
    there's **r** galore   Nic Leodhas (1)

rootabaga
    then this is the **R** country   Sandburg (3)

rope
    a **r** for a necklace   Kipling (14)

rotten
    world needs a few **r** people   Cushman (8)

routine
    r necessary to life   Konigsburg (18)

Rowley
    heigho says Anthony **R**   Nursery rhymes (17)

royalty
    r isn't allowed to hide   McKinley (7)

rub
    r a dub dub   Nursery rhymes (64)

rubber
    foam **r** son with no emotions   Park (2)

rule
    ancient **r** of Two times Two   Ciardi (3)
    r is jam tomorrow   Carroll (29)
    r of Four times Four   Ciardi (4)
    r of One times One   Ciardi (2)

rules
    r always come right if you wait   Grahame (2)
    simple little **r** and few   Belloc (12)

rummage
    nightly custom of mother to **r**   Barrie (3)

rumpus
    let the wild **r** start   Sendak (7)

run
    bunny who wanted to **r** away   Brown (7)
    grow hair faster than you **r**   Scieszka (4)
    he's since **r** off again   Lindgren, B. (2)
    motto of mongoose is **R** and find out   Kipling (5)
    see how they **r**   Nursery rhymes (77)

running
    takes all the **r** you can do   Carroll (24)

rye
    pocket full of **r**   Nursery rhymes (68)

◥ S

sacred
    ain't the book what's **s**   Fitzhugh (11)

sad
    began to think of things that were **s**   Lobel (22)
    need reason to be **s**   Sachar (3)
    to let a **s** thought get into your mind   Burnett (14)

sadness
    can't control your **s**   Park (3)
    don't have to spend money on **s**   Greene, B. (4)

safe
    better one **s** way   Aesop (23)
    brave from **s** distance   Aesop (11)
    don't feel so **s** being captain   Spinelli (4)
    knowing they were **s** and wrong   Norton (4)
    more important things than being **s**   Cushman (3)

sage
    not even the mention of **s** and onions   Potter (4)

sailed
    s away for a year and a day   Lear (9)
    s off in a wooden shoe   Field, E. (3)

sailor
    s chooses the wind   Avi (6)
    s was a dog Scuppers   Brown (8)

St. Ives
    as I was going to **S**   Nursery rhymes (4)

sale
    caps for **s**, fifty cents a cap   Slobodkina (2)

salt
    been spoiled till **s** won't save   Burnett (10)
    both **s** and sugar to make good [life] Blos (7)
    I love you as fresh meat loves **s**   Fairy tales (3)
    raw with just a pinch of **s**   Steig (6)
    Veruca **S** a girl who is spoiled   Dahl (9)

salty
    tastes a little bit **s** but tear-water tea Lobel (23)

Sam
> I am **S**, **S** I am   Seuss (19)
> I do not like that **S-I-am**   Seuss (20)

same
> all look the **s** when we turn off the light   Silverstein (12)
> house where everything is the **s**   Sandburg (1)
> **s** thing day after day is enemy   Hamilton (5)
> to river most things are **s**   Ciardi (6)

sand
> summer goes like the **s**   Hoban (18)

sand-pit
> getting rather tired of that **s**   Milne (12)

sandwich
> hippo **s** is easy to make   Silverstein (13)
> **s** pickle egg and milk come out even   Hoban (10)
> what became of the **s**   Lord, J. (2)

Santa
> one silver bell from **S**'s sleigh   Van Allsburg (4)

Santa Claus (subj.)
> bell still rings for me   Van Allsburg (5)

sap
> keep your **s** running   Bailey (3)

Sarah
> keep up your courage **S** Noble   Dalgliesh (1)

'satiable
> elephant's child full of **s** curiosity   Kipling (24)

satisfied
> she was not **s** even now   Fairy tales (8)

say
> child should always **s** what's true   Stevenson, R. (3)
> didn't seem to be a lot to **s**   Creech (2)

scare
> really exciting things **s** us   Dahl (13)
> smarter you are, more things can **s**   Paterson (3)

scared
> the matador was **s** stiff   Leaf (4)

scholar
> a diller, a dollar, a ten o'clock **s**   Nursery rhymes (13)

school
> Lower Trainswitch **S** for Locomotives   Crampton (3)
> never expected to use [imagination] in **s**   Cleary (6)
> never known what she was doing in **s**   Fisher (3)
> on Thursday there is never **s**   Collodi (8)

one little day home from s	Fitzhugh (8)
scared about what s would be like	Blume (6)
saddest shower night before s starts	Spinelli (8)
s just speeds things up	Sachar (2)
s most important thing ever happened	Conly (1)
show they think s is unimportant	Cleary (14)
Wayside S was built sideways	Sachar (1)

scientific
| s people always curious | Burnett (12) |

scion
| Miss Hickory had been a s | Bailey (6) |

scope
| more s for the imagination | Montgomery (1) |

scoreboard
| losing's just a number on a s | Krumgold (3) |

Scottie
| S dogs grow that way | Flack (1) |

sculpins
| catching s when everybody else | Aldrich (2) |

Scuppers
| sailor was a dog S was his name | Brown (8) |

sea
born at s in teeth of gale	Brown (8)
days at s when all you want	Fox, P. (1)
flounder flounder in the s	Fairy tales (7)
I too will live beside the s	Cooney (3)
life was like a s	Voigt (4)
s can swallow ships	Babbitt (1)
there is no s here but the land rolls	MacLachlan (9)
went to s in a sieve	Lear (11)
when I was down beside the s	Stevenson, R. (2)
you have to be out of the s	Steig (4)

seas
| is all the s were one sea | Nursery rhymes (32) |

seashells
| she sells s on the seashore | Nursery rhymes (66) |

seasons
| aren't we lucky the s are four | Lionni (6) |
| sing a song of s | Stevenson, R. (12) |

seasons (subj.)
| who scatters snowflakes | Lionni (6) |

second
s Strings to their Bows	Cresswell (2)
s to the right then straight	Barrie (9)
will make you a s-class citizen	Spinelli (1)

side
only one **s** to any question .... Stolz (7)

sideways
Wayside School was built **s** .... Sachar (1)

sieve
went to sea in a **s** .... Lear (11)

sighing
s like slow-leaking tire .... Gray, L. (2)

sight
no **s** so ugly as face in anger .... Fitzhugh (9)

silence
even the **s** was listening .... Dahl (14)
s can change you too .... MacLachlan (2)
s was as deep as death .... Dahl (14)

silence (subj.)
it wasn't that I was stupid .... Creech (2)
never miss chance to keep mouth shut .... Peck (2)

silent
to hear one must be **s** .... Le Guin (4)

silliness (subj.)
no reason why they should giggle .... Fisher (5)

silly
lot of serious things start **s** .... Babbitt (5)
s old Bear .... Milne (32)
s Sally went to town .... Wood (4)

silver
couldn't be sold for gold or **s** .... Burton (2)
one **s** bell from Santa's sleigh .... Van Allsburg (4)
s buckles on his knee .... Nursery rhymes (6)
time for the casting of **s** .... Forbes, E. (2)
with **s** bells and cockleshells .... Nursery rhymes (43)

Simon
simple **S** met a pieman .... Nursery rhymes (67)

simple
s little rules and few .... Belloc (12)
s Simon met a pieman .... Nursery rhymes (67)

simpleton
Jemima Puddle-Duck was a **s** .... Potter (4)

simplicity
true **s** is elegant .... Konigsburg (14)

sin
bottle up barrel of **s** .... Peck (6)
keep it from growing, that's a **s** .... Krumgold (1)
wages of **s** are hardest debts .... Stratton-Porter (3)

sparrow
    I said the s with my little bow   Nursery rhymes (84)

speak
    anybody picking on someone she'd s up   Estes (2)
    s when he is spoken to   Stevenson, R. (3)

speaking
    ways of s without words   Dalgliesh (3)

speck
    little s of a living thing   Steig (3)

speed
    so great was his s   Lobel (3)

spell
    somebody stumps you to s pneumonia   Fisher (4)

spelling
    my s is wobbly   Milne (39)

spend
    don't have to s money on sadness   Greene, B. (4)

spice
    sugar and s and all things nice   Nursery rhymes (82)

spices
    words like s   Aiken (2)

spider
    along came a s   Nursery rhymes (40)
    died by a s's cruel bite   Fairy tales (37)
    s didn't answer   Carle (1)
    there came a big s   Nursery rhymes (40)

spiders (subj.)
    Helen was too fast for him   Graham (1)

spilt
    sometimes it looked like s milk   Shaw (1)

spin
    my daughter can s straw into gold   Fairy tales (21)

spinach
    rowley-powley gammon and s   Nursery rhymes (17)

spindle
    prick herself with a s   Fairy tales (23)

spinning
    she was very busy s her web   Carle (1)

spirit
    hard times are about losing s   Hesse (2)
    welcome to the coming s   Ehrlich (2)

spiritual
    poet has **s** memory   Andersen (3)

spit
    if you **s** in the air   Cushman (10)

spoiled
    been **s** till salt won't save him   Burnett (10)
    s two birthday cakes   Cleary (2)

spoils
    ripe fruit soon **s**   Yorinks (1)

spook
    down **S** Hill   Berenstain (1)

spoon
    and the dish ran away with the **s**   Nursery rhymes (22)

sport
    why men are so fond of this **s**   Sewell (1)

sports (subj.)
    I'm really into violence   Blume (7)

spots
    white dog with black **s**   Zion (1)

spotted
    s or herbaceous backson   Milne (10)

spring
    found the corner that **s** was around   Lobel (9)
    s is wondrous necessity   Cleaver (4)
    three things to remember about **s**   MacLachlan (7)
    walk at my leisure toward a **s**   Saint-Exupery (11)
    wrong about swallows and **s**   Blos (4)

squash
    peaches came down **s**   Gage (1)

squirrel
    tail that belonged to a little red **s**   Potter (10)

stamping
    palace disappear by **s** his foot   Kipling (35)

stand
    oh no I can't **s** this   Murphy (1)
    only that a man can **s** up   Forbes, E. (3)
    united we **s**   Aesop (25)

star
    s-belly Sneetches   Seuss (45)
    s light **s** bright   Nursery rhymes (69)
    twinkle twinkle little **s**   Taylor, J. (1)

stars
    had bellies with **s**   Seuss (45)
    s are beautiful but not take active part   Barrie (6)

start
    way to **s** a day is this   Baylor (1)

starve
    soldier's job to **s** to death   Keith (1)

staying
    s on the rails no matter what   Crampton (3)

steady
    slow and **s** wins   Aesop (33)

steal
    where bears **s** ice cream   Duvoisin (4)

stealing
    like charity **s** begins at home   Blos (2)

steam shovel
    Mike Mulligan has a **s**   Burton (4)

stew
    good big supper of carrot **s**   Jackson, K. (2)
    rabbits don't like rabbit **s**   Kuskin (2)

stick
    s stock stone dead   Fairy tales (20)
    up **s** and bang him   Fairy tales (1)

sticky
    s bears is ninepence   Bond (3)

stile
    piggy won't go over the **s**   Fairy tales (17)

stodgy
    s parent is no fun at all   Dahl (15)

stomach
    everything more confusing on empty **s**   Alexander (5)

stone
    pulleth out this sword from this **s**   White, T. (4)
    third **s** came skipping back   Van Allsburg (3)

stops
    it **s** you right where you are   Babbitt (10)

store
    Christmas doesn't come from a **s**   Seuss (31)

stories
    mouse soup must be mixed with **s**   Lobel (21)
    swallows build to listen to **s**   Barrie (13)

sugar
    both salt and **s** to make good [life]   Blos (7)
    s and spice and all things nice   Nursery rhymes (82)

sugar-plums (sugarplums)
    s tumble of course to the ground   Field, E. (2)
    visions of **s** danced in their heads   Moore (2)

suicide
    committed **s** without killing myself   Aldrich (3)

suitcase
    on journey without **s**   Christiansen (1)

summer
    August hangs at top of **s**   Babbitt (9)
    here somes **s**   Silverstein (2)
    I tried on the **s** sun   Silverstein (4)
    one hot **s** in Itching Down   Lord, J. (1)
    s comes like hairy blanket   Napoli (1)
    s goes like the sand   Hoban (18)
    s sun was on their wings   Field, R. (5)
    s took all the lessons   Hoban (19)
    washing whole **s** down the drain   Spinelli (8)

sun
    greet the **s** with some kind of blessing   Baylor (1)
    I gather **s** rays for the winter   Lionni (3)
    I tried on the summer **s**   Silverstein (4)
    new **s** every day   Baylor (2)
    summer **s** was on their wings   Field, R. (5)
    s did not shine   Seuss (7)
    s is shining, that is magic   Burnett (13)
    s is so it can be a great day   Krauss (5)
    s has wonderfully glorious habit   George (4)

Sunday
    homework sits on top of **S**   Hoban (20)

sunlight
    things that grow upward like **s**   Voigt (10)

sunrise (subj.)
    way to start a day   Baylor (1)

sunset
    flamingo flying off into the **s**   Lewin (1)

supper
    good big **s** of carrot stew   Jackson, K. (2)

sure
    never doubt what nobody is **s**   Belloc (14)

swallow
    sea can **s** ships   Babbitt (1)

◣ T

tip
 t-tapping song-singing kind of day   Gray, L. (3)

tippets
 t for mice and ribbons for mobs   Potter (2)

tire
 sighing like slow-leaking **t**   Gray, L. (2)

tired
 too **t** from fighting the night   Ryan (1)
 what I am is **t** of jam   Hoban (13)

title
 when I type a **t** page   Byars (1)

toad
 ingenious Mr. **T**   Grahame (12)

today
 never jam **t**   Carroll (29)
 t is day tomorrow becomes   Babbitt (7)
 t was a difficult day   Henkes (5)

toe
 walk on your heel and favor your **t**   Paterson (8)

toes
 nothing so good for a Pobble's **t**   Lear (4)
 nothing tastes as good as **t**   Kuskin (4)
 how cold my **t** tiddely pom   Milne (1)
 Pobble was robbed of his twice five **t**   Lear (5)
 Pobble who has no **t**   Lear (3)
 Pobbles are happier without their **t**   Lear (6)

together
 place to be apart and time to be **t**   Grifalconi (1)

told
 George never said I **t** you so   Marshall (1)
 let people say I **t** you so   Butterworth (1)

tolerant
 nothing as **t** as kid you can whip   Fitzgerald (1)

Tom
 T T the piper's son   Nursery rhymes (81)

Tom Thumb
 here lies **T**   Fairy tales (37)
 I spy **T**   Ahlberg (1)

tomatoes
 t are the least of it   Levine (1)

Tommy
 little **T** Tucker sings for his supper   Nursery rhymes (41)

t worth counts for little   Field, R. (3)
what is **t** may not be clear   Ciardi (5)

Truffula
those trees, those **t** trees   Seuss (37)

trumpet
day deserves good loud **t**   Lobel (25)
sound upon the **t** the Heynal   Kelly (1)

trumpeter
ancient oath of the Krakow **t**   Kelly (1)

trust
do not **t** flatterers   Aesop (8)
don't **t** to those who promise   Collodi (3)

trusts
he who **t** a woman   Kipling (15)

truth
courage to appear with empty **t**   Demi (1)
t about the cat and pup   Field, E. (9)
t which I had learned   Gerrard (1)

try
t them and you may I say   Seuss (22)

tub
three men in a **t**   Nursery rhymes (64)
tonight we dance in the **t**   Wood (2)

tuffet
Little Miss Muffet sat on a **t**   Nursery rhymes (40)

tugboat
no place for a red-painted **t**   Crampton (1)

tug o' war
I will not play at **t**   Silverstein (9)

tule
ground-hugging California **t** fog   Fleischman, S. (1)

tumble
sugar-plums **t** of course to the ground   Field, E. (2)

turn
one bad **t** deserves another   Aesop (12)
one good **t** deserves another   Aesop (31)
then **t** not pale   Carroll (19)
t again Whittington   Fairy tales (6)

turtle
Yertle the **T** was king of the pond   Seuss (47)

turtles
all the **t** are free   Seuss (49)

Tweedle-dum
 way of **T** is not the way of Tweedle-dee   Kipling (7)

tweetle
 t beetle noodle poodle   Seuss (18)

twelve
 t little girls in two straight lines   Bemelmans (1)

twice
 large as life and **t** as natural   Carroll (35)

twinkle
 t t little bat   Carroll (12)
 t t little star   Taylor, J. (1)

twins
 trouble with being **t**   DeJong (1)

twist
 no more **t**   Potter (1)

two
 ancient rule of **T** times **T**   Ciardi (3)
 much more friendly with **t**   Milne (46)

two-headed
 only **t** beast in the world   Lofting (3)

type
 when I **t** a title page   Byars (1)

tyrant
 any excuse will serve a **t**   Aesop (2)

❚ U

ugly
 failure is the **u** duckling   Feiffer (4)
 no sight so **u** as face in anger   Fitzhugh (9)
 once you are real you can't be **u**   Williams, M. (3)
 u duckling   Andersen (11)

unbelievable
 so completely crazy it's **u**   Dahl (21)

unbirthday
 an **u** present   Carroll (32)

uncomfortable
 I know just enough to be **u**   Kipling (8)

uncommon
 not as much danger about **u** things   Hale, L. (5)

uncooperative
more time then usual in the **u** chair .... Henkes (3)

underground
once well **u** know exactly where you are .... Grahame (9)
took fear, misfortune and hid **u** .... Holman (1)

understand
grown-ups never **u** anything .... Saint-Exupery (1)
how animals **u** things .... Burnett (9)

understanding
u mother even though she was a cow .... Leaf (2)

understands
one only **u** the things one tames .... Saint-Exupery (8)

underwear
like having on raggedy **u** .... Myers (4)

unfair
after you have been **u** .... Barrie (16)

unforgivable
to forgive **u** is breath of life .... Morris (5)

unhappy
heart makes most people **u** .... Baum (12)

uninhabited
from the altogether **u** interior .... Kipling (20)

uninvited
u enemies of invited .... Konigsburg (26)

union
u gives strength .... Aesop (29)

unique
if you tame me, you will be **u** .... Saint-Exupery (6)
own story always seems **u** .... Kindl (1)

united
u we stand .... Aesop (25)

universe
vast living **u** .... Steig (3)

unless
u someone like you cares .... Seuss (39)
with one word, **u** .... Seuss (38)

unmix
painter must **u** [colors] .... Treviño (1)

up
general direction was **u** .... Holman (3)
u u u with a fish .... Seuss (9)

◣ V

◣ W

watched
w bloomer doesn't bloom · Kraus (1)

water
delicious is drink of cool w · Babbitt (8)
gliding on the w's face · Belloc (9)
to fetch a pail of w · Nursery rhymes (33)
w stops you right where you are · Babbitt (10)

waterbeetle
w here shall teach · Belloc (9)

watermelons
handles on w · Cushman (4)

waves
break now w and split your ribs · Fleischman, P. (1)

way
didn't have to get out of w for anybody · Merrill (3)
in the usual w, if you know what I mean · Milne (40)
w he can follow grows narrower · Le Guin (7)
whatever w a thing is done · Ciardi (2)
which w I ought to go · Carroll (6)

ways
he had his little w · Milne (14)

wayside
W School was built sideways · Sachar (1)

weakness
greatest victory won over own w · Morris (2)

wealth (subj.)
rich you will surely be · Alexander (8)

wear
but they can't make me w them · Viorst (3)

wearing
w out English language · Weller (2)

weasel
the monkey chased the w · Nursery rhymes (2)

weather
advice from friends like the w · Lobel (6)
football doesn't take any crap from w · Spinelli (2)
only thing different was its w · Barrett (1)

weave
w my tale but not embroider it · Konigsburg (17)

wee
cried w w w all the way home · Nursery rhymes (76)
w Willie Winkie · Nursery rhymes (83)

wished

might have **w** never to grow old   Blos (1)

wishes

rich people have penny **w**   Konigsburg (3)

w are funny, come true differently   Polacco (2)

w will not be rushed   Lobel (7)

wishing

anything worthwhile had for **w**   Alexander (18)

so busy **w** for good fortune   Alexander (21)

witch

Strega Nona which meant Grandma **W**   dePaola (3)

strict teacher who might be a **w**   Voigt (1)

there was this **w**   Balian (1)

Wicked **W** of the West   Baum (14)

witches

motto of all **w**   Dahl (22)

witching

w hour was special moment   Dahl (1)

wives

I met a man with seven **w**   Nursery rhymes (4)

nine hundred and ninety-nine **w**   Kipling (34)

wizard

very good man but very bad **w**   Baum (10)

wobbly

my spelling is **w**   Milne (39)

woke

w up found I'd turned into my mother   Rodgers (1)

woldwellers

w admired for knowledge   Babbitt (4)

wolf

Amaroq **w** my friend   George (2)

put your head inside **w**'s mouth   Aesop (6)

w in sheep's clothing   Aesop (15)

wolves

escaping goblins to be caught by **w**   Tolkien (5)

woman

he who trusts a **w**   Kipling (15)

more and not less **w**   O'Hara (1)

old **w** who lived in a shoe   Nursery rhymes (75)

w's hand and heart or child's presence   Porter (4)

women

battles are ugly when **w** fight   Lewis (4)

when **w** are advisers   Alcott (7)

w are houses for our children   Kindl (2)

women (subj.)
here in her world of men — O'Hara (1)
that kind of thinking — Spinelli (1)

wonder
how I **w** what you are — Taylor, J. (1)
may be **w** in money — Bagnold (4)

wondering
only when taking it easy, do **w** — Steig (1)

wondrous
spring is a **w** necessity — Cleaver (4)

wood
how much **w** would a woodchuck — Nursery rhymes (27)
once upon a time, a piece of **w** — Collodi (1)

wooden
sailed off in a **w** shoe — Field, E. (3)

woods
reality of the **w** — Paulsen (1)
the **w**, so many who enjoy it kill — Paulsen (11)

woodshed
I'll see you in the **w** after supper — Field, E. (15)

wool
have you any **w** — Nursery rhymes (5)

word
never use a simple **w** — Stolz (6)
[pen] makes written **w** cheap — Konigsburg (25)
when I use a **w** — Carroll (33)

words
anything with **w** except eat them — Fox, P. (6)
great assortment of four-lettered **w** — Konigsburg (23)
heat of all the **w** we had not spoken — Yolen (3)
I am gathering **w** — Lionni (5)
long **w** bother me — Milne (35)
regular **w** to stick in amongst cusses — Paterson (7)
sometimes **w** lie but song is true — Paulsen (2)
trees swayed by winds, men by **w** — Aiken (1)
ways of speaking without **w** — Dalgliesh (3)
when you go owling you don't need **w** — Yolen (4)
whether you can make **w** mean — Carroll (34)
w are like spices — Aiken (2)
w are source of misunderstandings — Saint-Exupery (9)
w began fights — Rawlings (4)
w have a life — MacLachlan (6)

words (subj.)
don't you know what "ther" means — Milne (28)
wrong to use too few, worse to use — Juster (3)

Wordsworth
 saw **W** once and Coleridge too   de la Mare (1)

work
 all **w** and no play   Nursery rhymes (3)
 do the **w** of it so well   MacDonald, G. (11)
 every man is obliged to **w**   Collodi (7)
 feels worse than sweat of **w**   Peck (3)
 how goes the **w**   Waddell (1)
 if you are willing to **w**   Stratton-Porter (2)
 to get an answer to prayer is **w**   Stratton-Porter (1)

working
 see all other fellows busy **w**   Grahame (4)

world
 maybe the **w** will get him first   Hoban (14)
 where the **w** is green and blue   Duvoisin (4)
 w is all one place   Alexander (20)
 w is so full of a number of things   Stevenson, R. (9)
 w needs a few rotten people   Cushman (8)

worm
 if you're a **w** sleep late   Silverstein (10)

worms (subj.)
 deep in our earth   Stevenson, J. (1)

worry
 w proves you care   Paterson (10)

worship
 man's **w** counts for naught   Peck (5)

worst
 Herdmans were **w** kids in history   Robinson (1)
 w things weren't outside of you   Voigt (11)

worth
 true **w** counts for little   Field, R. (3)

worthless
 ain't **w** if you can make person laugh   Paterson (14)

worthwhile
 anything **w** had for wishing   Alexander (18)

wounds
 he who leads bears **w** of all   Alexander (10)

writer
 life of **w** is absolute hell   Dahl (8)
 true friend and good **w**   White, E. (5)
 w has to force himself to work   Dahl (8)

writing
 come to **w** purely by chance   Howe (1)

this **w** business, pencils and what-not	Milne (49)
why is raven like **w** desk	Carroll (10)
w is like anything	Byars (3)

wrong

learn more being **w** for right reasons	Juster (9)
once you know something is **w**	Kerr (4)
only thing can do easily is be **w**	Juster (7)
whatever way thing is done is **w**	Ciardi (2)
who cares if question is **w**	Juster (6)
w thinking right for a smart kid	Voigt (7)
w to use too few [words]	Juster (3)
w to want a heart	Baum (12)
w will be right when Aslan comes	Lewis (2)

Wynken

W Blynken and Nod one night	Field, E. (3)
W and Blynken are two little eyes	Field, E. (4)

◣ Y

yak

commend me the **y**	Belloc (1)
where the **y** can be got	Belloc (2)

Yangtze

boat with two wise eyes on **Y** River	Flack (6)

year

this is **y** leaves will stay on trees	Holman (2)

years

hour or two off after hundred million **y**	Hoff (1)

yeller

we called him Old **Y**	Gipson (1)

yellow

man with the **y** hat	Rey (2)
road paved with **y** brick	Baum (3)
short hair was a dingy **y**	Gipson (1)
y fog hung so thick and heavy	Burnett (4)

yelp

very faint **y** as if some tiny person	Seuss (25)

yesterday

today is day **y** used to be	Babbitt (7)

yew

snippet snappet shapen **y**	Boston (1)

yield

y to all and soon have nothing	Aesop (24)

Yooks
   Y are not Zooks   Seuss (6)

York
   grand old duke of **Y**   Nursery rhymes (51)

you
   what **y** are lies with **y**   Stratton-Porter (2)

young
   to stay **y** is also not to change   Blos (1)
   y men never think about death   O'Dell (2)

youth
   I'm **y** I'm joy   Barrie (22)

❚ Z

Z
   most people stop with the **Z**   Seuss (44)

zeal
   z in learning never does harm   Spyri (1)

Zeee
   Z Is everyone still angry   Aardema (1)

Zeek
   Z Silver Moon was born   Ehrlich (1)

zoo
   having tea at the city **z**   DeRegniers (6)
   way people behave when not at **z**   Fatio (1)

Zook
   Z eats bread with the butter side down   Seuss (5)

TITLE INDEX

Locate the title by finding the author name or type of source in "Quotations by Author" and "Quotations from Traditional Sources."

"The Man and His Two Wives." Aesop.
"The Man and the Serpent." Aesop.
The Man in the Ceiling. Feiffer, Jules.
"The Man, the Boy, and the Donkey."
    Aesop.
Maniac Magee. Spinelli, Jerry.
Martin's Mice. King-Smith, Dick.
Marvin K. Mooney Will You Please Go
    Now! Seuss, Dr.
Mary Had a Little Lamb. Hale, Sara
    Josepha.
Mary Poppins. Travers, P. L.
The Matchlock Gun. Edmonds, Walter D.
Math Curse. Scieszka, Jon.
Matilda. Dahl, Roald.
May I Bring a Friend? DeRegniers,
    Beatrice Schenk.
Mick Harte Was Here. Park, Barbara.
"The Microbe." Belloc, Hilaire.
The Midwife's Apprentice. Cushman,
    Karen.
Mike Mulligan and His Steam Shovel.
    Burton, Virginia Lee.
"The Milkmaid." Nursery Rhymes.
"The Milkmaid and Her Pail." Aesop.
Millions of Cats. Gag, Wanda.
Mirette on the High Wire. McCully,
    Emily Arnold.
Miss Hickory. Bailey, Carolyn Sherwin.
Miss Nelson Is Missing. Allard, Harry.
Miss Rumphius. Cooney, Barbara.
"Miss T." de la Mare, Walter.
"Missing." Milne, A. A.
The Missing Milkman. Duvoisin, Roger.
The Missing Piece. Silverstein, Shel.
The Missing Piece Meets the Big O.
    Silverstein, Shel.
Misty of Chincoteague. Henry, Marguerite.
Molly's Pilgrim. Cohen, Barbara.
The Moon and I. Byars, Betsy.
Moon Man. Ungerer, Tomi.
The Moorchild. McGraw, Eloise.
A Moral Alphabet. Belloc, Hilaire.
More Beasts for Worse Children. Belloc,
    Hilaire.
Mother Goose. Nursery Rhymes.
Mother, Mother, I Want Another. Polushkin,
    Maria.
"The Mountain in Labor." Aesop.
The Mouse and His Child. Hoban, Russell.

The Mouse and the Motorcycle. Cleary,
    Beverly.
Mouse Soup. Lobel, Arnold.
"Mowgli's Brothers." Kipling, Rudyard.
"Mr. Fox." Fairy Tales.
Mrs. Armitage on Wheels. Blake, Quentin.
Mrs. Frisby and the Rats of NIMH.
    O'Brien, Robert C.
Mrs. Piggle-Wiggle. MacDonald, Betty.
Mrs. Tiggy-Winkle. See *The Tale of Mrs.*
    Tiggy-Winkle.
Muddigush. Knutson, Kimberley.
Mushroom in the Rain. Ginsburg, Mirra.
My Brother Sam Is Dead. Collier, James
    Lincoln & Christopher.
My Friend Flicka. O'Hara, Mary.
My Mama Had a Dancing Heart. Gray,
    Libba Moore.
My Rotten Redheaded Older Brother.
    Polacco, Patricia.
"My Shadow." Stevenson, Robert Louis.
My Side of the Mountain. George, Jean
    Craighead.
The Mysteries of Harris Burdick. Van
    Allsburg, Chris.

Nana Upstairs and Nana Downstairs.
    dePaola, Tomie.
The Napping House. Wood, Audrey.
National Velvet. Bagnold, Enid.
National Worm Day. Stevenson, James.
The Night Before Christmas. See *A Visit*
    from St. Nicholas.
"No Difference." Silverstein, Shel.
The Noisy Book. Brown, Margaret Wise.
Nonsense Alphabets. Lear, Edward.
Nonsense Songs and Stories. Lear, Edward.
Now We Are Six. Milne, A. A.
Number the Stars. Lowry, Lois.

"The Oak and the Reed." Aesop.
Oh, the Places You'll Go! Seuss, Dr.
Old Black Witch. Devlin, Wende and Harry.
"Old Mother Hubbard." Martin, Sarah
    Catherine.
"The Old Woman and Her Pig." Fairy Tales.
Old Yeller. Gipson, Fred.
On Beyond Zebra. Seuss, Dr.

BIBLIOGRAPHY

Aardema, Verna. *Why Mosquitoes Buzz in People's Ears: A West African Tale*. New York: Dial, 1975.

Aesop. *Aesop's Fables*. New York: Grosset & Dunlap, 1947.

———. *The Fables of Aesop*. Retold by Joseph Jacobs. New York: Macmillan, 1964.

———. *Tales from Aesop*. Written by Harold Jones. London, Julia MacRae, 1981.

Ahlberg, Janet, and Allan Ahlberg. *Each Peach Pear Plum*. New York: Viking, 1978.

Aiken, Joan. *The Last Slice of Rainbow and Other Stories*. New York: Harper & Row, 1985.

Alcott, Louisa May. *Little Women: Or Meg, Jo, Beth, and Amy*. New York: Crowell, 1955.

Aldrich, Thomas Bailey. *The Story of a Bad Boy*. Boston: Houghton Mifflin, 1951, c1869.

Alexander, Lloyd. *The Book of Three*. New York: Holt, Rinehart & Winston, 1964.

———. *The Cat Who Wished to Be a Man*. New York: Dutton, 1973.

———. *The Fortune-Tellers*. New York: Dutton, 1992.

———. *The High King*. New York: Holt, Rinehart & Winston, 1968.

———. *Westmark*. New York: Dutton, 1981.

———. *The Wizard in the Tree*. New York: Dutton, 1975.

Aliki. *We Are Best Friends*. New York: Greenwillow, 1982.

Allard, Harry. *Miss Nelson Is Missing*. Boston: Houghton Mifflin, 1977.

———. *The Stupids Die*. Boston: Houghton Mifflin, 1981.

Andersen, Hans Christian. *The Complete Fairy Tales and Stories*. Garden City, N.Y.: Doubleday, 1974.

The Arabian Nights. New York: Grosset & Dunlap, 1946.

Asbjørnsen, Peter Christen, and Jorgen E. Moe. *East of the Sun and West of the Moon and Other Tales*. New York: Macmillan, 1966.

Avi. *S. O. R. Losers*. New York: Bradbury, 1984.

———. *The True Confessions of Charlotte Doyle*. New York: Orchard Books, 1990.

Babbitt, Natalie. *The Eyes of the Amaryllis*. New York: Farrar, Straus & Giroux, 1977.

———. *Knee-Knock Rise*. New York: Farrar, Straus & Giroux, 1970.

———. *The Search for Delicious*. New York: Farrar, Straus & Giroux, 1969.

———. *Tuck Everlasting*. New York: Farrar, Straus & Giroux, 1975.

Bagnold, Enid. *National Velvet*. New York: Morrow, c1935.

Bailey, Carolyn Sherwin. *Miss Hickory*. New York: Viking, 1946.

Balian, Lorna. *Humbug Witch*. Watertown, Wis.: Humbug Books, c1965.

Bannerman, Helen. *The Story of Little Babaji*. New York: HarperCollins, 1996.

Baring-Gould, William S., and Ceil Baring-Gould. *The Annotated Mother Goose*. New York: Clarkson Potter, 1962.

Barrett, Judi. *Cloudy with a Chance of Meatballs*. New York: Atheneum, 1978.

Barrie, J. M. *Peter Pan*. New York: Viking Press, 1991.

Baum, L. Frank. *The Annotated Wizard of Oz*. New York: Clarkson Potter, 1973.

Baylor, Byrd. *The Way to Start a Day*. New York: Scribner, 1978.

Belloc, Hilaire. *The Bad Child's Book of Beasts, More Beasts for Worse Children, and A Moral Alphabet*. New York: Dover, 1961.

Bemelmans, Ludwig. *Madeline*. New York: Viking, 1939.

———. *Madeline and the Bad Hat*. New York: Viking, 1957.

———. *Madeline and the Gypsies*. New York: Viking, 1959.

———. *Madeline in London*. New York: Viking, 1961.

———. *Madeline's Rescue*. New York: Viking, 1953.

Berenstain, Jan, and Stan Berenstain. *Bears in the Night*. New York: Random, 1971.

———. *The Bike Lesson*. New York: Beginner Books, 1964.

Blake, Quentin. *Mrs. Armitage on Wheels*. New York: Knopf, 1987.

Blos, Joan W. *A Gathering of Days*. New York: Scribner, 1979.

Blume, Judy. *Are You There God? It's Me, Margaret*. New York: Bradbury, 1970.

———. *Freckle Juice*. New York: Four Winds, 1971.

———. *Superfudge*. New York: Dutton, 1980.

Bond, Michael. *A Bear Called Paddington*. Boston: Houghton Mifflin, 1958.

Bornstein, Ruth. *Indian Bunny*. New York: Children's, 1973.

———. *Little Gorilla*. New York: Clarion, 1976.

Boston, Lucy Maria. *The Children of Green Knowe*. San Diego: Harcourt Brace Jovanovich, 1983, c1955.

Bright, Robert. *Georgie*. New York: Doubleday, 1944.

Brink, Carol Ryrie. *Caddie Woodlawn*. New York: Macmillan, 1935.

Brittain, Bill. *The Wish Giver*. New York: Harper & Row, 1983.

Brooke, L. Leslie. *Johnny Crow's Garden*. London: Warne, 1903.

Brooks, Bruce. *Everywhere*. New York: Harper & Row, 1990.

———. *Vanishing*. New York: HarperCollins, 1999.

Brown, Margaret Wise. *Goodnight Moon*. New York: Harper, 1947.

———. *Little Fur Family*. New York: Harper & Row, 1946.

———. *The Noisy Book*. New York: Harper & Row, 1939.

———. *The Runaway Bunny*. New York: Harper & Row, 1942.

———. *The Sailor Dog*. New York: Golden Books, 1953.

Brunhoff, Jean de. *The Story of Babar, the Little Elephant*. New York: Random, 1933.

Burgess, Gelett. *Goops and How to Be Them*. Philadelphia: Lippincott, c1900.

Burnett, Frances Hodgson. *Little Lord Fauntleroy*. London: Puffin Books, 1981, c1886.

———. *The Little Princess*. Philadelphia: Lippincott, 1963.

———. *Sara Crewe: or, What Happened at Miss Minchin's.* New York: Putnam, 1981.

———. *The Secret Garden.* Philadelphia: Lippincott, 1949, c1938.

Burton, Virginia Lee. *Katy and the Big Snow.* Boston: Houghton Mifflin, 1943.

———. *The Little House.* Boston: Houghton Mifflin, 1942.

———. *Mike Mulligan and His Steam Shovel.* Boston: Houghton Mifflin, 1939.

Butterworth, Oliver. *The Enormous Egg.* Boston: Little, Brown, 1956.

Byars, Betsy. *The Moon and I.* Englewood Cliffs, N.J.: Julian Messner, 1991.

———. *The Summer of the Swans.* New York: Viking, 1970.

Caldecott, Randolph. *The Panjandrum Picture Book.* London: Warne, n.d.

———. *R. Caldecott's Second Collection of Pictures and Songs.* London: Warne, n.d.

Carle, Eric. *The Very Busy Spider.* New York: Philomel, 1984.

———. *The Very Hungry Caterpillar.* New York: Philomel, 1969.

Carroll, Lewis. *The Annotated Alice: Alice's Adventures in Wonderland, and Through the Looking Glass.* New York: Clarkson Potter, 1960.

Christelow, Eileen. *Five Little Monkeys Jumping on the Bed.* New York: Clarion, 1989.

Christiansen, C. B. *I See the Moon.* New York: Athneum, 1994.

Ciardi, John. *Fast & Slow.* Boston: Houghton Mifflin, 1975.

———. *Someone Could Win a Polar Bear.* Philadelphia: Lippincott, 1970.

Cleary, Beverly. *Beezus and Ramona.* New York: Morrow, 1955.

———. *Dear Mr. Henshaw.* New York: Morrow, 1983.

———. *A Girl from Yamhill: A Memoir.* New York: Morrow, 1988.

———. *The Mouse and the Motorcycle.* New York: Morrow, 1965.

———. *Ramona Quimby, Age 8.* New York: Morrow, 1981.

———. *Ribsy.* New York: Morrow, 1964.

———. *Strider.* New York: Morrow, 1991.

Cleaver, Vera, and Bill Cleaver. *Where the Lilies Bloom.* Philadelphia, Lippincott, 1969.

Coatsworth, Elizabeth. *The Cat Who Went to Heaven.* New York: Macmillan, 1958.

Coerr, Eleanor. *Sadako and the Thousand Paper Cranes.* New York:, Putnam, 1977.

Cohen, Barbara. *Molly's Pilgrim.* New York: Lothrop, Lee & Shepard, 1983.

Cohen, Miriam. *When Will I Read?* New York: Greenwillow, 1977.

Cole, Brock. *Celine.* New York: Farrar, Straus & Giroux, 1989.

Cole, Joanna. *The Magic School Bus at the Waterworks.* New York: Scholastic, 1986.

Collier, James Lincoln, and Christopher Collier. *My Brother Sam Is Dead.* New York: Four Winds, 1974.

Collodi, Carlo. *The Adventures of Pinocchio.* Garden City, N.Y.: Doubleday, 1960.

Conly, Jane Leslie. *Racso and the Rats of NIMH.* New York: Harper & Row, 1986.

Cooney, Barbara. *Hattie and the Wild Waves.* New York: Viking, 1990.

———. *Miss Rumphius.* New York: Viking, 1982.

Cooper, Susan. *The Dark Is Rising.* New York: Atheneum, 1978.

Craik, Dinah Maria Mulock. *The Little Lame Prince,* and *The Adventures of a Brownie.* Grosset & Dunlap, 1948.

Creech, Sharon. *Chasing Redbird.* New York: HarperCollins, 1997.

———. *Walk Two Moons.* New York: HarperCollins, 1994.

Cresswell, Helen. *Ordinary Jack.* New York: Macmillan, 1977.

Crews, Donald. *Freight Train.* New York: Greenwillow, 1978.

Crowe, Robert L. *Clyde Monster.* New York: Dutton, 1976.

Curtis, Jamie Lee. *When I Was Little: A Four-Year-Old's Memoir of Her Youth.* New York: HarperCollins, 1993.

Cushman, Karen. *The Ballad of Lucy Whipple.* New York: Clarion, 1996.

———. *Catherine Called Birdy.* New York: Clarion, 1994.

———. *The Midwife's Apprentice.* New York: Clarion, 1995.

Dahl, Roald. *The BFG.* New York: Farrar, Straus & Giroux, 1982.

———. *Boy: Tales of Childhood.* New York: Farrar, Straus & Giroux, 1984.

———. *Charlie and the Chocolate Factory.* New York: Knopf, 1964.

———. *Danny the Champion of the World.* New York: Knopf, 1975.

———. *Fantastic Mr. Fox.* New York: Knopf, 1970.

———. *James and the Giant Peach.* New York: Knopf, 1961.

———. *The Magic Finger.* New York: Harper & Row, 1966.

———. *Matilda.* New York: Viking, 1988.

———. *The Witches.* New York: Farrar, Straus & Giroux, 1983.

Dalgliesh, Alice. *The Courage of Sarah Noble.* New York: Scribner, 1954.

De Angeli, Marguerite. *The Door in the Wall.* New York: Doubleday, 1949.

DeFelice, Cynthia. *Weasel.* New York: Macmillan, 1990.

DeJong, Meindert. *The Wheel on the School.* New York: Harper & Row, 1954.

de la Mare, Walter. *The Complete Poems of Walter de la Mare.* New York: Knopf, 1970.

Demi. *The Empty Pot.* New York: Henry Holt, 1990.

dePaola, Tomie. *Nana Upstairs and Nana Downstairs.* New York: Putnam, 1973, 1998.

———. *Strega Nona: An Old Tale Retold.* Englewood Cliffs, N. J.: Prentice-Hall, 1975.

DeRegniers, Beatrice Schenk. *It Does Not Say Meow and Other Animal Riddles.* New York: Seabury, 1972.

———. *May I Bring a Friend?* New York: Atheneum, 1964.

———. *So Many Cats!* New York: Clarion, 1985.

Devlin, Wende, and Harry Devlin. *Old Black Witch.* Chicago: Encyclopaedia Brittanica, 1963.

Duvoisin, Roger. *Crocus.* New York: Knopf, 1967.

———. *Jasmine.* New York: Knopf, 1973.

———. *The Missing Milkman.* New York: Knopf, 1967.

———. *Petunia.* New York: Knopf, 1950.

Eastman, P. D. *Are You My Mother?* New York: Beginner Books. 1960.

Eckert, Allan W. *Incident at Hawk's Hill.* Boston: Little, Brown, 1971.

Edmonds, Walter D. *The Matchlock Gun.* New York: Dodd, Mead, 1941.

Egielski, Richard. *Buz.* New York: HarperCollins, 1995.

Ehrlich, Amy. *Zeek Silver Moon.* New York: Dial, 1972.

Emberley, Barbara. *Drummer Hoff.* New York: Simon & Schuster, 1967.

Emerson, Sally. *The Nursery Treasury.* New York: Doubleday, 1988.

Estes, Eleanor. *The Hundred Dresses.* New York: Harcourt, Brace, Jovanovich, 1944.

Ets, Marie Hall. *Gilberto and the Wind.* New York: Viking, 1963.

Family Treasury of Little Golden Books: 46 Best-Loved Stories. Selected and Edited by Ellen Lewis Buell. New York: Golden Books, 1998.

Fatio, Louise. *The Happy Lion.* New York: McGraw-Hill, 1954.

Feiffer, Jules. *The Man in the Ceiling.* New York: HarperCollins, 1993.

Field, Eugene. *Poems of Childhood.* New York: Airmont, 1970.

Field, Rachel. *Hitty Her First Hundred Years.* New York: Macmillan, 1929, 1957.

———. *Poems.* New York: Macmillan, 1957.

Fisher, Dorothy Canfield. *Understood Betsy.* Holt, Rinehart & Winston, 1972, c1945.

Fitzgerald, John D. *The Great Brain.* New York: Dial, 1967.

Fitzhugh, Louise. *Harriet the Spy.* New York: Harper & Row, 1964.

———. *The Long Secret.* New York: Harper & Row, 1965.

———. *Sport.* New York: Delacorte, 1979.

Flack, Marjorie. *Angus and the Cat.* New York: Doubleday, 1931.

———. *Angus and the Ducks.* New York: Doubleday, 1930.

———. *Ask Mr. Bear.* New York: Macmillan, 1932.

———. *The Story about Ping.* New York: Viking, 1933.

Fleischman, Paul. *The Half-a-Moon Inn.* New York: Harper & Row, 1980.

Fleischman, Sid. *The Ghost on Saturday Night.* Boston: Little, Brown, 1974.

———. *The Whipping Boy.* New York: Greenwillow, 1986.

Fleming, Ian. *Chitty Chitty Bang Bang.* Mattituck, N.Y.: Aeonian Press, 1974.

Forbes, Esther. *Johnny Tremain.* Boston: Houghton Mifflin, 1943.

Forbes, Kathryn. *Mama's Bank Account.* New York: Harcourt, Brace & World, c1943.

Foreman, Michael. *Michael Foreman's Mother Goose.* San Diego: Harcourt Brace Jovanovich, 1991.

Fox, Mem. *Tough Boris.* San Diego, Harcourt Brace Jovanovich, 1994.

Fox, Paula. *The Slave Dancer.* New York: Bradbury, 1973.

———. *Western Wind.* New York: Orchard, 1993.

Frasier, Debra. *On the Day You Were Born.* New York: Harcourt, Brace, Jovanovich, 1991.

Freeman, Don. *Corduroy.* New York: Viking, 1968.

———. *A Pocket for Corduroy.* New York: Viking, 1978.

Fritz, Jean. *The Cabin Faced West.* New York: Coward-McCann, 1958.

———. *Homesick: My Own Story.* New York: Putnam, 1982.

Gackenbach, Dick. *Harry and the Terrible Whatzit.* New York: Clarion, 1977.

———. *Poppy the Panda.* New York: Clarion, 1984.

Gag, Wanda. *Millions of Cats.* New York: Coward McCann & Geoghegan, 1928.

Gage, Wilson. *Squash Pie.* New York: Greenwillow, 1976.

Gardiner, John Reynolds. *Stone Fox.* New York: Crowell, 1980.

Gates, Doris. *Blue Willow.* New York: Viking, 1940.

George, Jean Craighead. *Julie of theWolves.* New York: Harper & Row, 1972.

———. *My Side of the Mountain.* New York: Dutton, 1959.

Gerrard, Roy. *Wagons West!* New York: Farrar, Straus & Giroux, 1996.

Giff, Patricia Reilly. *Lily's Crossing.* New York: Delacorte, 1997.

Ginsburg, Mirra. *Mushroom in the Rain.* New York: Macmillan, 1974.

Gipson, Fred. *Old Yeller.* New York: Harper & Row, 1956.

Godden, Rumer. *The Dolls' House.* New York: Viking, 1962.

Graham, Margaret Bloy. *Be Nice to Spiders.* New York: Harper & Row, 1967.

Grahame, Kenneth. *The Reluctant Dragon.* New York: Holt, Rinehart & Winston, 1983.

———. *The Wind in the Willows.* New York: Scribner, 1961.

Gramatky, Hardie. *Little Toot.* New York: Putnam, 1939.

Gray, Elizabeth Janet. *Adam of the Road.* New York: Viking, 1960.

Gray, Libba Moore. *Little Lil and the Swing-Singing Sax.* New York: Simon & Schuster, 1996.

———. *My Mama Had a Dancing Heart.* New York: Orchard, 1995.

———. *Small Green Snake.* New York: Orchard, 1994.

Greene, Bette. *Summer of My German Soldier.* New York: Dial, 1974.

Greene, Constance C. *Beat the Turtle Drum.* New York: Viking, 1976.

Grifalconi, Ann. *The Village of Round and Square Houses.* Boston: Little Brown, 1986.

Grimm, Jacob, and Wilhelm Grimm. *The Complete Brothers Grimm Fairy Tales.* New York: Gramercy Books, 1996.

———. *Fairy Tales of Brothers Grimm.* Retold by Neil Philip. New York: Viking, 1997.

———. *Favorite Fairy Tales Told in Germany.* Retold by Virginia Haviland. New York: Beech Tree, 1994.

———. *Grimms' Fairy Tales.* Translated by Peter Carter. Oxford: Oxford University Press, 1982.

———. *Household Stories.* Translated by Lucy Crane. London: Macmillan, 1882.

———. *The Juniper Tree and Other Tales from Grimm.* Translated by Lore Segal. New York: Farrar, Straus & Giroux, 1973.

Hadithi, Mwenye. *Hot Hippo.* Boston: Little, Brown, 1986.

Hale, Lucretia P. *The Complete Peterkin Papers.* Boston: Houghton Mifflin, 1960.

Hale, Sara Josepha. *Mary Had a Little Lamb.* New York: Scholastic,1990.

Hamilton, Virginia. *The House of Dies Drear.* New York: Macmillan, 1968.

———. *M. C. Higgins, the Great.* New York: Macmillan, 1974.

———. *Willie Bea and the Time the Martians Landed.* New York: Greenwillow, 1983.

——. *Zeely.* New York: Macmillan, 1967.

Harris, Joel Chandler. *The Complete Tales of Uncle Remus.* Boston: Houghton Mifflin, 1955.

Hedderwick, Mairi. *Katie Morag and the Two Grandmothers.* Boston: Little Brown, 1985.

Henkes, Kevin. *Chrysanthemum.* New York: Greenwillow, 1991.

——. *Jessica.* New York: Greenwillow, 1989.

——. *Julius, Baby of the World.* New York: Greenwillow, 1990.

——. *Lilly's Purple Plastic Purse.* New York: Greenwillow, 1996.

——. *Owen.* New York: Greenwillow, 1993.

——. *Sheila Rae, the Brave.* New York: Greenwillow, 1987.

——. *A Weekend with Wendell.* New York: Greenwillow, 1986.

Henry, Marguerite. *King of the Wind.* Chicago, Rand McNally, 1948.

——. *Misty of Chincoteague.* New York: Macmillan, 1947.

Hesse, Karen. *Out of the Dust.* New York: Scholastic, 1997.

Hill, Elizabeth Starr. *Evan's Corner.* New York: Viking, 1967, 1991.

Hite, Sid. *Answer My Prayer.* New York: Henry Holt, 1995.

Hoban, Russell. *A Bargain for Frances.* New York: Harper & Row, 1970.

——. *Best Friends for Frances.* New York: Harper & Row, 1969.

——. *A Birthday for Frances.* New York: Harper & Row, 1968.

——. *Bread and Jam for Frances.* New York: Harper & Row, 1964.

——. *Dinner at Alberta's.* New York: Crowell, 1975.

——. *Egg Thoughts and Other Frances Songs.* New York: Harper & Row, 1964, 1972.

——. *The Mouse and His Child.* New York: Harper & Row, 1967.

Hoberman, Mary Ann. *A House Is a House for Me.* New York: Viking, 1978.

Hoff, Syd. *Danny and the Dinosaur.* New York: Harper & Row, 1958.

Hoffman, Mary. *Amazing Grace.* New York: Dial, 1991.

Holman, Felice. *Slake's Limbo.* New York: Scribner, 1974.

Howe, Deborah, and James Howe. *Bunnicula: A Rabbit-Tale of Mystery.* New York: Atheneum, 1979.

Hunt, Irene. *Across Five Aprils.* Chicago: Follett, 1964.

——. *Up a Road Slowly.* Chicago: Follett, 1966.

Hurd, Edith Thacher. *Dinosaur My Darling.* New York: Harper & Row, 1978.

Hurwitz, Johanna. *Aldo Applesauce.* New York: Morrow, 1979.

Hutchins, Pat. *The Doorbell Rang.* New York: Greenwillow, 1986.

Irving, Washington. *Rip Van Winkle, and The Legend of Sleepy Hollow.* New York: Macmillan, 1966.

Jacobs, Joseph. *English Fairy Tales.* New York: Dover, 1967, c1898.

Jeter, Jacky. *The Cat and the Fiddler.* New York: Parents' Magazine Press, 1968.

Johnson, Crockett. *Harold and the Purple Crayon.* New York: HarperCollins, 1955.

——. *Harold's Circus.* New York: HarperCollins, 1959.

Jones, Diana Wynne. *The Homeward Bounders.* New York: Greenwillow, 1981.

Joosse, Barbara M. *Mama, Do You Love Me?* New York: Chronicle Books, 1991.

Joyce, William. *Bently & Egg.* New York: HarperCollins, 1992.

———. *Dinosaur Bob and His Adventures with the Family Lazardo.* New York: Harper-Collins, 1988.

Juster, Norton. *The Phantom Tollbooth.* New York: Epstein & Carroll, 1961.

Keith, Harold. *Rifles for Watie.* New York: Crowell, 1957.

Kellogg, Steven. *Can I Keep Him?* New York: Dial, 1971.

———. *The Island of the Skog.* New York: Dial, 1973.

Kelly, Eric P. *The Trumpeter of Krakow.* New York: Macmillan, 1928, 1966.

Kerr, M. E. *Gentlehands.* New York: Harper & Row, 1978.

Kimmel, Eric A. *Anansi and the Moss-Covered Rock.* New York: Holiday House, 1994.

———. *Anansi and the Talking Melon.* New York: Holiday House, 1988.

Kindl, Patrice. *The Woman in the Wall.* Boston: Houghton Mifflin, 1997.

King-Smith, Dick. *Babe the Gallant Pig.* New York: Crown, 1983.

———. *Martin's Mice.* New York: Crown, 1989.

Kipling, Rudyard. *The Jungle Book.* Garden City, N.Y.: Doubleday, c1893.

———. *Just So Stories.* New York: William Morrow, 1996.

———. *The Second Jungle Book.* Garden City, N.Y.:Doubleday, 1946, c1895.

Knight, Eric. *Lassie Come-Home.* New York: Holt, Rinehart & Winston, 1940.

Knutson, Kimberley. *Muddigush.* New York: Macmillan, 1992.

Konigsburg, E. L. *From the Mixed-Up Files of Mrs. Basil E. Frankweiler.* New York: Atheneum, 1967.

———. *A Proud Taste for Scarlet and Miniver.* New York: Atheneum, 1973.

———. *The View from Saturday.* New York: Atheneum, 1996.

Krasilovsky, Phyllis. *The Cow Who Fell in the Canal.* New York: Doubleday, 1957.

Kraus, Robert. *Leo the Late Bloomer.* New York: Windmill, 1971.

Krauss, Ruth. *The Carrot Seed.* New York: Harper & Row, 1945.

———. *A Hole Is to Dig: A First Book of Definitions.* New York: HarperCollins, 1952.

Krumgold, Joseph. *And Now Miguel.* New York: Crowell, 1953.

———. *Onion John.* New York: Crowell, 1959.

Kuskin, Karla. *The Philharmonic Gets Dressed.* New York: HarperCollins, 1982.

———. *Something Sleeping in the Hall.* New York: Harper & Row, 1985.

Lasker, Joe. *Lentil Soup.* Chicago: Albert Whitman, 1977.

Lawson, Robert. *Rabbit Hill.* New York: Viking, 1944.

Leaf, Munro. *The Story of Ferdinand.* New York: Puffin, 1977, c1936.

Lear, Edward. *The Complete Nonsense Book.* New York: Dodd, Mead, 1958.

Le Guin, Ursula K. *The Tombs of Atuan.* New York: Atheneum, 1974.

———. *A Wizard of Earthsea.* Berkeley: Parnassus, 1968.

L'Engle, Madeleine. *A Wrinkle in Time*. New York: Farrar, Straus and Giroux, 1962.

LeSieg, Theo. *I Wish That I Had Duck Feet*. New York: Beginner Books, 1965.

———. *Wacky Wednesday*. New York: Beginner Books, 1974.

Lester, Julius. *The Tales of Uncle Remus: The Adventures of Brer Rabbit*. New York: Dial, 1987.

Levine, Gail Carson. *Ella Enchanted*. HarperCollins, 1997.

Levy, Elizabeth. *Something Queer at the Ball Park: A Mystery*. New York: Dell, 1984, c1975.

Lewin, Hugh. *Jafta*. Minneapolis, Minn.: Carolrhoda Books, 1983.

Lewis, C. S. *The Lion, the Witch, and the Wardrobe*. New York: Macmillan, 1950.

———. *Prince Caspian: The Return to Narnia*. New York: Macmillan, 1951.

Lindgren, Astrid. *Pippi Longstocking*. New York: Viking, 1950.

Lindgren, Barbro. *The Wild Baby*. New York: Greenwillow, 1981.

Lionni, Leo. *A Color of His Own*. New York: Pantheon, 1975.

———. *Fish Is Fish*. New York: Pantheon, 1970.

———. *Frederick*. New York: Pantheon, 1967.

———. *Swimmy*. New York: Pantheon, 1968.

Lisle, Janet Taylor. *Afternoon of the Elves*. New York: Orchard, 1989.

Lobel, Arnold. *The Book of Pigericks*. New York: Harper & Row, 1983.

———. *Fables*. New York: Harper & Row, 1980.

———. *Frog and Toad All Year*. New York: Harper & Row, 1976.

———. *Frog and Toad Are Friends*. New York: HarperCollins, 1970.

———. *Frog and Toad Together*. New York: HarperCollins, 1971.

———. *Grasshopper on the Road*. New York: Harper & Row, 1978.

———. *Mouse Soup*. New York: Harper & Row, 1977.

———. *Owl at Home*. New York: Harper & Row, 1975.

———. *The Random House Book of Mother Goose*. New York: Random, 1986.

———. *Small Pig*. New York: Harper & Row, 1969.

———. *Uncle Elephant*. New York: HarperCollins, 1981.

Lofting, Hugh. *The Story of Doctor Dolittle*. Philadelphia: Lippincott, 1920.

Lord, Bette Bao. *In the Year of the Boar and Jackie Robinson*. New York: Harper & Row, 1984.

Lord, John Vernon. *The Giant Jam Sandwich*. Boston: Houghton Mifflin, 1972.

Lovelace, Maud Hart. *Betsy-Tacy*. New York: Crowell, 1940.

Lowry, Lois. *Anastasia Krupnik*. Boston: Houghton Mifflin, 1979.

———. *Number the Stars*. Boston: Houghton Mifflin, 1989.

Lyon, George Ella. *Borrowed Children*. New York: Orchard Books, 1988.

MacDonald, Betty. *Mrs. Piggle-Wiggle*. Philadelphia: Lippincott, 1947.

MacDonald, George. *At the Back of the North Wind*. New York: Morrow, 1919.

———. *The Lost Princess: A Double Story*. Grand Rapids, Mich.: William B. Eerdmans, 1992.

MacLachlan, Patricia. *Baby.* New York: Delacorte, 1993.

——. *Sarah, Plain and Tall.* New York: Harper & Row, 1985.

Marshall, James. *George and Martha Encore.* Boston: Houghton Mifflin, 1973.

——. *Yummers Too: The Second Course.* Boston: Houghton Mifflin, 1986.

Martin, Bill, Jr., and John Archambault. *Chicka Chicka Boom Boom.* New York: Simon & Schuster, 1989.

——. *Knots on a Counting Rope.* New York: Henry Holt, 1987.

Mayer, Mercer. *There's a Nightmare in My Closet.* New York: Dial, 1968.

McCloskey, Robert. *Blueberries for Sal.* New York: Viking, 1948.

——. *Homer Price.* New York: Viking, 1943.

——. *Make Way for Ducklings.* New York: Viking, 1941.

McCully, Emily Arnold. *Mirette on the High Wire.* New York: Putnam, 1992.

McGraw, Eloise. *The Moorchild.* New York: Margaret K. McElderry, 1996.

McKinley, Robin. *The Blue Sword.* New York: Greenwillow, 1982.

——. *The Hero and the Crown.* New York: Greenwillow, 1984.

Merrill, Jean. *The Pushcart War.* New York: William R. Scott, 1964.

Milne, A. A. *The House at Pooh Corner.* New York: Dutton, 1961, c1926.

——. *Winnie-the-Pooh.* New York: Dutton, 1926.

——. *The World of Christopher Robin: The Complete When We Were Very Young and Now We Are Six.* New York: Dutton, 1958.

Minarik, Else Holmelund. *Little Bear.* New York: Harper & Row, 1957.

Montgomery, Lucy Maud. *Anne of Green Gables.* New York: Grosset & Dunlap, c1908.

Moore, Clement Clarke. *The Night Before Christmas.* New York: Scholastic, 1985.

Morey, Walt. *Gentle Ben.* New York: Dutton, 1965.

Morris, Gerald. *The Squire's Tale.* Boston: Houghton Mifflin, 1998.

Mosel, Arlene. *Tikki Tikki Tembo.* New York: Henry Holt, 1968.

Moss, Lloyd. *Zin! Zin! Zin! A Violin.* New York: Simon & Schuster, 1995.

Munsch, Robert. *Love You Forever.* Willowdale, Ont.: Firefly Books, 1986.

——. *The Paper Bag Princess.* Toronto: Annick, 1980.

Murphy, Jill. *Peace at Last.* New York: Dial, 1980.

Myers, Walter Dean. *Fast Sam, Cool Clyde, and Stuff.* New York: Viking, 1975.

Napoli. Donna Jo. *The Magic Circle.* New York: Dutton, 1993.

——. *The Prince of the Pond, Otherwise Known as de Fawg Pin.* New York: Dutton, 1992.

——. *Zel.* New York: Dutton, 1996.

Nash, Ogden. *Custard the Dragon.* Boston: Little, Brown, 1959, c1936.

Naylor, Phyllis Reynolds. *The Agony of Alice.* New York: Atheneum, 1985.

——. *Shiloh.* New York: Atheneum, 1991.

——. *Witch's Sister.* New York: Atheneum, 1977.

Nesbit, Edith. *Five Children and It.* New York: Looking Glass (Random), 1948.

——. *The House of Arden.* New York: Books of Wonder, 1997, c1908.

Ness, Evaline. *Sam, Bangs, & Moonshine.* New York: Henry Holt, 1966.

Neville, Emily. *It's Like This, Cat.* New York: Harper & Row, 1963.

Nic Leodhas, Sorche. *Always Room for One More.* New York: Henry Holt, 1965.

Noble, Trinka Hakes. *The Day Jimmy's Boa Ate the Wash.* New York: Dial, 1980.

Nodset, Joan L. *Who Took the Farmer's Hat?* New York: Harper & Row, 1963.

Norton, Mary. *The Borrowers.* San Diego: Harcourt Brace, 1986.

Numeroff, Laura Joffe. *If You Give a Mouse a Cookie.* New York: HarperCollins, 1985.

O'Brien, Robert C. *Mrs. Frisby and the Rats of NIMH.* New York: Atheneum, 1972.

O'Dell, Scott. *Island of the Blue Dolphins.* New York: Dell, c1960.

——. *Sarah Bishop.* Boston: Houghton Mifflin, 1980.

——. *Sing Down the Moon.* Boston: Houghton Mifflin, 1970.

O'Hara, Mary. *My Friend Flicka.* Philadelphia: Lippincott, 1941.

O'Neill, Mary. *Hailstones and Halibut Bones: Adventures in Color.* Garden City: Double-day, 1961.

Oppenheim, Shulamith Levey. *The Hundredth Name.* Honesdale, Pa.: Boyds Mills, 1995.

Orr, Wendy. *Peeling the Onion.* New York: Holiday House, 1996.

Palmer, Helen. *A Fish out of Water.* New York: Beginner Books, 1961.

Park, Barbara. *The Kid in the Red Jacket.* New York: Knopf, 1987.

——. *Mick Harte Was Here.* New York: Apple Soup, 1995.

Parks, Van Dyke, and Malcolm Jones. *Jump! The Adventures of Brer Rabbit.* Adapted from *The Tales of Uncle Remus* by Joel Chandler Harris. San Diego: Harcourt Brace Jovanovich, 1986.

Paterson, Katherine. *Bridge to Terabithia.* New York: Crowell, 1972.

——. *Flip-Flop Girl.* New York: Dutton, 1994.

——. *The Great Gilly Hopkins.* New York: Crowell, 1978.

——. *Jacob Have I Loved.* New York: Crowell, 1980.

——. *Jip: His Story.* New York: Dutton, 1996.

Paulsen, Gary. *Brian's Winter.* New York: Delacorte, 1996.

——. *Dogsong.* New York: Bradbury, 1985.

——. *Hatchet.* New York: Puffin, 1988.

——. *Woodsong.* New York: Bradbury, 1990.

Peck, Robert Newton. *A Day No Pigs Would Die.* New York: Knopf, 1972.

——. *Soup.* New York: Knopf, 1974.

Pene DuBois, William. *Bear Party.* New York: Viking, 1951.

——. *The Twenty-One Balloons.* New York: Viking, 1947.

Perrault, Charles, and Madame D'Aulnoy. *The Sleeping Beauty and Other Classic French Tales.* New York: Children's Classics, 1991.

Petersham, Maud, and Miska Petersham. *The Circus Baby.* New York: Macmillan, 1950.

Pilkey, Dav. *When Cats Dream.* New York: Orchard, 1992.

Pinkwater, Daniel Manus. *Aunt Lulu.* New York: Macmillan, 1988.

———. *The Big Orange Splot.* New York: Hastings House, 1977.

———. *Borgel.* New York: Macmillan, 1990.

———. *The Hoboken Chicken Emergency.* New York: Prentice Hall, 1976.

Piper, Watty. *The Little Engine That Could.* New York: Platt & Munk, 1961.

Polacco, Patricia. *My Rotten Redheaded Older Brother.* New York: Simon & Schuster, 1994.

Polushkin, Maria. *Mother, Mother, I Want Another.* New York: Crown, 1978.

Porter, Eleanor H. *Pollyanna.* New York: Grosset & Dunlap, 1946.

Potter, Beatrix. *The Tailor of Gloucester.* New York: Warne, 1968, c1901.

———. *The Tale of Jemima Puddle-Duck.* New York: Warne, c1908.

———. *The Tale of Mrs. Tiggy-Winkle.* New York: Warne, c1905.

———. *The Tale of Peter Rabbit.* New York: Warne, c1902.

———. *The Tale of Squirrel Nutkin.* New York: Warne, c1903.

Prelutsky, Jack. *A. Nonny Mouse Writes Again!* New York: Knopf, 1993.

———. *Poems of A. Nonny Mouse.* New York: Knopf, 1989.

———. *Ride a Purple Pelican.* New York: Greenwillow, 1986.

Preston, Edna Mitchell. *The Sad Story of the Little Bluebird and the Hungry Cat.* New York: Four Winds, 1975.

Ransome, Arthur. *Swallows and Amazons.* Philadelphia: Lippincott, 1931.

Raskin, Ellen. *The Westing Game.* New York: Dutton, 1978.

Rawlings, Marjorie Kinnan. *The Yearling.* New York: Scribner, 1939.

Reid Banks, Lynne. *The Indian in the Cupboard.* New York: Doubleday, 1980.

Rey, H. A. *Curious George.* Boston: Houghton Mifflin, 1941.

———. *Curious George Rides a Bike.* Boston: Houghton Mifflin, 1952.

Ringgold, Faith. *Tar Beach.* New York: Crown, 1991.

Robinson, Barbara. *The Best Christmas Pageant Ever.* New York: Harper & Row, 1972.

Rodgers, Mary. *Freaky Friday.* New York: HarperCollins, 1972.

Rowling, J. K. *Harry Potter and the Chamber of Secrets.* New York: Arthur A. Levine, 1999.

Ryan, Cheli Duran. *Hildilid's Night.* New York: Macmillan, 1971.

Rylant, Cynthia. *Henry and Mudge in Puddle Trouble.* New York: Bradbury, 1987.

———. *The Relatives Came.* New York: Bradbury, 1985.

Sachar, Louis. *Sideways Stories from Wayside School.* New York: Knopf, 1990.

Saint-Exupery, Antoine de. *The Little Prince.* New York: Harcourt, Brace & World, 1943.

Sandburg, Carl. *Rootabaga Stories.* New York: Harcourt Brace, 1922.

Schwartz, Amy. *Bea and Mr. Jones.* New York: Bradbury, 1982.

Scieszka, Jon. *The Stinky Cheese Man and Other Fairly Stupid Tales.* New York: Viking, 1992.

———. *The True Story of the 3 Little Pigs, by A. Wolf.* New York: Viking, 1989.

Seeger, Pete. *Abiyoyo.* New York: Macmillan, 1986.

Sendak, Maurice. *Chicken Soup with Rice*. New, York: Harper & Row, 1962.

———. *In the Night Kitchen*. New York: Harper & Row, 1970.

———. *Pierre: A Cautionary Tale in Five Chapters and a Prologue*. New York: Harper & Row, 1962.

———. *Where the Wild Things Are*. New York: Harper & Row, 1963.

Seuss, Dr. *And to Think That I Saw It on Mulberry Street*. New York: Vanguard, 1937.

———. *Bartholomew and the Oobleck*. New York: Random, 1949.

———. *The Butter Battle Book*. New York: Random, 1984.

———. *The Cat in the Hat*. New York: Random, c1957.

———. *The Cat in the Hat Comes Back*. New York: Beginner Books, 1958.

———. *Daisy-Head Mayzie*. New York: Random, 1994.

———. *Did I Ever Tell You How Lucky You Are?* New York: Random, 1973.

———. *Fox in Socks*. New York: Beginner Books, 1965.

———. *Green Eggs and Ham*. New York: Beginner Books, 1960.

———. *Horton Hatches the Egg*. New York: Random, c1940.

———. *Horton Hears a Who!* New York: Random, 1954.

———. *How the Grinch Stole Christmas*. New York: Random, 1957.

———. *I Had Trouble in Getting to Solla Sollew*. New York: Random, 1965.

———. *The Lorax*. New York: Random, 1971.

———. *Marvin K. Mooney Will You Please Go Now!* New York: Ransom, 1972.

———. *Oh, the Places You'll Go!* New York: Random, 1990.

———. *On Beyond Zebra*. New York: Random, 1955.

———. *The Sneetches and Other Stories*. New York: Random, 1961.

———. *Yertle the Turtle and Other Stories*. New York: Random, 1986.

Sewell, Anna. *Black Beauty*. New York: Dodd, Mead, 1941.

Sharmat, Mitchell. *Gregory the Terrible Eater*. New York: Four Winds, 1980.

Sharp, Margery. *The Rescuers*. Boston: Little, Brown 1959.

Shaw, Charles. *It Looked Like Spilt Milk*. New York: Harper & Row, 1947.

Sidney, Margaret. *Five Little Peppers*. New York: Macmillan, 1962.

Silverstein, Shel. *The Giving Tree*. New York: Harper & Row, 1964.

———. *A Light in the Attic*. New York: HarperCollins, 1981.

———. *The Missing Piece*. New York: Harper & Row, 1976.

———. *The Missing Piece Meets the Big O*. New York: HarperCollins, 1981.

———. *Where the Sidewalk Ends*. New York: Harper & Row, 1974.

Slepian, Jan. *Back to Before*. New York: Philomel, 1993.

Slobodkina, Esphyr. *Caps for Sale*. New York: HarperCollins, c1940.

Smith, Dodie. *The Hundred and One Dalmatians*. New York: Viking, 1957.

Smith, Doris Buchanan. *A Taste of Blackberries*. New York: Crowell, 1973.

Snyder, Zilpha Keatley. *Below the Root*. New York: Atheneum, 1975.

——. *The Egypt Game.* New York: Dell Yearling, 1986, c1967.

Spinelli, Jerry. *Crash.* New York: Knopf, 1996.

——. *Maniac Magee.* Boston: Little, Brown, 1990.

——. *Who Put That Hair in My Toothbrush?* Boston: Little, Brown, 1984.

Spyri, Johanna. *Heidi.* Racine, Wis.: Whitman, 1950.

Steel, Flora Annie. *English Fairy Tales.* New York: Mayflower, 1979, c1918.

Steig, William. *Abel's Island.* New York: Farrar, Straus & Giroux, 1976.

——. *Amos & Boris.* New York: Farrar, Straus & Giroux, 1971.

——. *Caleb and Kate.* New York: Farrar, Straus & Giroux, 1977.

——. *Doctor De Soto.* New York: Farrar, Straus & Giroux, 1982.

Stevenson, James. *National Worm Day.* New York: Greenwillow, 1990.

Stevenson, Robert Louis. *A Child's Garden of Verses.* New York: Delacorte, 1985.

Stolz, Mary. *The Bully of Barkham Street.* New York: Harper & Row, 1963.

——. *Cezanne Pinto: A Memoir.* New York: Knopf, 1994.

Stratton-Porter, Gene. *A Girl of the Limberlost.* New York: Grosset & Dunlap, c1909.

Swift, Hildegarde, and Lynd Ward. *The Little Red Lighthouse and the Great Gray Bridge.* New York: Harcourt, Brace & World, 1942.

Taylor, Mildred. *Roll of Thunder, Hear My Cry.* New York: Dial, 1976.

——. *Song of the Trees.* New York: Dial, 1975.

Thayer, Jane. *The Puppy Who Wanted a Boy.* New York: William Morrow, 1985.

Thomas, Patricia. *"Stand Back," Said the Elephant, "I'm Going to Sneeze!"* New York: Lothrop, Lee & Shepard, 1971.

Thompson, Kay. *Eloise: A Book for Precocious Grown Ups.* New York: Simon & Schuster, 1955.

Thurber, James. *The Thirteen Clocks.* New York: Simon & Schuster, 1950.

Titus, Eve. *Anatole.* New York: McGraw-Hill, 1956.

Tolkien, J. R. R. *The Hobbit.* Rev. ed. New York: Ballantine, 1982.

Travers, P. L. *Mary Poppins.* New York: Harcourt, Brace & World, 1962.

Treviño, Elizabeth Borton de. *I, Juan de Pareja.* New York: Farrar, Straus & Giroux, 1965.

Udry, Janice May. *A Tree Is Nice.* New York: Harper & Row, 1956.

Ungerer, Tomi. *Moon Man.* New York: Harper & Row, 1975.

——. *The Three Robbers.* New York: Atheneum, 1962.

Van Allsburg, Chris. *Jumanji.* Boston: Houghton Mifflin, 1981.

——. *The Mysteries of Harris Burdick.* Boston: Houghton Mifflin, 1984.

——. *The Polar Express.* Boston: Houghton Mifflin, 1985.

Viorst, Judith. *Alexander and the Terrible, Horrible, No Good, Very Bad Day.* New York: Atheneum, 1972.

——. *I'll Fix Anthony.* New York: Harper & Row, 1969.

——. *The Tenth Good Thing about Barney.* New York: Atheneum, 1971.

Voigt, Cynthia. *Bad Girls.* New York: Scholastic, 1996.

———. *Dicey's Song.* New York: Atheneum, 1982.

———. *Homecoming.* New York: Atheneum, 1983.

———. *A Solitary Blue.* New York: Atheneum, 1983.

———. *Tree by Leaf.* New York: Atheneum, 1988.

Waber, Bernard. *The House on East 88th Street.* Boston: Houghton Mifflin, 1962.

Waddell, Martin. *Farmer Duck.* Cambridge, Mass.: Candlewick, 1991.

Weller, Frances Ward. *Boat Song.* New York: Macmillan, 1987.

White, E. B. *Charlotte's Web.* New York: Harper, 1952.

White, T. H. *The Sword in the Stone.* New York: Philomel, 1993.

Wiggin, Kate Douglas. *Rebecca of Sunnybrook Farm.* Boston: Houghton Mifflin, 1903.

Wilder, Laura Ingalls. *Little House in the Big Woods.* New York: Harper & Row, 1971.

Wildsmith, Brian. *What the Moon Saw.* Oxford: Oxford University Press, 1978.

Williams, Jay. *Everyone Knows What a Dragon Looks Like.* New York: Four Winds, 1976.

Williams, Linda. *The Little Old Lady Who Was Not Afraid of Anything.* New York: Crowell, 1986.

Williams, Margery. *The Velveteen Rabbit.* New York: Avon, 1975.

Wojciechowska, Maia. *Shadow of a Bull.* New York: Atheneum, 1972.

Wood, Audrey. *King Bidgood's in the Bathtub.* San Diego: Harcourt Brace Jovanovich, 1985.

———. *The Napping House.* San Diego, Harcourt Brace Jovanovich, 1984.

———. *Silly Sally.* San Diego: Harcourt Brace Jovanovich, 1992.

Wrede, Patricia C. *Calling on Dragons.* San Diego: Harcourt Brace Jovanovich, 1993.

———. *Dealing with Dragons.* San Diego: Harcourt Brace Jovanovich, 1990.

Yates, Elizabeth. *Amos Fortune Free Man.* New York: Dutton, 1950.

Yee, Wong Herbert. *Big Black Bear.* Boston: Houghton Mifflin, 1993.

———. *Fireman Small.* Boston: Houghton Mifflin, 1994.

Yep, Laurence. *Dragonwings.* New York: Harper & Row, 1975.

Yolen, Jane. *Eeny, Meeny, Miney Mole.* San Diego: Harcourt Brace Jovanovich, 1992.

———. *Owl Moon.* New York: Philomel, 1987.

Yorinks, Arthur. *Hey, Al.* New York: Farrar, Straus & Giroux, 1986.

———. *Louis the Fish.* New York: Farrar, Straus & Giroux, 1980.

Zemach, Harve. *The Judge.* New York: Farrar, Straus and Giroux, 1969.

Zimmerman, H. Werner. *Henny Penny.* New York: Scholastic, 1989.

Zion, Gene. *Harry the Dirty Dog.* New York: HarperCollins, 1956.

Zolotow, Charlotte. *William's Doll.* New York: HarperCollins, 1972.